The Wolf Man's Magic Word:
A Cryptonymy

Nicolas Abraham
Maria Torok

The Wolf Man's Magic Word:

A Cryptonymy

Translated by Nicholas Rand
Foreword by Jacques Derrida

Theory and History of Literature, volume 37
University of Minnesota Press, Minneapolis

The University of Minnesota Press gratefully acknowledges
assistance to translation of this book by the George Lurcy
Charitable and Educational Trust.

Published by the University of Minnesota Press
2037 University Avenue Southeast, Minneapolis MN 55414.
Published simultaneously in Canada
by Fitzhenry & Whiteside Limited, Markham.
Printed in the United States of America.

Library of Congress Cataloging-in-Publication Data

Abraham, Nicolas.
  The Wolf Man's magic word.

  (Theory and history of literature ; v. 37)
  Translation of: Cryptonymie.
  Includes index.
  1. Pankejeff, Sergius, 1887–1979.
2. Psychoanalysis—Case studies. 3. Neuroses—
Case studies. 4. Freud, Sigmund, 1856–1939.
Aus der Geschichte einer infantilen Neurose.
I. Torok, Maria. II. Title. III. Series.
RC506.A1813   1986   616.89'17   86-7030
ISBN 0-8166-1421-0
ISBN 0-8166-1422-9 (pbk.)

The following permissions were obtained for the quotation of selected passages:

From *The Wolf-Man by the Wolf-Man*, edited by Muriel Gardiner. Copyright © 1971 by Basic Books, Inc., Publishers. Reprinted by permission of Basic Books and of Chatto & Windus: The Hogarth Press.

From *The History of an Infantile Neurosis*, Vol. XVII, *The Standard Edition of the Complete Psychological Works of Sigmund Freud*, translated and edited by James Strachey. Reprinted by permission of Sigmund Freud Copyrights Ltd., The Institute of Psycho-Analysis, and the Hogarth Press.

From *The Collected Papers of Sigmund Freud*, Vols. 3 and 5, edited by James Strachey. Copyright © 1959 by Basic Books, Inc., Publishers, by arrangement with The Hogarth Press, Ltd., and the Institute of Psycho-Analysis, London. Reprinted by permission of the publisher.

From *An Outline of Psychoanalysis* by Sigmund Freud. Translated by James Strachey. Copyright © 1949 by W. W. Norton & Company, Copyright © 1969 by The Institute of Psychoanalysis and Alix Strachey. Reprinted by permission of the publisher.

From *New Introductory Lectures on Psychoanalysis by Sigmund Freud*. Translated by James Strachey. Copyright © 1965, 1964 by James Strachey. Reprinted by permission of the publisher.

Theory and History of Literature
Edited by Wlad Godzich and Jochen Schulte-Sasse

Contents

Foreword:
Fors: The Anglish Words
of Nicolas Abraham and Maria Torok
Jacques Derrida

Translated by Barbara Johnson

> From then on, that particular pleasure, jealously preserved in his *inner safe*, could only be subject to total disavowal. In addition, not having himself been included in the scene . . . .
>
> The intervention of the mother, with her Russian words, and then of the nurse with her English words, closed two doors for him at the same time.
>
> *The Wolf Man's Magic Word*
>
> But thanks to this subterfuge, the text of the drama being written *behind* his *inner safe* will play itself out *in front*, on the *outer safe*, so to speak.
>
> Nicolas Abraham, *The Case of Jonah*

What is a crypt?

What if I were writing on one now? In other words on the *title* of the book alone, on the outer partition of its very first and entirely obvious readability?

Translator's note. The word *fors* in French, derived from the Latin *foris* ("outside, outdoors"), is an archaic preposition meaning "except for, barring, save." In addition, *fors* is the plural of the word *for,* which, in the French expression *le for intérieur,* designates the inner heart, "the tribunal

Less still: on the first detachable fragment of a title, on its broken symbol or its truncated column—cryptonymy, still minus a name? What if I vaulted to a stop, immobilizing myself and you, reader, in front of a word or a thing, or rather in front of the place of a word-thing, as Nicolas Abraham and Maria Torok present it for us to decipher: the crypt of cryptonymy?

For I shall not engage myself further.

In place of another here the first word is—crypt.

Then it won't have been, in principle, the first. It won't have taken place as such. Its rightful place is the other's. The crypt keeps an undiscoverable place, with reason.

What is a crypt?

All that can be said against a preface, I have already said. The place of what absence—of what of whom of what lost text—does the preface claim to take? Thus disposing and predisposing [of] a first word that does not belong to it, the preface—a crypt in its turn—will take the form of what pre-serves (and ob-serves me here), the irreplaceable.

I shall not engage myself beyond this first word in (the) place of an other. Not even beyond a first piece of a word, that which remains of a *symbol* (one

of conscience," subjective interiority. The word *fors* thus "means" both interiority and exteriority, a spatial problematic that will be developed at great length here in connection with the "crypt." In the translation I have tried to convey this double-edged meaning by translating *le for intérieur* as "the inner safe" and by using the word "save" to mean, among other things, "except for." Another thing the title *Fors* suggests is *Fore*word (*Hors*-livre), which is in fact the function of this text: It was written as an introductory essay to the book by the late analyst-poet-translator Nicolas Abraham and his colleague Maria Torok entitled *Cryptonymie: Le verbier de l'Homme aux loups* (Paris: Aubier-Flammarion, 1976), typically referred to here as *The Magic Word*. This book is a collection of analytical writings dealing mainly with the "Wolf Man," a Russian émigré who was a patient of Freud and other analysts and who, late in life, wrote his own memoirs (translated into English by Muriel Gardiner as *The Wolf-Man by the Wolf-Man*. New York: Basic Books, 1971). Freud's analysis of the Wolf Man, which is reprinted by Gardiner, can be found in volume 17 of *The Standard Edition of the Complete Psychological Works* under the title *The History of an Infantile Neurosis*. The present translation of Professor Derrida's introduction was sponsored by the Kanzer Seminar on Psychoanalysis and the Humanities at Yale University. It first appeared in *The Georgia Review* XXXI, no. 1 (Spring 1979): 64–116.

The word "Anglish" [*anglés*] is a portmanteau word combining "angled" and "English." The expression also alludes to the French poet Mallarmé's strange book *English Words*, in which lists of words are grouped according to their initial sounds in order to demonstrate the "motivation" of the sign, the nonarbitrary relation between the signifier and the signified, the essential core of meaning conveyed by letters alone.

All references in *Fors* are to original editions. Since the publication of *Cryptonymie*, the works of Nicolas Abraham have been collected in *L'écorce et le noyau* (1978), *Jonas* (1981), and *Rythmes: De l'oeuvre, de la traduction et de la psychanalyse* (1985), all published by Aubier-Flammarion.

of the objects of the book) in the name of an engagement, of what is engaged and bound, within the very partition of the title: the name "crypt" even before any cryptonymy. I'll stop here, already (*vault* to a stop), setting down on the edge of the crypt the little blank stone of a scruple, a voiceless word for thought alone, on the sole path, in order to engage others to it, of a crypt.

What is a crypt?

Not a crypt *in general*, but *this* one, in its singularity, the one I shall keep coming back to? The form of this question will henceforth precede those that, ever since philosophy began, have been called *first*: what, originally, is a Thing? What is called Thinking? The Wolf Man's Verbarium (here I'm vaulting ahead) indicates that the Thing is to be thought out *starting from* the Crypt, the Thing as a "crypt effect." The Verbarium no longer conforms to any law and order — certainly not to philosophical order, which thus finds itself moved, to the point of no return, by a psychoanalytical lever — but neither does it abide by the common order of psychoanalysis. *This* crypt no longer rallies the easy metaphors of the Unconscious (hidden, secret, underground, latent, other, etc.), of the prime object, in sum, of any psychoanalysis. Instead, using that first object as a background, it is a kind of "false unconscious," an "artificial" unconscious lodged like a prothesis, a graft in the heart of an organ, within the *divided self.* A very specific and peculiar place, highly circumscribed, to which access can nevertheless only be gained by following the routes of a different topography.

To invert the order of questions, no longer to consider the name "crypt" as a metaphor in any ordinary sense, would perhaps be to go on — starting with psychoanalysis and, within it, starting from a new cryptology — to an *anasemic*[1] retranscription of all concepts, to that "radical semantic change that psychoanalysis has introduced into language."[2] About this anasemic "conversion" that procedes by "designifying," along the lines of an "antisemantics," more remains to be said. But it must nevertheless be designated immediately as the very condition of the whole enterprise, its element and its method. Instead of claiming to have access to this crypt through the ordinary meaning or common figure of a crypt, we must bend with a movement that it would be too simple, linear, and unilateral to think of as the *opposite* of that type of access, as I hastily described it above, as if, by anasemia, the movement consisted of going *back* toward the rightful place and the proper meaning from *out* of this crypt. Nevertheless, *it remains* that the question "What is a crypt?" can no longer, it seems to me, be posed.

Neither a metaphor nor a literal meaning, the displacement I am going to *fol-low* here obeys a different *tropo*graphy. That displacement takes the form of everything a crypt implies: *topoi, death, cipher.* These things are the crypt's *same.* They can be neither dissociated nor hierarchically ordered. They do not form a multiplicity of separable predicates, the contingent or essential attributes of a crypt. Their being together did not just happen; their *unity* is irreducible only with respect to the crypt they constitute through and through: That unity is only *thinkable* from out of *this* crypt, here.

1. *Topoi* [*Les Lieux*]

What is a crypt? No crypt presents itself. The grounds [*lieux*] are so disposed as to disguise and to hide: something, always a body in some way. But also to disguise the act of hiding and to hide the disguise: the crypt hides as it holds. Carved out of nature, sometimes making use of probability or facts, these grounds are not natural. A crypt is never natural through and through, and if, as is well known, *physis* has a tendency to encrypt (itself), that is because it overflows its own bounds and encloses, naturally, its other, all others. The crypt is thus not a natural place [*lieu*], but the striking history of an artifice, an *archi-tecture*, an artifact: of a place *comprehended* within another but rigorously separate from it, isolated from general space by partitions, an enclosure, an enclave. So as to purloin *the thing* from the rest. Constructing a system of partitions, with their inner and outer surfaces, the cryptic enclave produces a cleft in space, in the assembled system of various places, in the architectonics of the open square within space, itself delimited by a generalized closure, in the *forum*. Within this forum, a place where the free circulation and exchange of objects and speeches can occur, the crypt constructs another, more inward forum like a closed rostrum or speaker's box, a *safe*: sealed, and thus internal to itself, a secret interior within the public square, but, by the same token, outside it, external to the interior. Whatever one might write upon them, the crypt's parietal surfaces do not simply separate an inner forum from an outer forum. The inner forum is (a) safe, an outcast outside inside the inside. That is the condition, and the stratagem, of the cryptic enclave's ability to isolate, to protect, to shelter from any penetration, from anything that can filter in from outside along with air, light, or sounds, along with the eye or the ear, the gesture or the spoken word.

Caulked or padded along its inner partition, with cement or concrete on the other side, the cryptic safe protects from the outside the very secret of its clandestine inclusion or its internal exclusion. Is this strange space *hermetically* sealed? The fact that one must always answer *yes* and *no* to this question that I am deferring here will have already been apparent from the topographical structure of the crypt, on its highest level of generality: The crypt can constitute its secret only by means of its division, its fracture. "I" can *save* an inner safe only by putting it inside "myself," *beside(s)* myself, outside.

What is at stake here is what takes place secretly, or takes a secret place, in order to keep itself *safe* somewhere in a self. Before knowing whether such a fort is hermetic, let us set aside the name *hermetics* to designate the science of cryptological interpretation. It is not a form of hermeneutics, as we shall see, and it begins with a reconnaissance of the territory [*lieux*].

Before turning our minds to the break-in technique that will allow us to penetrate into a crypt (it consists of locating the crack or the lock, choosing the angle of a partition, and forcing entry), we have to know that the crypt itself is *built* by violence. In one or several blows, but whose marks are at first soundless. The first hypothesis of *The Magic Word* posits a preverbal traumatic scene that would have been "encrypted" with all its libidinal forces, which, through their contradiction, through their very opposition, support the internal resistance of the vault like pillars, beams, studs, and retaining walls, leaning the powers of intolerable pain against an ineffable, forbidden pleasure, whose locus [*lieu*] is not simply the Unconscious but the Self.

That supposes a redefinition of the Self (the system of *introjections*) and of the fantasy of *incorporation*. The Wolf Man would have had to have incorporated within him, in his Self, his older sister: his sister as seduced by the father and trying to repeat the same scene with her brother. And by the same token, the Wolf Man, the brother, would also have had to have incorporated the father's place, the paternal penis confused with his own. The violence of the mute forces that would thus be setting up the crypt does not end with the trauma of a single unbearable and condemned seduction scene—condemned to remain mute, but also condemned as a building is condemned, by official order of the court. A forum is always defined, from the start—and this will be concretely verified in this case—as a politico-judicial instance, something more than a dueling ground, but like a dueling ground requiring a *third*, a witness; a tribunal preparing a case, summoning before it for indictments, statements of counsel, and sentencing, a multiplicity of persons called up by *sub poena*. But here the inner safe cannot be called the "jury box" of consciousness,[3] even though it is enclosed within the forum of the self. The seduction scene alone is not sufficient. What is needed, still mute, is the contradiction springing from the incorporation itself. It ceaselessly opposes two stiff, incompatible forces, erect against each other: "deadly pleasure" . . . "two contradictory demands: that the Father's penis should neither *come* [*ne jouisse*] . . . nor go [*ni ne périsse*]." Without this contradiction within desire, nothing would be comprehensible: neither the relative solidity of the crypt—what architects call "the resistance of the materials" that balances the pressures, repels intrusions, foresees collapse, or in any case delays it, tries to compute, like miners, the moment a shaft should be allowed to cave in—nor the hermeticism and the indefatigable effort to maintain it, nor the failure of that effort, the permeation from within or from without, seeping through the crypt's partitions, passing from one part of the divided Self to the other, engraving itself upon several surfaces along the angular lines that we will identify later and that always follow the division of a "fantasmatic double(ness)," each fantasy being "double and opposed."

The "indelible mark" (a mark that is at first prelinguistic) left by the incorporation of the seductress sister forms a contradiction, enclosed, entombed, encysted inside the Self. This is not a solution, rather the opposite of one, but it allows for the easing of the conflict (by feigning its internalization) between the aggressiveness and the libido that are directed toward the Object. The crypt is always an internalization, an inclusion intended as a compromise, but since it is a parasitic inclusion, an inside heterogeneous to the inside of the Self, an outcast in the domain of general introjection within which it violently takes its place, the cryptic safe can only maintain in a state of repetition the mortal conflict it is impotent to resolve.

Introjection/incorporation: Everything is played out on the borderline that divides and opposes the two terms. From one safe, the other; from one inside, the other; one within the other; and the same outside the other. Before ever deciding to take a new look at the case of the Wolf Man, Nicolas Abraham and Maria Torok had submitted the concept of introjection to a rigorous reelaboration. First introduced by Ferenczi in 1909, and later seen tracing its problematic way through the works of Freud, K. Abraham, and Klein, introjection, as defined by Ferenczi, is the process by which autoerotic cathexes are extended. By including the object—whence the name introjection—the process expands the self. It does not retreat; it advances, propagates itself, assimilates, takes over. "I emphasized the idea of 'inclusion' in order to say that I conceive of all object-love (or all transference), both in a normal subject and in a neurotic . . . , as an enlargement of the Self, that is, as an introjection. Basically, a person's love can be directed only toward himself. Insofar as he loves an object, he adopts it as a part of his Self" (Ferenczi). Referring to this definition, Maria Torok goes on to point out that introjection includes not only the object but also the instincts and desires attached to it.[4] In contrast to the widespread tendency to confuse the terms introjection and incorporation, she traces a rigorous demarcation between them. That boundary is indispensable to the localization of the crypt, for it surrounds, within the Self (the set of introjections), the cryptic enclave as an extraneous or foreign area of incorporation. According to Freud's *Mourning and Melancholy* (which was written between the Wolf Man's first analysis and the publication of *The History of an Infantile Neurosis*, the two texts being more or less contemporaneous), the process of incorporation into the Self provides an economic answer to the loss of the object. The Self tries to identify with the object it has "incorporated." Thanks to what Maria Torok calls "temporization," the self recuperates its previous cathectic investments from the lost object, while waiting for a libidinal reorganization. Sealing the loss of the object, but also marking the refusal to mourn, such a maneuver is foreign to and actually opposed to the process of introjection. I pretend to keep the dead alive, intact, *safe (save) inside me*, but it is only in order to refuse, in a necessarily equivocal way, to love the dead as a living part of me, dead *save in me*, through the process of introjection, as happens in so-called normal mourning. The question could of course be raised as to whether or not "normal" mourning preserves the object *as other* (a living person dead) inside me. This question—of the general appropriation and safekeeping of the other *as other*—can always be raised as the deciding factor, but does it not at the same time blur the very line it draws between introjection and incorporation, through an essential and irreducible ambiguity? Let us give this question a chance to be reposed. For Maria Torok, "incorporation, properly speaking," in its "rightful semantic specificity," intervenes at the limits of introjection itself, when introjection, for some reason, fails. Faced with the impotence of the process of introjection (gradual, slow, laborious, mediated, effective), incorporation is the only choice: fantasmatic, unmediated, instantaneous, magical, sometimes hallucinatory. Magic (the Wolf Man himself will resort to a "magic word" to silently commemorate—his word is also a "word-thing" and a "mute word"—the act of incorporation)—magic is already recognized, in the 1968 article, as the very element of incorporation. Anasemia of reading: The new concept of incorporation thus tells us more about magic than the ordinary conception of magic—which everyone thinks he is sure of—reveals about an aspect of incorporation. The inaugural text about the "exquisite corpse" also identifies the *secret* or *cryptic* character of incorporation. With the real loss of the object having been rejected and the desire having been maintained but at the same time excluded from introjection (simultaneous conservation and suppression, between which no synthesis is possible), incorporation is a kind of theft to reappropriate the pleasure object. But that reappropriation is simultaneously rejected: which leads to the paradox of a foreign body preserved as foreign but by the same token excluded from a self that thenceforth deals not with the other, but only with itself. The more the self keeps the foreign element as a foreigner inside itself, the more it excludes it. The self *mimes* introjection. But this mimicry with its redoubtable logic depends on clandestinity. Incorporation negotiates clandestinely with a prohibition it neither accepts nor transgresses. "Secrecy is essential," whence the crypt, a hidden place, a disguise hiding the traces of the act of disguising, a place of silence. Introjection speaks; "denomination" is its "privileged" medium. Incorporation keeps still, speaks only to silence or to ward off intruders from its secret place. What the crypt commemorates, as the incorporated object's "monument" or "tomb," is not the object itself, but its exclusion, the exclusion of a specific desire from the introjection process: A door is silently sealed off like a condemned passageway inside the Self, becoming the outcast safe: "A commemorative monument, the incorporated object marks the place, the date, the circumstances in which such-and-such a desire was barred from introjection: like so many tombs in the life of the Self" (Torok, "Maladie du deuil"). The crypt is the vault of a desire. Like the *conceptual* boundary line, the *topographical* divider separating introjection from incorporation is rigorous in principle, but in fact it does not rule out all sorts of original compromises. The ambiguity I mentioned earlier (reappropriation of the other *as* other) actually makes the compromise irreducible. Although it is kept secret, the fantasy of incorporation can and even must "signify," in its own way, the introjection it is incapable of: its impossibility, its simulacrum, its displacement. Of course, if one starts out with the possibility of compromise and passageways, and with the structural semi-permeability of the partition (which "the existence of such a vault is designed to block"[5]), rather than with the partitions themselves and the spaces they divide, one could be tempted to see a simple polarity, a polarized system (introjection/incorporation) rather than the intractable, untreatable rigor of their distinction. But in actual clinical practice, one has to be sensitive to the sometimes massive, spectacular opposition between *tendencies* in a bipolar mechanism, in all the compromises and negotiations it permits. And these tendencies can be analyzed only be starting out with a rigorous dissociation, even if the purity of such a dissociation remains in fact only a theoretical ideal.

The possibility of this dissociation, whose line of fracture takes the very form of a cryptic space (not a simple opposition but the excluding inclusion of one safe within the other), propagates and diffuses its effects on the entire topography and on the whole of metapsychological conceptuality. Putting an end to the vague notion of "panfantasism," it allows for a strict delimitation of what a "fantasy" is. Incorporation is of the order of a fantasy. What is the criterion? A fantasy *does not coerce*, it does not impose, as Reality[6] does (Reality as redefined in a metapsychological sense, with but an anasemic relation to the traditional philosophical, judicial, scientific, etc., uses of the word), from within or from without, any topographical transformation. In contrast with Reality, the fantasy tends to maintain the order of the *topoi*. All the clever tricks it can deploy obey a conservative, "narcissistic" finality. It is precisely this kind of resistance, refusal, disavowal, or denial that designates Reality as such: Reality is that which would require a change of place, a modification of the topography. This definition serves as a keystone: in the architecture of the crypt, doubtless, but also in the theoretical construction of *The Magic Word*: "It is admitted that it [the fantasy], whether or not it is conscious, has as its function to maintain the topography in the same position. The Wolf Man's fantasies cannot be without relation to the contents of the crypt, and that relation can even be one of preservation, of conservation."

Reality, that about which nothing should ever be known or heard of, would thus be in an essential relation with the secret. "The metapsychological concept of Reality refers back, in the psychic apparatus, to the place where the secret is buried."[7] The concept of Reality is thus indispensable to the *situation* of the crypt. And by the same token it is necessary to a sort of structural *multiplicity* in the cryptic incorporation: The crypt must always incorporate *more than one* and behave toward it in *more than one way*. *More than one*: The secret of the cryptophore must be shared, at least with a "third"; that is what makes a secret a secret. *More than one way*: The incorporated third is held *in* so as to be crossed *out*, kept alive so as to be left for dead; the excluded third parties are suppressed but for that very reason implicated, enveloped by the scene: " . . . a third party the locus of an undue pleasure and . . . other third parties, left out, and thus − by that very pleasure − suppressed."[8] From out of the Wolf Man's crypt a whole assembly of witnesses will be summoned (the *forum*) but also a whole strategy of testifying will be deployed. Anyone will be *cut off* at any time: Witnesses will testify by interrupting, butting in, taking the words out of each other's mouth, blurting out confessions through a kind of infallible inadvertence, confirming by cross-checking, being wounded on the angular cutting edge of the partitions that carve up the *forum*. The topography is fragmented by the secret. The cryptic enclave, between "the dynamic unconscious" and the "Self of introjection," forms, inside the self, inside the general space of the self, a kind of pocket of resistance, the hard cyst of an "artificial unconscious." The interior is partitioned off from the interior. The most inward safe (the crypt as an artificial unconscious, as the Self's artifact) becomes the outcast (*Hormis*: except for, save, *fors*), the outside (*foris*) with respect to the outer safe (the Self) that includes it without comprehending it, in order to comprehend *nothing* in it.[9] The inner safe (the Self) has placed itself outside the crypt, or, if one prefers, has constituted "within itself" the crypt as an outer safe. One might go on indefinitely switching the place names around in this dizzying topology (the inside as the outside of the outside, or of the inside; the outside as the inside of the inside, or of the outside, etc.), but total con-fusion is not possible. The parietal partitions are *very* solid. Maintained by "conservative repression," the dividing wall is *real*.[10] So is the inclusion. Doubtless the Self *does* identify, in order to resist introjection, but in an "imaginary, occult" way, with the lost object, with its "life beyond the grave." Doubtless this "endocryptic identification" designed to keep the topography intact and the place safe, remains fantasmatic, cryptofantasmatic. But the *inclusion* itself is real; it is not of the order of fantasies. The same can be said of the partitions set up for that purpose, and thus of all the divisions in the topographical structure.

The elements of this topographical analysis had been brought out *before* but also, from 1968 to 1975, *through* a new reading of the case of the Wolf Man. The original premises were confirmed, enriched, sharpened by the test. By the time *The Magic Word* was finished, a whole theory of the symbol (which had been in the process of elaboration for more than fifteen years)[11] could be measured against the hypothesis of the cryptic cleft inside the Self and of the "particular type of unconscious." The "fractured symbol" marked with "indetermination" by the absence of its other part, of its unconscious "cosymbol," can undergo a "supplementary" break: no longer the break that affects the original unity of the presymbolic order and that gives rise to the unconscious, but the break that would "fragment the symbolic raw material" until it constituted a subject particularly resistant to analysis, a subject carrying within him a "puzzle of shards about which we would know nothing: neither how to put it together nor how to recognize most of the pieces." The cryptic fortress protects this analysis resister by provoking the symbolic break. It fractures the symbol into angular pieces, arranges internal (intrasymbolic) partitions, cavities, corridors, niches, zigzag labyrinths, and craggy fortifications. Always "anfractuosities," since they are the effects of breakages: Such are the "partitions of the crypt." Thenceforth the wall to pass through will be not only that of the Unconscious (as is the case with the *single* word-thing or repressed cosymbol) but the angular partition within the Self. *That* is the "supplementary" hypothesis. It requires (as in the blackness and rarefied air of all crypts the image of a night light, its flame flickering with the slightest draft) that some sort of *lucidity* light up the inner partition of the splintered symbol. Within the crypt, in the Self, a "lucid, reflecting instance" enlightens the crossing of the dividing wall and oversees the disguises, "each fragment being conscious to itself and unconscious to the 'noncrypt' (what is outside the crypt)" " . . . these are the particularities that govern the intrasymbolic and not cosymbolic [i.e., belonging in the Unconscious] relations of the *word*."

When one part of the self that is split by the crypt speaks to the other in order to say, *like* an unconscious, in the manner of the unconscious, *Wo Ich war soll Es werden*,[12] it is a stratagem for keeping *safe* a place or rather a no-place in the place, a "maneuver to preserve this no-place in the spot where the most extreme pleasure can no longer occur, but due to which that pleasure can occur elsewhere." This place, the place of the excluded word-thing, of the nonsymbolizable, is subject to a "true repression" that thrusts it into the Unconscious, from out of which we will see it act, live, return. But in order to explain the disguises (verbal, visual, or symptomatic) under which it then returns, this symmetrical unconscious cosymbol must also, in its topographical structure (and we are concerned only with the latter for the time being), be fragmented, cleft by a dividing line that prolongs the dividing line of the symbol, of the intrasymbolic place. That is one of the most difficult, concentrated passages in *The Magic Word*, it seems to me, — the most pregnant, one might say, with the whole problematic's actual and future elaboration. It is here that *the Thing* is named, named in the text; it is called Thing but also unnamable Word-Thing, the "mute word." *Thing* would be that formation that is "complementary in the Unconscious" to a cosymbol fractured along the *same* line as the symbol. The "Thing in the cryptic Unconscious" implies, if not a crypt in the Id, at least a "divided Id," corresponding to the crypt in the Self. The topography is "twice cleft." "This must be admitted, otherwise the word *tieret*, the Thing, would not need to come back as an undecipherable symbol."

One cannot gain access to the thought about the Thing without a thought about the Topos and, within it, as an essential possibility, about the Crypt. But no topocryptography can exist in the absence of the determination of this singular "beyond-place" or "no-place" [*non-lieu*]. The topography of the safes requires us to think—we have just confirmed this—about a no-place or non-place within space, a place as no-place. It is necessary to keep, *save* (except for, *hormis*, *fors*) (,) in a no-place the *other* place. And according to the judicial mind set present to any thought about the *Thing* [*chose*, *causa* (also "thing" in Old English means "assembly"—Trans.)] (its anasemic determination is no longer contained within an area of discourse called "law"), the no-place, nongrounds, *non-suit* [*non-lieu*] is designed to indicate, at the close of a hearing, that no suit ever took place, that the suit *should not have taken place*, or *should have not taken place*. It is not an acquittal. It is more or less than the acquittance of a debt, or of a crime, or of a forbidden pleasure. It indicates that the space of acquittal or engagement should never even have been drawn up. The trauma and the "contradictory" incorporation should (not) have taken place. The topography of the crypt follows the line of a fracture that goes from this no-place, or this beyond-place, toward the other place; the place where the "pleasure's death" still silently marks *the* singular pleasure: safe.

2. Death (*Atopos*)

Thus, the cryptic place is also a sepulcher. The topography has taught us to take a certain nonplace into consideration. The sepulchral function in turn can signify something other than simply death. A crypt, people believe, always hides something dead. But to guard it from what? Against what does one keep a corpse intact, safe both from life and from death, which could both come in from the outside to touch it? And to allow death to take no place in life?

When the word-thing *tieret* is buried (in the unconscious, in fact, as the cryptic Unconscious's Thing), it is "interred with the fallacious fiction that it is no longer alive." The inhabitant of a crypt is always a living dead, a dead entity we are perfectly willing to keep alive, but *as* dead, one we are willing to keep, as long as we keep it, within us, intact in any way save as living.

The fact that the cryptic incorporation always marks an effect of impossible or refused mourning (melancholy *or* mourning) is ceaselessly confirmed by *The Magic Word*. But at the same time the incorporation is never finished. It should even be said: It never finishes anything *off*. First, for the following general reason: It is worked through by introjection. An inaccessible introjection, perhaps, but for which the process of incorporation always carries within it, inscribed in its very possibility, the "nostalgic vocation."[13] Next, because it always remains contradictory in its structure: By resisting introjection, it prevents the loving, appropriating assimilation of the other, and thus seems to preserve the other *as* other (foreign), but it also does the opposite. It is not the *other* that the process of incorporation preserves, but a certain topography it keeps safe, intact, untouched by the very relationship with the other to which, paradoxically enough, introjection is more open. Nevertheless, it remains that the otherness of the other installs within any process of appropriation (even before any opposition between introjecting and incorporating) a "contradiction," or better, or worse, if contradiction always carries with it the *telos* of an *Aufhebung*, let us call it an undecidable irresolution that forever prevents the two from closing over their *rightful, ideal, proper* coherence, in other words and at any rate, over *their death* ("their" corpse). Finally, whatever the redoubtable difficulties of the idiom, the incorporation that gives rise to the Wolf Man's crypt is contradictory in the very singularity of its libidinal content: "a contradiction within the very desire" of the man who wanted his father and sister dead. Once he had incorporated his sister—"the only way to love her in order to keep from killing her and to kill her in order to keep from loving her"—he had to incorporate the person who seduced her: the father. The identification between the two penises both internalizes the contradiction and makes it insoluble. The incorporated object (Father-Sister) must be both killed and kept safe so as to prevent it from carrying off the "common penis into the grave." One could say that the cryptic forum is the general theater of all the maneuvers, of all the transactions made to prevent the contradiction from turning into a catastrophe, into one of the two catastrophes between which one has but to choose. In fact, beyond all the catastrophes (which could euphemistically be called "secondary") that recurred periodically in the Wolf Man's life, it must first be recognized that the crypt is itself the catastrophe, or rather its monument. In trying to destroy it—this is what is so catastrophic—he can only consolidate it.

That is, for example, how the *nose language* functions. "The crypt on his nose like a rebus" is the symptom of the sought-for but impossible compromise. We will find out later what word is being paraded around here. For the time being we shall consider only the contradiction between the libidinal forces that enter into its composition. When Freud, in 1923, seems to him in danger of dying, the Wolf Man tries to *save the analyst* threatened by death, to save Father whose place Freud has taken by saving Sister from suicide (she occupies the same place as that later occupied by Ruth Mack Brunswick), by curing her. The Therapist, whom he has also set up within him, will be saved if he saves his sister on the night before her suicide, when she was blaming the pimples on her face as the cause of her feeling of desperation. But in attempting to cure her (to cure himself and to cure everyone else), he is also trying to "make Father die by bringing him back to life." The terrifying logic of this insoluble contradiction is that the Wolf Man can only wish to eliminate the crypt (the incorporation of the Father-Sister couple), or even express that wish to the analyst, by killing within him all the dead figures, which are thus still alive and consequently intolerable, that is to say (without saying), by silently consolidating the crypt. The crypt is thus built (whence it derives both the hermeticism of a stronghold or strongbox—safe—and a certain ceaselessly threatening instability) through the double pressure of contradictory forces: It is erected by its very ruin, held up by what never stops eating away at its foundation. Whence, to this day, the indefatigable vigilance employed in accomplishing the impossible murder and, simultaneously, in saving from an inevitable murder, already perpetrated, the couple—a dead man and a live girl, a living man and a dead girl—a living death outside him inside him, within his most outcast inner safe. His force and his fortress are made of their death as much as of their life. This tireless compulsion is shown, in *The Magic Word*, *working*, always the same, throughout all the clinical material, the verbal or preverbal marks, the symptoms, the dreams, the representations of words or things. In constructing the crypt, in letting the crypt construct and consolidate itself, the Wolf Man wants to save the living death he has walled up inside him. That is, *himself*—the lodging, the haunt of a host of ghosts, and the *dramatic* contradiction of a desire, a desire that is, however, no longer even his.

Along the way, we have seen, he wanted to save two of his analysts (a Father and a Sister, separately or combined), and even to save the perpetuation of the analysis. To save the analyst, and even the analysis, what does that mean? Are there not at least two rescues in this case, or two salvations, one of which mimes the other in order to avoid it, just as incorporation simulates introjection, for which it has a "nostalgic vocation"? But where does the logic of such a simulacrum lead us?

Look at the writing of *The Magic Word*: It is a singular tale, certainly, the tale of the *drama* of the Wolf Man, but also the pulsing, rhythmic, step-by-step tale of the act of deciphering, decrypting, itself dramatic, the tale of a tale, of its progress, its obstacles, its delays, its interruptions, its discoveries all along a labyrinth; of its entrance hall, its corridors, its angles. The analysts' desire (there are two analysts and the question of desire becomes less simple than ever) is fully engaged in the tale; it is never left obscure. That desire invests the entire space, is part of the operation, and even gives it its first push.

And that desire is also the desire to save. To save whom, to save what? Not the Wolf Man: It is too late. A short discussion, near the end, asks: "*Can the Wolf Man be analyzed, and how?*" It notes the difficulty of recognizing a "true transference" from the moment that the Wolf Man "was his sister." It would have been necessary to challenge the "judicial instance" that set Sergei up as the judge over the criminal father. Without expecting any transference, it "would have been necessary" to put in question the "juridical code" on which the blackmail of the governess with her English words depended, to set in opposition the analytical comprehension of the father to a repressive juridicality and reach back all the way to an analysis of the grandparents, or even of the paternal great-grandparents. The only occurrence of the word *safe* [*for*] is in this chapter where we see sketched out, insofar as it is read with another kind of analytic attention and an anasemic vigilance, the whole politico-judicial scope of this "case."

To save, then, not the Wolf Man (he was born Christmas Day, 1886, and has just signed his memoirs) but his analysis. Plus two analysts: not Freud and Ruth Mack Brunswick but the co-signers of *The Magic Word*: "An irresistible force pulls us: to save the analysis of the Wolf Man, to save ourselves."

At regular intervals, a narrator or a speaker steps forward on the stage and says "we" (the couple who signed *The Magic Word*), as in a Poe story or a Brecht play: to sum up, to measure the step reached, to present the hero of the action, that is, of a *drama*. For example, the italicized paragraph, as the curtain rises upon what is "Behind the inner world," at the beginning of the second chapter. The desire of the two "authors," of their double unit, is assumed in the first person plural, even if, outside the italics, that double unit uses the third person. The assumed desire is indeed that of *saving* not the Wolf Man but his analysis and "ourselves," the two, or the three, of them finding themselves here bound beneath the seal of a contract to be deciphered.

The Wolf Man's *drama* remains incomplete for its *hero*. But once set in motion, its *action* cannot be stopped; it must proceed *in us* inevitably to its *final outcome*. And here *our* dissatisfaction, spurred on by a providential *deus ex machina*, expounds, imagines, dreams. An irresistible force pulls *us*: to *save* the analysis of the Wolf Man, to *save ourselves*. With time the fourth act opens within us, stretches before us, and *in us* comes to fulfillment, bringing *salvation*.

1. An Impromptu Walk through a Verbarium: Cryptonyms and What They Hide

The authors arrived at this very juncture in the process of their writing, and planned to take up Freud's text again with their point of view — incorporation — in mind, when it occurred to them to consult a Russian dictionary. (emphasis mine)

In unfolding the "drama" of the Wolf Man, in deciphering the monumental record of his history, in reconstituting the hieroglyphic code (which he had to invent in order to say without saying the interdict) (they allude at one point to Champollion and the Rosetta stone), the two analysts constructed: the analysis of a crypt, of course, of a cryptography, with its language and its method; but also, inseparably, the crypt of an analysis, its "decrypted" (deciphered) crypt, its crypt in the act of decrypting, the commemorative monument of what must be kept alive and seminally active. The most precious thing of all, without doubt. Both for them and for us, even if it cannot be exactly the same thing in each case. What it was for them is held in reserve by their very designation of it, but they do not attempt, as is so often the case, to withhold it in principle from the reader, to count it out of the scene. They even offer it, at one point, to a "third ear." In saving itself, the force of their double desire is no less part of the scene. It is part of what is shown there and part of what, as is always the case with force, escapes representation.

The Wolf Man's Magic Word reads like a novel, a poem, a myth, a drama, the whole thing in a plural translation, productive and simultaneous. I am not here defining the forms or genres that would *lend themselves* (let themselves be borrowed) to a psychoanalytic exposition. I am pointing out, in the invisible intersection of these apparently formal necessities, what is unique about a procedure that has to invent its own language. And certain readers (the quick-witted type) will perhaps be surprised not to find in the style of *The Magic Word* any of the prevalent mannerisms of this or that French discourse today: within the psychoanalytic agora, outside it, or in that intermediary zone that expands so rapidly. Neither in its most exposed simplicity, its serenity (for example, we know that we are looking for something from which nothing will turn us away), and its smile (I know the patient smile of the authors, their indulgent, pitiless, and truly analytic lucidity before all kinds of dogmatism, banality, theoretical boastfulness, and conformity, the search for cheap thrills. "Hey, come on, what, or whom, is he afraid of? What does he want? What is he trying to do to us *now*?"), nor in the elliptical refinement of the most daring subtlety does this "style" resemble anything that a French reader could expect to recognize of a program he would find reassuring. A certain foreign body is here working over our household words. And, the familiar program holding no secrets for him, that foreigner will have already foreseen all the modes of refusal (internal expulsion or incorporation) that might hasten to lock him up. The feeling of foreignness does not come from the authors' mother tongue or their polyglotism, nor from the most active, insistent "references" (Freud, Ferenczi, K. Abraham, Hermann, Klein, poets from France, England, Hungary, etc.). It is attached to the Thing they are occupied with.

And *The Magic Word* calls us in turn with a tale: the tale of a novel, a poem, a myth, a drama, the whole thing translating into French what was first the analytic translation (the active hollowing-out that produces a crypt that is simultaneously attacked in the three languages that are building it), the analytic translation, that is, of a text (the Wolf Man's real "drama") that itself already constituted a cryptic translation.

First consequence: the genesis. *The Magic Word* does not present itself as a catalogue, a taxonomy, a lexical table where all the verbal species would be fixed and ordered. On the contrary, the whole thing begins at the moment the "material" is explained through the laws of its vital functioning, at the moment one refuses "to be content with a catalogue of deciphered hieroglyphics," where the genetic constitution of this cryptography is analyzed in its history starting with preverbal events, then verbal events of a singular type, where the laws of formation or displacement (in a topographical or in an economical sense), of contradiction or temporization, come to account for what has been able to *function* as a verbarium, a dictionary in several languages manipulated with an agility all the more stupefying—bordering on the incredible—for having set each language at an angle with *itself* as much as with the other two, all linear correspondence being thus effectively shattered.

But its genesis is not enough to characterize the "form" of this book. The tale recounts, certainly, besides the genesis of the "case," its own *history as a story*, staging its speakers and marking all the genres employed in this double articulation: the *novel* (family saga, the adventures of one or more subjects in a modern European society traversed by several wars or revolutions), the *drama* (a "hero" who is legion, an "action" in four acts, and even a "dramaturgy of the Unconscious on Ruth Mack Brunswick's couch," several theatrical scenes, a "recognition scene" and even a "denouement," but only, it is true, for the speakers), or the *poem* (the production of a work as language, "a single poem for several voices," as it is called, a "poem of life" in which, in addition to the Wolf Man himself, all the analysts known or unknown to him will have participated) or the *myth* (reconstruction of an immemorial origin, *in illo tempore*), or *translation* (circulation among types of writing, corporeal marks, whether verbal or not, which form a more or less [as always] idiomatic corpus and which call for the production of *another* kind of writing to translate them). But if this description is still insufficient, it is because it does not explain the necessity of this recourse to all these "forms." That necessity, it seems to me, springs in the final analysis from the *cryptic* structure of the ultimate "referent." The referent is constructed in such a way as never to present itself "in person," not even as the object of a theoretical discourse within the traditional norms. The Thing is encrypted. Not *within* the crypt (the Self's safe) but *by* the crypt and *in* the Unconscious. The "narrated" event, reconstituted by a novelistic, mytho-dramatico-poetic genesis, never appears. It requires, in addition to the temporality of deferred action on which *The History of an Infantile Neurosis* so frequently insists, that "transphenomenal" approach we recognized earlier as the most continuous movement of this research. At the very moment one recognizes that an analysis on the basis of "documents" (in this case as in the case of Schreber) is a translation of an "established" text into an "invented" text (unveiling and "creation"), at the very moment the distinction between the original and its second version is maintained, it must be made clear that that original is only an *asymptotic* place of "convergences" among all the possible translations and betrayals" [*traduttore, traditore*—Trans.], an interminable approximation of the idiom (interminable for the "original" text itself). And it must especially be made clear that the original is already marked with "fiction." If fiction already opens the possibility of an "original," the account that "translates" the original must for its part move forward "in the mode of fiction"; even if the story cannot be reduced simply to a fiction, it is like an "imaginary voyage." It is in this mode that it is related to the event that instituted the crypt, to what took (chose) [its] place outside space (the reproduction, already, with the younger brother, of a seduction scene that linked the sister to the father and that inaugurates, in an intolerable libidinal contradiction, the "first incorporation" of the crypt). The no-place proper to this arch event is here called "a conjuncture, as mythical as one likes," a "zero hour" of contradiction, a "hypothetical zero hour." The postscript to the first part emphasizes the "entirely fictional"[14] character of the preceding reconstitution. That reconstitution was about a "mythical person." We should not take this type of remark as merely the rhetoric of a prudent, modest self-irony. But neither should we hasten to oppose "science," "truth," or the "real" to this fiction. "Fictive" does not mean "gratuitous," adds the postscript. To be constrained by a certain internal logic in the original still remains the rule of translation, even if that original is itself constructed, by the structure of the "original" event, as a "cryptomythic" system. A certain type of verification is constantly at work, whose procedures can depend only on new anasemic and metapsychological stipulations, notably the new topographical definitions of the Thing, Reality, Fantasy, etc. These stipulations are both produced and tested by this type of work. By their very nature they exclude gratuitousness, they leave no freedom for reordering the story or for tampering with the internal necessity of the translations.

That a "story" [*récit*] will be produced seems everywhere inevitable and this inevitability stands in need of some explanation. "Psychoanalysis lithographica"[15] also takes the form of an autobiographical, autoanalytic narrative, even at the very moment it is forcing (into existence? open?) *another* crypt, without claiming to "confirm or invalidate (my) construction, on the level of factual reality." It is at first a "how I wrote 'Psychoanalysis lithographica,'" how I deciphered the extraordinary cryptogram "archeopterix" (central to the first dream) into its anagram "cryptorchia," and then proceeded (almost without any extratextual referent) to set up the libidinal organization that long ago decided and fixed the "genotypical" correspondences between the two "grammatosomes" (*archeopterics* and *cryptorchia*). There too, as in *The Magic Word* (the two developments overlapped and the same concepts are tried out in both texts), it is English words that pave the way. "The discovery of English as a cryptic language was a crucial step" (*The Magic Word*). In one case the English governess; in the other, an English-speaking doctor. There too, with the extra piece of luck that the word "crypt" should have been *part* of the word that was disguised, kept secret, encrypted (a crypt within a crypt, a name within a name, a body within the body), *crypt* as part of *cryptorchidie,* — the account of the analysis "from documents" also recounts from the *other* side, the object's side, that mythical founding event, that "advent" that demands from the very beginning an encrypted account, to the extent that it requires, in its very possibility, secrecy. The emphasis is mine: "It could not have *taken place* without the obligation that it be kept secret." "Psychoanalysis lithographica" frequently comes back to the necessity of "the poetic," of a "poetic truth" that loses nothing in breaking with "veracity," the scientistic, naively objectivist, or realist form of epistemological consensus. The question here is not one of reaching a perfectly matching equivalence [*adéquation*] with any "hidden reality" (although . . . , he says, smiling, "sometimes a coincidence . . . "), but rather of finding out *through what*, by what means or process, the analyzed person's discourse "becomes a work of art." "And now that has been done, it seems to me." But only another work of art, in its turn, could answer that question, and *do it*. Now *that* has been done.

Nicolas Abraham never ceased to feel the necessity, within the new type of scientific mode of verification required by psychoanalysis, of a mytho-poetic text. In 1962, his introduction to *Thalassa* [16] conveys, as through a network of translations, the Ferenczian dream of psychoanalysis as a "universal science," bioanalysis, and a new kind of philosophy capable of dealing with the questions that the writer of the introduction, very present throughout even if he says at the end that he "effaces himself," will never abandon: "the structure of the initial symbol," the "topology and physiology of symbolic sets," the "transphenomenal meaning of phenomena," etc. Such an introduction introduces *itself*, of course, sets itself on stage, steps *to the fore* [in English in the original], without holding back the "jubilant" affect, the "joy," the "deliverance" provoked by the collapse, at last, of an "impervious wall within the self." It is not yet the wall of a crypt, but only what separates still another form of rationality from a form of irrationality. But the affect is recognizable: the joy of saving or delivering something by blowing up an internal partition, of putting an end to a kind of artificial hermeticism "within the self," or rather, of putting an end to an artifact, the *quasi-natural*, though accidental, production of an artifice or of an artificial mechanism. This is the condition necessary for "scientific truth and poetic truth" to be seen as belonging to the "same essence." But inversely, the practical (practicing) discovery of this common essence will be able to knock down walls. Thus understood, *this* poetic truth neither leads us astray into the gratuitousness of literary estheticism, nor does it lead us back to the simple unveiling of a presence, to the intuition of the "thing itself" of philosophers and phenomenologists. This truth is "poetic" in the sense that it writes a text on and in a text, a hieroglyph upon a hieroglyph, a symbol (in a very specific sense of the word, determined by the whole of the research, which should not be assimilated too easily) on a symbol. The body already signs even before any "proper" name: "The language of bodily organs and functions would thus in turn be a set of symbols referring back to an even more archaic language, *and so forth*. This being posited, it would seem logically flawless to consider the organism as a *hieroglyphic text*, deposited in the course of the history of the species and which an appropriate investigation should be in a position to decipher. . . . We might add that the psychoanalytic method too proceeds by going back and forth inces-

santly between the outside and the inside, and that there is in principle no difference between the verbal behavior of a patient, the efforts of a paramecium faced
with an obstacle, the inflammatory reaction of a tissue to a chemical aggression,
and even the normal functioning of the cardiac muscle" (Ferenczi, *Thalassa*,
emphasis mine). And ten years earlier: " . . . nothing exists that is not a symbol." Or: "The *symbolized* is always the symbol of an earlier symbolized [*un
symbolisé inférieur*]."[17] The hieroglyphic model at work *everywhere* (it is often
evoked in *The Magic Word*) is more, and other, than an analogical model. It implies on the one hand, of course, that the ultimate object still remains, even as
a "proper" name or body, a text *to be deciphered*, but it also implies that that
writing is not essentially verbal or phonetic, whatever the *economic* importance
and complexity of phonetization may be. We shall nevertheless avoid the sim-
plistic, "scripturalistic" interpretation; we shall avoid omitting the "subject's
operation" or the operative functioning of the symbol: We shall avoid turning
the object-text into a substance, the "symbol-thing considered as a hieroglyphic,
or symbolic text" into a "dead symbol" (Abraham, *Le Symbole*). If these things
were not avoided, we would be faced with nothing but a "catalogue of hieroglyphics," to which *The Magic Word* can in no way be reduced: At the very moment *The Magic Word* isolates a unique "word-thing" hitherto considered dead
or lethargic, it explains the symbol's operative genesis, its vibrant, vigilant effectiveness, from the point of view of psychoanalysis, and not of philosophy, lexi-
cology, or archeology as such.

There is an extraordinary continuity, a striking coherence between the 1961
program and all the *anasemic* research of the later work. From the very first
page of the 1961 manuscript, in the first paragraph ("The Text of the Symbol")
of the first chapter ("Psychoanalysis and Transphenomenology of the Symbol"),
one recognizes *The Magic Word's* milieu: "We are accustomed to approaching
symbols as an archaeologist struggles to decipher documents in an unknown language. What is given is a thing that contains meaning. We live with the handy
prejudice that all one has to do is attach the meaning to the thing, its support,
join the semantic significations to the hieroglyphics, in order to pride oneself on
one's success in the act of deciphering. But all this process really accomplishes
is to convert one system of symbols into another, which then in turn becomes
accountable for its secret. The reading of a symbolic text does not in reality stop
at the observation of a one-to-one correspondence between terms. To fully complete the work of deciphering, one must restore the entire functional circuit,
which implies and implicates a multiplicity of teleological subjects, and within
which the symbol-thing acts as a mere relay. In other words, *to understand a
symbol is to place it back into the dynamism of an intersubjective functioning*."

In thus turning back toward the faraway premises of *The Magic Word*, I do
not mean to indulge in the facile retrospection of the *already*, in the idea of a
continuous teleology or of a future perfect. The 1961 manuscript was indeed an

indispensable step in a long elaboration. Nicolas Abraham, who was, as they say, formally educated as a philosopher, extremely attentive to problems of aesthetics, language, translation, poetics and poetic translation, read Husserl as no one, it seems to me, was reading him at that time. As was his habit, gently, obstinately, and with a tranquil sense of irony (in my memory, restricted here to a kind of parenthetical shorthand, this period is called "la rue Vézelay," two years after our meeting at a colloquium [18] where we began a dialogue that went on for almost twenty years between us, along various paths-parallel, tangential, intersecting-and through many transverse translations, within which was maintained, like a living breath of friendship, that mobile reserve that I would describe in a word dear to Nicolas Abraham and Maria Torok, as can be seen in their writings: the "authentic" [and all its synonyms] as opposed to the "alienated," to "empty words," to the "hollow words that move the ideologues, the utopians, the idolators"[19], Nicolas Abraham rejected, without letting himself be turned off by, what was then taking over as a dogma, a facile answer, an oversimplification: the incompatibility of Husserlain phenomenology with the discoveries of psychoanalysis. How could transcendental idealism, phenomenological reduction, or the return to the original givens of conscious perception, it was asked, possibly have anything in common, or anything reconcilable, with psychoanalysis? The question was not illegitimate, but it hardened into a slogan and into a misapprehension. Nicolas Abraham sought on the contrary, patiently, an effective passageway *through* phenomenology, a rigorous determination of what lay beyond it, a reinterpretation of its *content* (notably that of genetic phenomenology, through the themes of intersubjectivity, time, iteration, teleology, the original hulé, etc.) and of its *method* (intentional analysis, transcendental reduction, the discounting of already constituted theses and objects, the return to the actual constituting operations, etc.): These were the conditions for a critical break with every sort of presupposition or naiveté, whose traces psychoanalysis itself, even today, is still unevenly maintaining. A break, in particular, with every sort of psychologism.

This "transphenomenology" called for in 1961 is still at the heart of the project of arch-psychoanalysis defined by the "Introduction to Hermann."[20] Of course, the transphenomenological concept of the "hieroglyph" has been greatly enriched and complicated since that time, the notion of the "secret" has been given a new topographical or metapsychological status, the symbol-thing's role is no longer simply that of a "relay," or in any case its mediation in *The Magic Word* takes on a form that the 1961 manuscript does not expressly anticipate, the teleology of desire has become more contradictory and twisted. And most important, the two notable structures of displacement and decentralization in the more recent writings—the *crypt* as a foreign body included through incorporation in the Self, and the *ghost* effect, more radically heterogeneous insofar as it implies the topography of an *other*, of a "corpse buried in the other"[21]—these

two structures did something more, and other, than simply complete or compli-
cate the anticipations of a program. They introduced into it an essential unruli-
ness [*déportement*]. A general restructuring was required and immediately un-
dertaken, more productive than ever, refusing the artificial incorporation of the
two new structures, which would have eliminated their newness and the risks
involved in the process of restructuring.

Whereas the transphenomenological project of 1961 was still negotiating, so
to speak, with phenomenology, or at least on its fringes, "The Shell and the Kernel" ["L'écorce et le noyau"] (1968) marks, with a much more incisive gesture,
the heterogeneity of the two approaches. I would say that this heterogeneity
comes from *heterogeneity* itself, from otherness: not so much the commonly accepted otherness of the Unconscious but, more radically, the otherness that will
soon make possible the definition of the crypt as a foreigner in the Self, and especially of the heterocryptic ghost that *returns* from the Unconscious *of* the other,
according to what might be called the law of *another generation*. The phenomenology of the ego or of the transcendental alter ego, governed by the principle
of principles (the intuition of presence in self-presence), could only block the
way. In 1968 "Husserl's misconception [*contresens*] concerning the unconscious" is explicitly analyzed. It is true that Nicolas Abraham uses, as did Husserl at times to designate acts of reduction, of placing out of consideration or
in parenthesis, the word *conversion* when he is talking about the transformation
that psychoanalysis brings about or should bring about: notably in its language,
in its relation to language and to the tradition of concepts. Anasemia reverses
meaning and the meaning of meaning, and thus is indeed a sort of conversion,
but what is at stake behind this word is something entirely other than what is
at stake in a phenomenological reduction. What has to be found out here is what
happens when, beneath the paleonymy of inherited concepts, beneath the same
old words, the "radical semantic change that psychoanalysis introduced into language" ("L'écorce et le noyau") comes about. That change is never clear-cut,
unequivocal, homogeneous. It has to work with all sorts of remnants, precisely
because of the identity of the old names. It produces and keeps up the "innumera-
ble misconceptions and absurdities [*contresens*] on which psychoanalytic literature feeds." What can be understood, for example, under the word "pleasure",
of a "pleasure" that would not be felt as such, but (cf. *Beyond the Pleasure Principle*) as pain? (Let me note in passing that Maria Torok supplies an answer to
this exemplary question in her essay on the "exquisite corpse.") The theory of
anasemia is designed to define in a *systematic* way (system alone can here limit
the ceaselessly recurring ambiguity) the law of this semantic conversion. It is
a kind of theory of errata [*contresens*]. In French, the metapsychological capital
letters (the Unconscious, Perception-Conscious, the Self, Pleasure, etc.) refer,
through their artifice, to a semantic transformation foreign to phenomenological
reduction and to the quotation marks that indicate it. The domain of psychoanal-

ysis extends to the "ground of not-thought [*impensé*]" ("L'écorce et le noyau") of phenomenology. And yet this strange foreignness inhabits the same words, disguises itself in the same language and in the same discursive system. Whence the question asked in "The Shell and the Kernel": "It is within this hiatus, within this non-presence of the self to itself, the very condition of reflexivity, that the phenomenologist is standing without knowing it, to scrutinize, from the point of view of this *terra incognita*, his only visible horizon, that of the inhabited continents. Whereas the domain of psychoanalysis is situated precisely on that 'ground of not-thought' of phenomenology. To note this is already to designate, if not to resolve, the following problem: How can we include in a discourse, *any* discourse, that which, being the very condition of discourse, would by its very essence *escape* discourse? If non-presence, the core and ultimate reason behind all discourse, becomes speech, can it—or should it—make itself heard in and through self-presence? This is how the paradoxical situation inherent in the psychoanalytical problematic appears." The captialized words must thus both "designify" and refer back to the "foundation of meaning," by means of figures "absent from rhetorical treatises." We could take as a first example of this the very "figure" of the-shell-and-the-kernel. From the time it appeared in the theory of nuclearity (1961 manuscript) to its occurrence in the essay of the same name, it had undergone a long anasemic operation.

This problematic is indispensable to any revolution (theoretical or otherwise) that tries to define rigorously the strategy of its own discourse, the *form* of its irruption or its break into traditional discursive space. The irruption itself cannot be reduced to that strategy alone, of course, but neither can it, without that strategy, without that new type of "critique," protect itself against mystifications, obscurantism, and pseudo-revolutionary catchwords.

In the "Introduction to Hermann," the *anasemic* program is systematized under the name of arch-psychoanalysis. In addition to the inherent richness of that "Introduction" (presentation, parenthemes, and glossary), a reading of the "Remarks concerning the reading of Hermann, anasemia and arch-psychoanalysis" can give every moment an insight into *The Magic Word*: For example, on the subject of *topography* or *topoi* [*lieux*], we see that these words must be taken neither literally nor figuratively but as an "allusion to that without which no meaning-neither literal nor figurative-could come into being." "What we will call (intrapsychic) *topos* is the condition in us that enables us to speak of any *place* whatsoever; we will call (intrapsychic) *force* that without which we would not understand any phenomenon of *intensity*. . . . These terms attempt the impossible: to grasp through language the very source from which language emanates. . . . A psychoanalytical theory is recognized as such precisely to the extent that it operates by means of anasemias." The condition necessary in order that this "impossible," "indescribable," "transphenomenal" "X ignotum" give rise to anasemic concepts is that the phenomenon be recognized as a symbol and, by that

FOREWORD □ xxxiii

very fact, as requiring a transphenomenal *complement*. In its singular case, *The Magic Word* strictly obeys this general rule.

The "form" of the "Introduction to Hermann" is no less remarkable. It is divided: two introductions in one, a "fictive monologue" to begin with, the narration of a "poem," a poem that itself recounts the "once upon a first time," the "inaugural event" that, however "u-topian" or "u-chronological" it may have been, nevertheless "really took place": the "deciphered" poem of what took place without taking place, without having ever been present, "of what has never been." There is a memory left of what has never been, and to this strange rememoration [*anamnèse*] only a mythical narrative is suitable, a poetic narrative, but a narrative belonging to the age of psychoanalysis, arch-psychoanalysis and anasemia, "as fantastic as a fairy tale," perhaps, but "as rigorous as mathematics."

The signature, if one could still use the expression, on this arch-poem telling the arch-event of the traumatic "tearing away," vacillates between the names Imre Hermann and Nicolas Abraham: it authenticates at any rate "the autotestimony of the super(hu)manized psychoanalyst I have become." In deciphering Hermann's poem, the "translator" has written another. Through the rigorous faithfulness of the transcription, another text emerged, the same but another. One can no more separate the concept of anasemia from a certain concept of translation than one can dissociate Nicolas Abraham the analyst from Nicolas Abraham the theoretician of arch-psychoanalysis or Nicolas Abraham the poet-translator. This will perhaps become clearer when one reads the "mimed poesies" (1954), *The Case of Jonah* or *Hamlet's Ghost.*[22] Each time, the poetic translation or the psychoanalytic interpretation clears a new path for the other, orients the other without any unilateral privilege. The work of poetry writing (translating) presupposes a psychoanalytic reading, in its singular precision and in the generality of its laws (for example, the theory of the "ghost"). But the poetic translation is not an *application*, nor a *verification*, a follow-up; it belongs to the process of analytic deciphering in its most active, inaugural, groundbreaking phase. And this analytico-poetic transcription does not put the presumed author of a text on the couch, but rather the work itself. Nicolas Abraham often insists on this: "The privileged patient is none other than the poem" (*The Case of Jonah*), "the work of art (and not the artist!)."[23]

Thus, whenever *The Magic Word* proposes an operation of *translation*, that proposition can be understood in the context of this vast anasemic space.

This space is worked through from all directions, invested with the scientific value of mythical tales, with analytico-poetic transcriptions, with the project of a new psychoanalytic aesthetic and a new theory of poetic rhythm or rhyme, with a metapsychological remodeling, etc.

Three more words in connection with anasemia: the *narrative account* [le récit], the *angle*, and the *sepulcher*.

1. Even before all the reasons that impose a "narrative" or quasi-autobiographical form on this work, to the point of superposing the form of an "account" on everything – the poem, the drama, the novel, the translation (I have just indicated some of those reasons, and connected them with the new topography of an event that took place without ever having been) – the account will have been called for *within* the concept, within the workings of the concept, *by the anasemic structure*. That structure describes a story or a fable *within* the concept; the story is described as a path followed backward by the structure in order to reach all the way back beyond the origin, which is nonetheless not in any way a proper, rightful, literal meaning. The concept is re-cited in the course of this journey.

2. Anasemia creates an angle. Within the word itself. While preserving the old word in order to submit it to its singular conversion, the anasemic operation does not result in a growing explicitness, in the uninterrupted development of a virtual significance, in a regression toward the orginal meaning, as would be the case if it followed the style of phenomenology. If anasemia "goes back to the source" of meaning, as is said in "The Shell and the Kernel" and in the "Introduction to Hermann," that source is *preoriginal*. A change of direction abruptly interrupts the continuity of the process of becoming explicit and imposes on it an anasemic angulation: the effect and the *condition* of psychoanalytic discourse itself.

3. If the anasemic process inaugurates a mytho-poetic arch-psychoanalytic science that diverts its account toward *another* event that takes place where it has never been, this is because the loss of the object (for example, in the arch-trauma of tearing away, even before the distinction between mourning and the refusal or sickness of mourning) does not simply play one role among many. It is "from out of" [*depuis*] the possibility of this "loss" or of the "death" of the subject (these words to be read anasemically), from out of the possibility of a sepulcher, in one form or another, that the entire theoretical space is redistributed. The anasemic account thus has an essential relation to a sepulcher. *A fortiori* in the case (of the Wolf Man) where the trauma did not take place only once: One can less than ever dispense with a narrative account.

Thus we come back to the crypt as a sepulcher. Back to that singular crypt we have never really left.

To track down the path to the tomb, then to violate a sepulcher: that is what the analysis of a cryptic incorporation is like. The idea of violation [*viol*] might imply some kind of transgression of a right, the forced entry of a penetrating, digging force, but the violated sepulcher *itself* was never "legal."[24] It is the very tombstone of the illicit, and marks the spot of an extreme pleasure [*jouissance*], a pleasure entirely *real* though walled up, buried alive in its own prohibition. When the process of introjection is thwarted, a contradiction sets in, as we have seen, and with it that opposition of forces that constructs the crypt, props up the partitions, organizes a system of transactions, a kind of market, inside it, evaluates the *rates* of pleasure or pain (this is by definition the *forum* or *for*, the *mar-ket*place where jurisdiction, laws, rates and proportions [*fur*: the expression *au fur età mesure* is redundant][25] are determined). The very thing that provokes the worst suffering must be kept alive. The outpouring of the libido at the moment of loss (whose intensity sometimes rises to the point of orgasm) is repressed, not in and of itself, as such, but in its ties with the dead. The mourning sickness takes root in this "supplementary repression," censuring its relation to the moment of orgasmic hallucination and to the "illegitimate delectation [*volupté*]."[26] The "conservative" repression installs in the Unconscious what takes on for the Self the appearance of an exquisite corpse: apparently illegible and devoid of meaning, blurring the records by the segmented accumulation of pieces of folded sentences (the "surrealistic" effect) but also infallibly designating, when the flattened piece of paper loses its creases and reveals its challenge to semantics, the corpse of an exquisite pleasure, disguised by repression as an exquisite pain, the singular, precise, chosen (exquisite) spot where the repressed is to be exhumed. That is the spot where the therapist "must operate in order to dig up the repressed." "The pain of the self-torture which puts us on the track of the vault where the buried desire is lying (a 'here lies' in which the name of the deceased long remains illegible) is also an invitation to the analyst to proceed with the exhumation, while at the same time giving him the type of tactic appropriate to this stage of analysis: 'Accuse me'" ("Maladie du devil").

In 1968 Maria Torok had thus identified the theoretical strata on the basis of which, some years later, the analysis of the Wolf Man was to become possible: the opposition (both internal *and* external) between the process of introjective inclusion and the fantasy of incorporation; the crypic structure of incorporative inclusion (the vault, the recumbent effigy, the exquisite corpse, the localized reversal of pleasure into pain, the insoluble contradiction within desire as the "cement of imaginal fixation," the specificity of analysis as an "exhumation," etc.).

What essential particulars will be required in order to adapt these general premises to the case of the Wolf Man? What intermediary schemes? They concern most importantly the function of the Self and of language in the psychic organization of the cryptophore.

The Self: a cemetery guard. The crypt is enclosed within the self, but as a foreign place, prohibited, excluded. The self is not the proprietor of what he is guarding. He makes the rounds like a proprietor, but only the rounds. He turns around and around, and in particular he uses all his knowledge of the grounds to turn visitors away. "He stands there firmly, keeping an eye on the comings and goings of the nearest of kin who claim—under various titles—to have the right to approach the tomb. If he agrees to let in the curious, the injured parties, the detectives, it will only be to serve them with false leads and fake graves."[27]

As for language, it inhabits the crypt in the form of "words buried alive" ("De la topique réalitaire"), defunct words, that is, words "relieved of their communicative function." They no longer point to the desire via the prohibition, as in hysterical repression, which they therefore threaten to the extent that they no longer carry on the effect of prohibition. They mark, on the very spot where they are buried alive, "preserved," the fact that the desire was in a way satisfied, that the pleasurable fulfillment *did take place*.

Beyond these intermediate schemes, an essential feature distinguishes the case of the Wolf Man: the supplementary relay or delay of a *procuration*. The word does not, as I recall, appear in *The Magic Word*, but twice, in connection with the Wolf Man, in "Introjection-Incorporation" and in "The Lost Object— Me." The Wolf Man's crypt does not shelter his own lost and incorporated object, as a melancholic's crypt would, but the illegitimate object of another, of his sister, of his sister seduced by his father. Thus, if a cemetery guard, though lacking ownership of the tombs, is at least entitled to his position, the Wolf Man, on the other hand, is only a proxy (by procuration) in the position of guard.[28] At least as far as the relaying of the seduction is concerned. Hysterical to the extent that he is disappointed not to have been himself seduced by the father, he keeps the secret, he does not denounce, he does not betray, in those extraordinary "testimony" scenes, in order to "supplant" his sister. The words of his account will serve, according to this or that angle, both to speak out *and* to keep still, in order to experience maximum pleasure.

3. The Cipher (Mortgage)

A crypt, then, according to the angle of the words.

To crypt: I do not think I have yet used it as a verb. To crypt is to cipher, a symbolic or semiotic operation that consists of manipulating a secret code, which is something one can never do alone.

Up to now we have recognized the crypt as (1) a certain organization of places [*lieux*] designed to *lead astray* and (2) a topographical arrangement made to keep (conserve-hidden) the *living dead*. But the notion of a cipher, a code, had not yet seemed indispensable to the definition of the crypt: as if the ghostly bodies, the mere silhouettes, could go on floating past each other through the funereal silence of the grounds without ever exchanging a sign.

Nevertheless, what we now read here is a "crypted" text written on the very partitions of a crypt, a crypt on a crypt. But the partition does not preexist, it is made out of the very material of the text. The cipher is not deciphered *on* a parietal surface.

In postponing access to the ciphering agency of the secret code, it is mainly the "verbal" nature of the cryptic operation that we have not yet been able to situate in its necessity. And yet, on first reading, the most theatrical discovery of the crypt effects, in *The Magic Word*, seems to involve verbal machinery or machinations, often lexical or even nominal. A machine, yes, and a calculating shrewdness; the *mêkhanê* was indeed a theater of words if what the authors invoked as the *deus ex machina* of their discovery, just an instant before the denouement, first took on the form of a dictionary. More than one dictionary. But who is holding the dictionaries? Who keeps them? And can all this really be kept, in the final analysis, in the hold of a dictionary?

The longest part of *The Magic Word* discusses *sentences* of dreams with a *dialogue* structure. Everything seems to be decided, in the interpretation, from step to step, according to what one would call language criteria: the masking of the archeonyms under the cryptonyms, the return of the childhood knowledge of English, a (conscious-unconscious) translation machine almost perfect in its finality, the operation of certain words in the wolf nightmare, etc. And finally, what must be kept *absolutely* secret, *tieret*, is still a word, isn't it? a particular species of word, certainly, a mute thing too, but still "something" that could not take "place," it seems, without language? Whence, one would say once again, the necessity that the story become, infinitely enveloped in itself, the story of a story, etc. Already doubled since it recounts the history of the decipherment at the same time as it tells the object deciphered, it uncovers in that object the structure of a story. Not only, as a supplementary medium, because the documentary material takes the form of stories (notably accounts of dreams), but because the "event," the drama it re-counts is itself recognized by the analysts as a story of words, of words exchanged: words exchanged among several subjects in the dream itself, and words exchanging themselves with one another to lead the analyst astray, one word for the other from one safe to another.

Thenceforth, one will ask, isn't the crypt's cipher formed out of verbal, even nominal material? The answer to this question cannot be a simple yes or no, and its very formulation must be displaced by the object and protocol of the book itself.

The essential limitations of what I would call a "linguisticistic" reading of *The Magic Word* seem to me posted on the theoretical base of the enterprise.

1. The eventual autonomization of language strictly speaking, of *verbal* language, is comprehended, thus limited from the very beginning, from the first general premises, as an *oral moment* in the process of introjection. The mouth's empty cavity begins as a place for shouts, sobs, as "deferred filling," [29] then it becomes a place for calling the mother, then, gradually, according to the progress of introjection or autoaffection, it tends toward "phonic self-filling, through the linguo-palato-glossal exploration of its own void." One would thus witness a "progressive *partial* substitution" (emphasis mine): the "satisfactions of the mouth, full of the maternal object," would be replaced, *partially*, by "satisfactions proper to the mouth emptied of that object but filled with words addressed to the subject. . . . To learn to fill the mouth's void with words is actually a first paradigm of introjection. . . . Thus the absorption of food in a literal sense becomes introjection in a figurative sense. To pass from one to the

other is to succeed in transforming the presence of the object into an auto-apprehension of its absence. The language which is substituted in that absence, as a *figure* of presence, can only be comprehended within a 'community of empty mouths'" ("Introjecter-Incorporer").

On the borderline between the outside and the inside, itself a system of edges, the buccal orifice plays this paradigmatic role in introjection only to the extent that it is *first* a silent spot in the body, never totally ceases to be silent, and only "speaks" through supplementarity. This general rule also informs the additional limitation and the *catastrophic* reversal that will occur with the fantasy of incorporation. That fantasy transforms the oral metaphor presiding over introjection into a *reality*; it refuses to accept (or finds itself prohibiting), along with introjection, the metaphor of the substitutive supplement, and actually introduces an *object* into the body. But the fantasy involves eating the object (through the mouth or otherwise) in order *not* to introject it, in order to vomit it, in a way, into the inside, into the pocket of a cyst. The metaphor is taken *literally* in order to refuse its introjective effectiveness—an effectiveness that is always, I would be tempted to add, a form of idealization. If, on the one hand, incorporation could be said to resemble, paradoxically enough, an act of vomiting to the inside, then on the other hand a successful necrophagy in which the dead would be assimilated, and in which there would be an "alimentary communion among the survivors," would be a "preventative measure of anti-incorporation" (ibid.) No one will ever have asked the dead person how he would have preferred to be eaten: Everything is organized in order that he *remain* a missing person in both cases, having vanished, as *other*, from the operation, whether it be mourning *or* melancholy. Departed, nowhere to be found, *atopique*.

In order for the introjective metaphor to be taken literally, the limit prohibiting introjection has to be situated in the mouth—as the very paradigm of introjection. No longer able to articulate certain forbidden words, the mouth takes in—as a fantasy, that is—the unnamable thing. It is only from that point on that incorporation passes through a crypt of language (whence the "linguisticistic" effect), but this is only because the forbidden moment of the oral function had *first* been a "substitute" for or a "figure" of a wordless presence. If some sort of metaphorization had not preceded it (in the body), the process of demetaphorization [30] (which is also a hypermetaphorization) could not have pretended to ingest the unnamable thing—another way of getting rid of it. The dead object must remain dead, must be kept in his place as dead; this must always be verifiable. He must not come back, not bring back with him the trauma of loss. He must pledge, on his own, warmly, to occupy his place as dead, not to budge from it. He must thus engage himself alive. That presupposes a contract: unilateral, as is always (or never) the case. The crypt is perhaps itself that contract with the dead. The cryptophore engages itself toward the dead, grants the dead, as collateral, a mortgage within itself, a pledge within the body, a cys-

tic pocket both visible (blatant) and secret, the spot where a thanato-poetic pleasure can always catch fire again. Whence the *double* desire, the mortal contradiction assigned by every crypt. In order to keep life safe and put the dead
in one's pocket (in a "matchbox," says Genet in *Pompes funèbres*), that pocket
has to be sewn in a place near the *pudenda*, an extra flap of cloth where the most
precious thing is kept: money, a title, an active share in the stock market. Also
a hold over its carrier for his own blackmail by another who always leaves one
without resources when at night, around every corner, behind every angle in the
road, he comes to threaten a desire: your wallet or your life.

That presupposes that the cryptophore, having taken the bite (the bit) without
being able to digest it, forced to keep it in accessible and impossible reserve,
must constantly betray the cipher that seals and conceals it. To keep life safe and
put death in one's pocket, to stay death in the very sentence that decrees it: as
in Blanchot's title *L'Arrêt de mort* (*Death Sentence* and *Stay of Death*) – perhaps
a truly cryptic story.

2. In spite of its enormous range, the whole machinery of the stratagems of
language, the entire crypto*nymy* reconstituted by *The Magic Word*, would be entirely lacking in any functional relation either to the Wolf Man's drama or to the
drama of analysis, without the *instigating* force of the reconstructed or conjectured trauma, without the organization of the libidinal forces, without the
positions of the characters, without a desire doubly erect and bound within the
"unlivable contradiction of the zero hour," without the economic function, without the "economically contradictory reasons" that maintain the traumatic scene
"with its hidden words" and its excluded word; all these are so many constraining
forces ("force est . . . " says *The Magic Word* repeatedly) that do not as such
require any verbalization. It is in fact precisely *because* the verbal instance is
only a derivative effect that the word-thing could constitute itself as such, re-
become a kind of thing after the repression that cast it out. It is the topographical
possibility of the crypt, the line of demarcation that it institutes between the process of introjection and the fantasy of incorporation, which would account for,
but is not restricted to, the verbal function.

But one thing must be made clear: If it is true that nothing in this cryptonymy
is purely verbal, it is nevertheless also true that nothing appears as a thing given
directly to perception. Perception itself, like all mute pictures, falls under the
law of the cipher. All is cryptic, "hieroglyphic." Words and things are but pawns
on a chessboard. Nothing there can be perceptible or verbalizable from the first,
through and through. Without this general "hieroglyphia," we could never even
understand the mere possibility that a crypt could take place, that its fantasy
could be something other than a phenomenal or epiphenomenal illusion, that its
inclusion could be real and its effectiveness so resistant.

Within these strict limits, the "verbarium" proper conserves its vast crypto-
nymic scope, richness, and capacity for proliferation.

The first part of this book, "The Magic Word," provides the general matrix of the analysis. It is subdivided into two chapters corresponding to two phases of the research, the positioning of the investigatory apparatus and data, then the discovery. The first chapter reconstructs a traumatic scenography and the incorporation that accompanies it. It appears not to resort to any fact of language or any verbal material. All we learn in it is why the Wolf Man's desire had to remain "mute." A certain "nose language" *is* analyzed, but this is still (provisionally) a symptom in which no word can yet be read, a symptom made to be illegible in a lexical framework: a sort of writing without language, a "billboard" or "open book" covered with unpronounceable signs. The proposed translation is thus not yet that of a *rebus*. Another allusion to a mute hieroglyphic: the "mauve-colored stones" of a certain dream that "like the Rosetta stone, are awaiting their Champollion." The following chapter does not contradict the schema thus mapped out. But without hiding a certain rearrangement of the investigatory apparatus and a noticeable modification in the procedure, this time it does bring in verbal material. That material unfurls in a proliferating mass, but it is always contained, oriented, *comprehended*, at the most determinate moments of the interpretation, by the general structure of the previously recognized organization of the investigation. Why does this happen, and how?

Why: in order to explain that certain words, as a means of autotherapy, were both able and obliged to be treated as things, or even as Objects. That was indispensable to the fantasy of incorporation and to the topographical requirements already defined. If indeed the Wolf Man went on to a cryptic incorporation (the hypothesis of the first chapter), he had to have behaved in *just such a way* with words.

How: The analysts begin, at both ends of the first verbal chain to be reconstituted, with two silent scenes, two visible (visualized) "tableaux" that had to have as their end the transformation of words into things and that thus, inversely, must be read as *rebuses*. Two "images," one phobogenic, the other erogenic. We cannot yet know whether they are complementary. On the one hand, we have the original dream. Schematically: The *six* in the six wolves (the number is maintained even though it had been corrected as seven and sketched as five), is translated into Russian (*shiest*, perch, mast and perhaps sex, close to *shiestiero* and *shiestorka*, "the six," the "lot of six people," close to *siestra*, sister, and its diminutive *siestorka*, sissy, toward which the influence of the German *Schwester* had oriented the decipherment). Thus, within the mother tongue, through an essentially verbal relay this time, the sister is associated with the phobic image of the wolf. But the relay is nevertheless not semantic: It comes from lexical contiguity or a formal consonance. If one passes through the virtual expression *siestorka—buka* (siswolf) as deformed, in the nightmare of the star and the half-moon, into *zviezda-luna*, one would perhaps begin to see a confirmation.

But the sister-wolf association seems to break down in the nightmare about the skyscraper. The sister, it seems, is no longer there. The wolf *is* there, at least in the German word for skyscraper *Wolk*enkratzer, or in the other Russian word for wolf (not *buka* this time but *Volk*). However, if it is thus attested, the presence of the wolf is no longer associated with that of the sister, but only (as in the French name *Grateloup* [literally, Scrapewolf], which I propose as a substitute for skyscraper) with the semantic family that certain languages group under the intitial sounds *gr, kr, skr*, (the mechanism that interests us here in this "case" is that of these "motivations," whatever one may think about linguistic motivation in general): the Russian *skreb*, which is the root of *skrebok*, scraper-eraser, *skroït*, to sharpen, *skrip*, scraping sound, the German *Krebs*, cancer, which is like *skreb* backward, etc. The *Grateloup* family, apparently having no connection with the sister, is less unrelated, *in its name*, to her hypochondriac fears concerning the nose (scratches, scars, cancer) no doubt associated, along both semantic and phonic paths *at the same time*—quasi-homonyms *and* quasi-synonyms (the *play* between the two, without any absolute privilege of *either* the signifier or the signified, is an indispensable part of the mechanism)—with lupus seborrheus. The hypothesis according to which the sister (the seduced seductress) was replaced in her absence by this lexical abundance around the focus *Grateloup* (scrape, scratch, scar) excluded, because of the very abundance and mobility of the substitutive vocabulary, the possibility that any single word with one single meaning could have been replaced by another, according to some simple metonymic displacement. The rich, orderly polysemia of an unspeakable (hidden, crypted) word had to be lurking behind a regular—in spite of a certain amount of play—series of *cryptonyms*. But what was that unspeakable word?

At this point we take up the chain from the other end. We follow it in the direction of a second mute scene, a second visualized tableau. Grusha, the floor scrubber, with her bucket and broom, seen from the rear, and the compulsive return to this erogenic image. It is a *rebus* of a particular kind. As soon as, in contrast with Freud, we focus on the act of *rubbing*, and turn our attention to the Russian words for that act (*tieret, natieret*), we will see that the catalogue of uses (allosemes) of these two words provides us with the whole range of associations and dissociations among the ideas of rubbing and/or wounding= scratching (*tieret*: 1. to rub, 2. to grind, 3. to wound, 4. to polish; *natieret*: 1. to rub down, 2. to rub, scrub, wax, 3. to scrape or wound oneself). The skyscraper as *Grateloup* could thus relate the wolf to the pleasure obtained by rubbing. The word *tieret*, forbidden because it would betray the scene of the encrypted desire, would be replaced not by a single other word, nor by a thing, but by translations, into words or into rebus symptoms, of one of its allosemes. Cryptonymy would thus not consist in representing-hiding one word by another, one thing by another, a thing by a word or a word by a thing, but in picking out from the extended series of allosemes, a term that then (in a second-degree distancing) is translated into a synonym. The scar, for example, (real in the symptom) is the bodily, visible, theatrical representation of a synonym of one of the magic word's allosemes (to scratch or wound oneself).

It is as though the cryptonymic translation, playing with the allosemes and their synonyms (always more numerous in their open series than is indicated by a dictionary), swerves off at an angle in order to throw the reader off the track and make its itinerary unreadable. An art of chicanery: judicial pettifogging or sophistic ratiocination, but also [*chicane* = maze] a topographical stratagem multiplying simulated barriers, hidden doors, obligatory detours, abrupt changes of direction [*sens*], all the trials and errors of a game of solitaire meant both to seduce and to discourage, to fascinate, and fatigue.

It is because of the angular, zigzagging procedure of this cryptonymy, and especially because the allosemic pathways in this strange relay race pass through nonsemantic associations, purely phonetic contaminations, it is because these associations in themselves constitute words or parts of words that act like visible and/or audible bodies or things, that the authors of *The Magic Word* are hesitant to speak of metonymic displacement here, or even to trust themselves to a catalogue of rhetorical figures.

That supposes that each lexical element, whether or not it is repressed (in the strict sense of the word) as (a) thing, has an angular, if not crystalline, structure, like a cut gem, and maintains, with its allosemes or other words, contact—a contiguity sometimes semantic, sometimes formal—according to the most *economical* line or surface. One of the first consequences of this placement is the recognition of the cryptonymic character of certain meanings that had hitherto been interpreted uncircuitously and inflexibly: for example, the threat of castration. The terms in which that threat is evoked would themselves be but "cryptonyms of repressed pleasure words." The type of repression that chases the pleasure word toward the Unconscious where it functions like a thing (rather than like the representation of a thing) is different from neurotic repression: No verbalization is possible as such, which must mean that the trauma must have not taken place: no-place in any safe. Chronic constipation at most symbolizes this "retention of saying," this impossibility of expressing, of placing words on the market. In place of verbal symbolization, the floor scrubber scene makes *tieret* visible, the erogenic fantasy translates the taboo word as a rebus, and from then on functions as an undecipherable fetish.

The "word" *tieret*, subjected to a "true repression" that banishes it into the Unconscious, can thus only have the status of a word-thing. From out of the Unconscious, the *tieret*, as a Thing of the cryptic unconscious, a cosymbol marked by the *same* dividing line as the symbol broken by the crypt, can return along two routes that attest to its *double density*: the route of the alloseme that crosses the border of the Unconscious directly in order to fix itself in a tableau or a symptom (for example, in an erogenic tableau: the woman scrubbing the floor), or the route of the alloseme's synonym in the case where, as a *word* (conscious or unconscious, illuminated by the lucid reflecting agency of the crypt), it crosses the intrasymbolic crack, the partition of the crypt, without passing through the Unconscious. It is then disguised as a cryptonym in the strict sense, that is, in the form of the word. This machinery would attest to the existence of the crypt in the divided self but also to "another fate of the same word": its fetishization in the Unconscious. In both cases, the crossing of an interrupting partition follows an angular detour. That is due to the fact that the partition itself was constructed by joining polygonal or even polyhedral pieces together. Not only because of polyglotism, the dialogue between mother and nurse in the Wolf Man's dreams, but because, already within a single language, every word multiplies its faces or its allosemic sides, and multiplies the allosemic multiplication by further crossing formal grafts and combining phonic affinities.

A single example. I lift it, out of so many others, from the middle of that prodigious interpretation of dreams that *The Magic Word* deploys into an immense polyphonic poem. This interpretation of dreams, it should not be forgotten, draws its cryptonymic (in the strict sense, intrasymbolic and lexical) inferences from the hypothetical matrix: the crypt in the Self and the repression of a single word-thing *tieret* into the Unconscious. Here is the example: In order that, in the sentence *Ich stehe vor dem Kasten*, the phrase "I am standing" should mean "I am telling a lie," at least *three* combined operations are necessary: (1) A system of reversals proper to this dream. The mainspring of these reversals cannot be linguistic (neither semantic nor formal) and in another dream, *I am standing up* will indeed mean *I am not lying down* whereas here it "means" *ich liege, I am lying down*. (2) A translation from one language [German] into another [English] in the ordinary sense. Here the same *meaning* is maintained in another discourse: synonymy: *ich liege = I am lying down*. (3) A formal equivalence (a homonymic contamination, if you like) within the English language: *I am lying*, I am in a supine position; *I am lying*, I am telling an untruth. These operations belong to three essentially different systems. The passage from one technique to another is part of a particular stratagem but its possibility belongs to the hieroglyphic's polyhedral structure.

In some ways *The Magic Word* seems to implicate and develop certain Freudian propositions: less those concerning the Wolf Man himself than those touching on the splitting of the ego (*Fetischismus*, 1927; *Die Ichspaltung . . .* , 1938), or earlier, on the topographical distribution of the representations of words (the preconscious-conscious system) and the representation of things (the unconscious system). In fact, the very possibility of the cryptic structure within the divided self, as well as the analysis of the partitions in the intrasymbolic surface, proposes a total rethinking of the concept of *Ichspaltung*. Especially when, given that *tieret* is not simply the representation of a word in the Unconscious, that it is not even a representation nourishing a mnemic trace, but, in the new sense of the unconscious cosymbol, the Thing, we recognize it neither as a word nor as a thing. In the Unconscious, this "word" is a "mute word," absolutely heterogeneous to the functioning of other words in other systems. How would one be able to contain, within the opposition between words and things, the trace this "word" constitutes of an event that has never been present? The Thing does not speak and it is not a thing. Its testamentary structure organizes all the funereal pomp and circumstance of the cryptic functioning. That structure requires an entirely different graphology, an entirely other topology, an entirely new theory of the symbol.

That new theory is dealt with in the last chapter ("The Broken Symbol"). We find in it, sometimes to the letter (the process of "indetermination," the "complete symmetrical core," etc.), the program of 1961. It is now confirmed that whereas the archeonyms, the "original words" that never announce themselves openly, produce the "speech" of a "word"—not rhetorical figures but what we will here call "rhymes" (semantic or formal, through meaning, sight, or sound, or even through the absence of any rhyme), an entire poetics in fact calls for a translator-poet-psychoanalyst—*tieret*, on the other hand, *tieret* alone produces no speech at all. The pleasure it gives rise to is only that of a living tableau. But *tieret* is not contrasted with this tableau-fetish in the way that the thing itself is traditionally opposed to *its* fetish. This Thing is not the thing-in-itself philosophers speak of. It is a mark or a cipher, a piece of a cipher that can only be translated into a vast interminable sentence or into the scene of a tableau with more than one subject, more than one object, more than one entrance or exit. A trace with no present in its wake, *a Thing*, *ein Ding*, *une Chose* without a cause, "Cause" to be designified in the crypts of anasemia.

With the edification of the crypt completed, it must now be sealed. The exit will have had to be condemned and signed.

But with what name?

No crypt without edification: an edifice, an edifying speech. Take a look at the one he signs, under the title *Memoires*, with the name the Wolf Man. It consolidates the crypt: to lead the reader astray with the stamp of the final seal. But if the edification of such a safe implies more than one, always—who signs and with what ciphered seal?

He had edified a crypt within him: an artifact, an artificial unconscious in the Self, an interior enclave, partitions, hidden passages, zigzags, occult and difficult traffic, two closed doors, an internal labyrinth endlessly echoing, a singular discourse crossing so many languages and yet somewhere inside all that noise, a deathly silence, a blackout. He will die with or through the crypt within him.

As he saw it, first, as he lives it still, for he is still alive at the very moment I write this without knowing.

But who, he? Who *returns* here? where? to whom? to what?

Will it have ended up working well for him, this cryptic machination? If yes, no, if no, yes. To this day his cryptonyms had so successfully disguised his identity, scrambled the tracks of his real name (and first and foremost in the very eyes of him who says *I*), that it seemed the goal had been attained. Everything had worked out very well. But also very badly: What was kept safe was the monument of a catastrophe and the permanent possibility of its return. And it is to the extent that the crypt *closed badly* that a chance still remained: the proof. But one can never sufficiently ponder the fact that the proof came, for him, too late.

For him, but who? Would he ever have been able to read what is written *here* on his own crypt? Would it all come back to him? A ghost returning from where?

Something like his proper name is what his cryptonyms kept secret. Cryptonymy is said first of his proper name.

The Thing (*tieret*) would perhaps be the Wolf Man's name if there were any such thing here as a name or a proper name. He *gave* himself no name. *Beneath* the patronymic he received from civil society without having been present to the certification of his birth, *beneath* the second name he pretended to adopt from the international psychoanalytic society and with which he signs his memoirs and his will, another cryptonym, he seems to call himself by the name of the Thing. When in secret he dares, barely aware of it, to *call himself*, when he wishes to call himself and to call his wish by its (his) name, he calls himself by the unspeakable name of the Thing. He, but who? The Thing is part of a symbol. It no longer calls itself. The entire body of a proper name is always shattered by the *topoi*. As for the "word" that says the Thing in the word-thing, it is not even a noun but a verb, a whole collapsed sentence, the operation of a sentence and the sentence of an operation engaging several subjects, several instances, several name bearers, several places, a desire excluded precisely by that which inhabits it like a voluble contradiction, forbidding him to call himself simply, identically, by a single glorious word. And to sign one single time with only one hand, in a single continuous stroke, without breaking the seal.

If it did not enter into the possibility of such structures and such topographical machinations, the problematic of name effects and signature effects would circle around and miss the places (taking place and no-place) where everything is decided. It would continue to let us believe that the *I* signs when it authenticates the seal of an "I sign," that a proper-name phenomenon stops at what goes back to the father, to the name given by the legal father: Sergei P., or by the father of psychoanalysis: the Wolf Man. And even under the cover of these two battle names, "he" kept more than one in reserve. More than one password. In spite of its exclusive privilege, *tieret* is not the only one. The edifice of the name is supported by at least three columns:

"The Wolf Man created a magic word that, without betraying anyone, allowed him to obtain actual or sublimated sexual satisfaction: that would be the word *tieret*. But he also had a lot of other secrets . . . *goulfik*, 'fly' [of a pair of pants], the father's occult attribute, the real name of his ideal, transformed into *Wolf*, his cryptic family name. In the same fashion, he carries inside him a third disguised word, the name of his vocation as a witness: *vidietz.* . . . These three words . . . seem to constitute the three invisible but solid columns that the Wolf Man edified upon his impossible desire to occupy one place or the other in the scene he witnessed, his true 'primal scene.' These three columns have supported, for some eight decades, a booby-trapped life still struggling under the influence of the inaugural infantile hypnosis."

Little has been said about the mother's name. *The Magic Word*'s authors mention at one point the fact that, with respect to the seduction scene between father and daughter, the Wolf Man and his mother were "both under the same sign." In a certain way the Wolf Man also occupies his mother's place. Freud spoke of the Wolf Man's "identification with his mother." Within the range of this common position, the Wolf Man also signs with her name; he calls himself his mother. And in the dream of the icons, it is upon her that he confers the task of fulfilling "his own desire."

For the same reasons, a problematic of the *sign's* "motivation" or "arbitrariness," of the "mimetic" powers or illusions of language, if it did not pass through this new logic of name effects or signature effects, would simply bypass what effectively produces *both* the effect of arbitrariness *and* the effect of motivation. That problematic would to this day remain enclosed within the narrow limits: the conscious representations of "words" and "things" for a self speaking within the "internal" system of language. Within the strict limits of this "internal" functioning governed by the principle of the arbitrariness of the sign, no effect, even an illusory one, of motivation is explainable. Mallarmé's *English Words*, that strange dream of ordering the system of mimetic motivations in a language, would remain less than a game, less than "a neat little potboiler . . . about which the less said the better," an aberration with no foundation or future. But the situation would be quite different if we focused on what is produced in speech or in writing by a *desire for idiom* or an *idiom of desire*. There, a system is wrenched open within the system, general (national) codes are diverted and exploited, at the cost of certain transactions, in a type of economy that thenceforth is neither purely idiomatic (the absolutely undecipherable) nor simply commonplace (conventional and transparent).

The Wolf Man's Magic Word shows how a sign, having become arbitrary, can remotivate itself. And into what labyrinth, what multiplicity of heterogeneous places, one must enter in order to track down the cryptic motivation, for example in the case of *TR*, when it is marked by a proper-name effect (here, *tieret*), and when, consequently, it no longer belongs simply to the internal system of language. Such motivation does nevertheless function within the system and no linguistic consciousness can deny it. For example, when *Turok* (Turk, the Turkish flag in the dream of the moon with a star) says (?), means (?), translates (?), points out (?), represents (?), or *in any case* also imitates, induces the word-thing *tieret*. *For example*. In this connection, let me refer the reader to the note entitled "To weep on the tomb of a poet" (the title of a poem by Lermontov); or to the paragraph in "Introjection-Incorporation" on the sister's suicide from mercury poisoning (thing and word, *rtout*), which the Wolf Man seeks, hermetically of course, to hide from Freud: by saying that she shot herself; or again the note on the case of the hidden *TR* that tells of "the central importance for the Wolf Man of the root *tr, tor* (*tor*: the past tense of the verb *tieret*)"; or yet again the Wolf Man's letter telling of his interest in comparative linguistics and noting in passing: "I have become aware of the Germanic root of certain Russian words. For example the first name *Trude* comes from the Germanic *Trud*, which means 'force.' This old Germanic word is very likely the root of the Russian *Trud*, since in Russian *trud* designates the 'effort' one needs in order to work." (I leave an elliptical pause here for those who, like me, might be interested in the great chain: *Ich stehe*: *Ich liege*: *I am lying*, not to speak of *truth* and all its "rhymes," collected at the end of *The Magic Word*, and finally *Trud*, force, and thus an entire history of being.)

As for the secret seal of this or that proper name, the act of decrypting would be impossible, the very temptation would be prohibited, if the analyst's own desire was reluctant to engage itself, as was said earlier, and if he did not also work doubly, in his own name, on his own name.

But here, in this case, by what name should the analyst be called?

And if—verification made—a proper name is already never just one single simple vocable, if it always describes, beneath the articulation of a sentence and a scene, a multiple economy of places, instances, and safes, what happens, what supplementary complication, when the analyst is several? Double, which in no way limits, on the contrary, that plurality? When the analyst does not say *I* but, as we see it here, a distinctly *un*editorial *we*?

To whom? To what does a name go back? But a *present* going back, a going back in the present, a bringing back to the present, to whatever kind of haunting return or *unheimlich* homecoming—isn't all that already the law of the name?

In rushing, at the risk of cutting off, the question "Who signs here?" I am not asking, that goes without saying, *which* of the two, but how are they *first-named*, in their proper and common name(s): Nicolas Abraham and Maria Torok?

Striking demonstration of *Cryptonymy*: the crack in a symbol, the upright column of a name, for example, or the blank voice of a scruple, always extends out on the other side, beyond the Self.

I am thinking (detached illustration) of the paleontologist standing motionless, suddenly, in the sun, bewitched by the delicate stay of a word-thing, an abandoned stone instrument, like a tombstone burning in the grass, the double-edged stare of a two-faced Medusa.

And then I can feel, on the tip of my tongue, the angular cut of a shattered word.

Why try to say—what Nicolas Abraham lived, in his own name, what he saw in a name, in Marika Torok. And in others, among them his friends.

In you, anonymous reader in this much-sealed case.

Acknowledgments

This translation of *The Wolf Man's Magic Word* is dedicated to the memory of my professor and friend Paul de Man who recognized, before anyone else on this continent, the revolutionary nature of Abraham and Torok's works and promoted their publication. Special thanks are due to Lindsay Waters, former editor at the University of Minnesota Press, for his enthusiastic support of this project. Professors Esther Rashkin of Dartmouth College and Marian Rothstein of the University of Wisconsin-Madison have graciously read the manuscript and vastly improved the quality of my English rendition. My thanks go to the editors at the University of Minnesota Press as well as to my typist, Jacqueline Johnston, whose cheerful competence in dealing with extraordinarily difficult material coming to her from overseas surpassed all my expectations. Finally, I wish to express my gratitude to the Graduate School of the University of Wisconsin-Madison for its generous award of a research grant during my first semester of teaching there. Many others, friends in Europe and America as well as colleagues in Madison, know the due measure of my warm recognition of their encouragement.

Nicholas Rand

Translator's Introduction: Toward a Cryptonymy of Literature

1. A Theory of Readability

The University of Minnesota Press's decision to include *The Wolf Man's Magic Word* in its Theory and History of Literature Series may at first seem surprising, especially if the book is perceived as merely a psychoanalytic study of Freud's most famous patient. Sections of it were indeed delivered as lectures (from 1970 onward) to clinicians and later appeared in French psychoanalytic journals. In its French edition, with a foreword by Jacques Derrida, the book is part of a philosophical series (*Philosophie en effet*). Finally, in Germany it has been published in Ullstein's popular *Materialien* series and aimed, under the heading of Psychology and Education at students and instructors (*für Schüler und Lehrer*). The variety of fields in the history of the book's publication is certainly no accident. The editorial difficulty in classifying this work is an indication of its pivotal position at the juncture of philosophy, psychoanalysis and literature. Close scrutiny of *The Wolf Man's Magic Word* shows it to be not only a revolutionary approach to psychoanalysis but also a turning point in the history of literary criticism and the many other disciplines dealing with issues of interpretation.

Literature, philosophy, psychoanalysis, and pedagogy are only useful names for delimiting the areas of inquiry that converge in *The Wolf Man's Magic Word* and that stand to benefit from its single most important contribution: a theory of readability. A theory of readability does not define the act of reading but rather attempts to create avenues for reading where previously there were none. More radically, it demonstrates that interpretation is possible even in the face of obvious obstruction. Such a theory is primarily concerned with converting obstructions into guides to understanding. Whereas most contemporary critical approaches deal with the perception and production of meaning, or alternatively, with its potentially indefinite deferral, the theory of readability implied in *The Wolf Man's Magic Word* proposes ways in which significance can be conjectured despite its apparent absence. Rather than analyze the vicissitudes of meaning (which may include its negation) within a signifying process, Abraham and Torok's theory of readability begins by addressing the problem of establishing a signifying process.

2. The Wolf Man and Psychoanalysis in the Mirror of Narratology

The Wolf Man was born in czarist Russia, settled in Vienna two years after the outbreak of the Revolution, and died there in 1979 at the age of ninety-two. During most of his adult life he underwent various forms of psychoanalysis. His existence must therefore be considered unique in the development of the "talking cure." The Wolf Man, whose real name was Sergei Constantinovitch Pankeiev, seems to have been Freud's test case for the establishment of psychoanalysis as a transmissible school of thought. In 1918, following a crisis occasioned by the first major dissensions within the then-budding psychoanalytic movement, Freud devoted an entire work—*The History of an Infantile Neurosis*—to the Wolf Man's case. With this study of an *infantile* neurosis (i.e. a neurosis that emerges in childhood), Freud sought to provide exemplary proof of his belief that forgotten childhood disturbances during the development of the sexual instincts can lead to psychopathology. *The History of an Infantile Neurosis* was intended to shore up the cardinal tenets constituting psychoanalysis as Freud had invented it—the unconscious, infantile sexuality, and the Oedipus complex—against attacks by his former disciples, Jung and Adler, both of whom disputed the primacy of infantile sexuality and the Oedipus complex. The Wolf Man's case was called upon in the context of this debate to demonstrate three interconnected axioms that, to Freud's mind, epitomized the distinction between psychoanalysis and all other forms of psychic treatment: (1) neuroses in adults result from the vicissitudes of infantile sexuality; (2) a childhood neurosis, possibly unnoticed, must have preceded the adult one; and (3) finding the disturbing factors in the progress of infantile sexuality and elaborating them through transference leads to their dissolution, that is, to a cure of the adult neurosis.

> It will have been easy to guess from my account that the patient was a Russian. I parted from him, regarding him as cured, a few weeks before the unexpected outbreak of the Great War. . . . He then came to Vienna and reported that immediately after the end of the treatment he had been seized with a longing to tear himself free from my influence.

After a few months' work, a piece of transference which had not been overcome was successfully dealt with. Since then the patient has felt normal and has behaved unexceptionably, in spite of the war having robbed him of his home, his possessions, and all his family relationships. (*The History of an Infantile Neurosis*, in vol. 17 of *The Standard Edition of the Complete Psychological Works of Sigmund Freud*. 24 vols. Translated from the German under the general editorship of James Strachey. London: Hogarth Press, 1966, pp. 121–22)

The History of an Infantile Neurosis marked the public and triumphant aspect of the Wolf Man's existence in Freud's works. A more private and more disruptive existence is evident in several other major essays by Freud. Though rarely identified as such, the Wolf Man is recognizable in *The Uncanny (1919), Fetishism* (1927), *New Introductory Lectures to Psychoanalysis* (1932), *Analysis Terminable and Interminable* (1937), and *The Splitting of the Ego in the Process of Defense* (1938). The Wolf Man's repeated appearances in these works have been interpreted by Abraham and Torok as a clear indication of the complex role he continued to play in Freud's conception of psychoanalysis after *The History of an Infantile Neurosis*.

"From 1910 well into Freud's extreme old age, the case of this enigmatic Russian — bewitched by some secret — never stopped haunting him, drawing from him theory upon theory because he could not deliver the key words to the poem" (Abraham and Torok, "A Poetics of Psychoanalysis: The Lost Object — Me," *Sub-Stance* 43[1984]:4). Implicit here is the idea that Freud's initial analysis of the Wolf Man in fact failed to eradicate the adult neurosis. The Wolf Man returned to Vienna in 1919 with the same anal symptoms that had tortured him throughout his childhood and his early sessions with Freud in 1910. He was analyzed repeatedly by Freud's pupil, Ruth Mack Brunswick (1926–27; 1938), helped by Muriel Gardiner and a host of other analysts. The Wolf Man became an anomaly. His neurosis persisted even though its precipitating causes were fully understood. Freud wrote in *Analysis Terminable and Interminable*:

In these last months of his treatment he was able to reproduce all the memories and to discover all the connections which seemed necessary for the understanding of his early neurosis and mastering his present one. When he left me in the midsummer of 1914, with as little suspicion as the rest of us of what lay so shortly ahead, I believed that his cure was radical and permanent. (*Standard Edition*, vol. 23, p. 217)

The case of the Wolf Man (as presented in *The History of an Infantile Neurosis*) should have provided a complete paradigm for the definition and practice of psychoanalysis, but it rebelled against both. The frequent and fragmentary reappearance of the Wolf Man's clinical material cannot therefore be read as proof of the universal validity of Freud's theories elaborated in connection with his patient. Rather, it stands as evidence of Freud's unacknowledged awareness that the case had not been resolved and was in need of further work. Freud's overt response to seeing the living challenge (the Wolf Man) to his "fool-proof" paradigm (*The History of an Infantile Neurosis*) consisted of viewing the paradigm as healthy. He used material from it for further theoretical elaborations and attempted to attribute the Wolf Man's relapses to a transferential residue of the analytic relationship and to the lifeless remnants of the patient's childhood history still waiting to be eliminated.

> In a footnote added to this patient's case history in 1923, I have already reported that I was mistaken. When, towards the end of the war, he returned to Vienna, a refugee and destitute, I had to help him to master a part of the transference which had not been resolved. This was accomplished in a few months, and I was able to end my footnote with the statement that "since then the patient has felt normal and has behaved unexceptionably, in spite of the war having robbed him of his home, his possessions, and family relationships." Fifteen years have passed since then without disproving the truth of this verdict; but certain reservations have become necessary. The patient has stayed on in Vienna and has kept a place in society, if a humble one. But several times during this period his good state of health has been interrupted by attacks of illness which could only be construed as offshoots of his perennial neurosis. Thanks to the skill of one of my pupils, Dr. Ruth Mack Brunswick, a short course of treatment has on each occasion brought these conditions to an end. . . . Some of these attacks were still concerned with residual portions of the transference. . . . In other attacks, however, the pathogenic material consisted of pieces of the patient's childhood history, which . . . now came away—the comparison is unavoidable—like sutures after an operation, or small fragments of necrotic bone. I have found the history of this patient's recovery scarcely less interesting than that of his illness. (*Standard Edition*, vol. 23, pp. 217–18)

Necrotic bone in a live organism is probably as good a metaphor as any to describe "the history of the Wolf Man's recovery" as it related to the history of psychoanalysis up to 1937. Faced with the "interminable" history of his patient's recovery, Freud understandably must have wished for the spontaneous evacuation of the "residue" that deadened psychoanalytic tissue.

Although the Wolf Man's "attacks of illness" continued to assault the model of psychoanalysis proclaimed by *The History of an Infantile Neurosis*, the exemplary qualities of this case history have been used by literary critics—even elaborated as fiction. Peter Brooks states at the beginning of his essay, "The Fictions of the Wolf-Man": "The case history of the Wolf-Man's story . . . suggests a paradigm for the status of modern [narrative] explanation" (*Diacritics*

9[1979]:74). The emphasis has shifted significantly from what must have been the primary aim of Freud's demonstration in 1918—the understanding of infantile and adult neuroses in terms of the vicissitudes of sexual instincts developing into and/or regressing from specific phases of organization during childhood—to issues of fictionality.

> I want to consider how the narrativity of the structure of explanation deployed in this non-fictional genre, the case history, necessarily implicates the question of fictions through the very plotting of that narrativity and what this implies about the nature of modernist narrative understanding. (Brooks, *Reading for the Plot*. New York: Knopf, 1984, pp. 270-71)

Both Brooks and Jonathan Culler, the latter in an essay entitled "Story and Discourse in the Analysis of Narrative" (*The Pursuit of Signs*. Ithaca, N.Y.: Cornell University Press, 1981) take their cue from two additions made by Freud to the case history of the Wolf Man concerning his "intention of pursuing the discussion of the reality of 'primal scenes' " (*Standard Edition*, vol. 17, p. 57). Juxtaposing the initial summaries of the problem by Culler and Brooks, the issue seems to be whether the Wolf Man's main nightmare and his subsequent neurosis produced their own fictitious origin, or whether the nightmare and the neurosis indeed resulted from a prior and real event. In other words, is the organization of a narrative sequence, such as the case history, the effect of a primal event or its cause?

> One may maintain the primacy of the event; it took place at the appropriate moment and determined subsequent events and their significance. Or one can maintain that the structures of signification, the discursive requirements, work to produce a fictional or tropological event. At this point Freud admits the contradiction between these two perspectives, but refuses to choose between them. (Culler, *Pursuit of Signs*, p. 180)

The question of choice between trauma and fantasy, an issue in psychoanalysis in Freud's lifetime and beyond, is thrown into acute relief by these narratological excursions. For Freud either neurosis sprang from unconscious fantasies produced by conflicting infantile sexual instincts pressed up against factors inhibiting their full expansion, or psychopathology was the product of traumas, that is, outside intrusions (in the form of child abuse and/or seduction) that upset the natural course of sexuality. Freud never decided conclusively for or against one of these two modes. Narratological studies have highlighted a major split in psychoanalytic theory showing that the Wolf Man's case history relies on two discordant lines of argument. Oscillating between the primacy of trauma or that of fantasy, Freud's elaborations in *The History of an Infantile Neurosis* confound the logic of their own hierarchy by alternatively assigning priority to mutually exclusive entities.

3. Cryptonymy: A Design in Fiction or Reality?

The Wolf Man's Magic Word stakes out its territory in the space between fantasy and trauma, fiction and reality. The intermediary space between such alternatives is the original creation of the Wolf Man. Abraham and Torok begin by suggesting this within the context of a historical understanding of psychoanalysis.

> *The History of an Infantile Neurosis* is one of the most intriguing works by the inventor of psychoanalysis. Polemical in its explicit purpose, it also reflects another debate, that of the author with himself. Throughout this stirring account and within the meanderings of the theoretical discussion, attentive readers will sense a doubt—it is Freud's doubt regarding his own statements. Whether he deals with the unique process that plays a part in this treatment, or with the application to this case of established insights, Freud's exposition is marred by an insidious incredulity. These unconscious doubts are certainly not foreign to the new turn in Freudian theory taking place about this time. . . . Thus originated a certain malaise that has haunted psychoanalytic theory ever since. The first or second topography—the early or the later Freud? This frequently invoked alternative suggests a break. It marks instead a moment of isolation. We shall attempt to link the theories, the two eras, by going back to what we consider to be the very moment of the "break": the analysis of the Wolf Man.

In *The Wolf Man's Magic Word*, linking fantasy and trauma, fiction and reality, means reading a life-long poem and, at first, envisioning a human life as the creation of a readable poem. Abraham and Torok's analysis of the Wolf Man ends with a table of lexical items in several languages (Appendix: The Wolf Man's Verbarium), and with a short prose poem evoking the action of the Wolf Man's words. The poem is a token of the Wolf Man's "life-poem" elaborated throughout the authors' study.

> We know now which words spoke and how. We also surmise what robbed the words of their power to tell, what crushed them into words without grasp, silenced them into words beyond grasp.
> These words we grasped them, we restored to them their grasp.
> Their rhymes within him, within us.
> His laughter: his words brought to light, "cracking words" that restore life. Word of magic, word of panic, word of iniquity
> . . . inseparable companions, they create and recreate the poem of the tomb deep within. Black, their humor rises, white, their

pain recoils, but for pleasure they are mute. From beyond the
tomb, pleasure . . . nevertheless!
In his place, oh my brother, what would you do?

This poem represents in miniature the progression of *The Wolf Man's Magic
Word*. Taken together with the Verbarium, it suggests that the Wolf Man is a
collection of poetic devices, a compendium of rhymes, puns, silent distortions,
and secret verbal contortions. The Verbarium presents the rudimentary elements
of a personal dictionary with headings such as *The Words or Archeonyms, The
Rhymes*, and *Translation of the Rhymes into German and English*. "Verbarium"
itself (also in the book's original title: *Le Verbier de l'Homme aux loups*) is
coined by the authors from the French *verbe* (word or verb) and *herbier* (herbarium). The progressive elaboration of a dictionary leads the authors to construct,
dream by dream and symptom by symptom, a dialogue—not an event—at the
base of the Wolf Man's "nightmare of the wolves." The dialogue itself is about
truth and falsehood, in poetic terms, about the discrepancy between *Dichtung*
and *Wahrheit*. Whereas Freud conjectured a primal scene or primal fantasy—of
a coitus performed from behind by the parents and witnessed by the child of
eighteen months at the cost of deferred neurotic effects—Abraham and Torok
construct a precise verbal exchange, a kind of lawsuit, investigating the real or
fictional status of an event, alleged by only one of the participants in the dialogue. The Wolf Man's dreams and symptomatology are thus construed as the
splinters, distorted beyond recognition, of a bewildering dialogue. The genre
shifts accordingly. The analysis of the nightmare of the wolves does not result
in a narrative. The principle of etiological explanation based on an ordered temporal sequence cannot apply here, for the "origin" itself is a debate, a conflict
between two parties, that results in immobility rather than progression.

Understandably, Freud desires to know whether he has discovered the
decisive event of his patient's past . . . or whether the parents' behavior was in no way decisive, since whatever they did could be transformed by the tropes of fantasy into what the forces of signification in
the narrative required. . . . In one sense, however, Freud is right,
for the two alternatives give us very similar narratives. If one opts for
the production of the event by forces of signification . . . the primal
fantasy . . . can be efficacious only if the imagined event functions
for the 4 year old as a real event from his past. And if . . . we opt
for the reality of the primal scene . . . this event would not have had
the disastrous consequences it did unless the structures of signification
which make it a trauma for the Wolfman . . . were as suited to it as
to make it in some sense necessary. . . . But however close these
two accounts may be, the fact remains that from the point of view of
narratology . . . the difference between an event of the plot and an
imaginary event is irreducible. (Culler, *Pursuit of Signs*, p. 181)

What Culler terms "the urgency of choice" between real or imagined events defines quite precisely the Wolf Man's life-long predicament as elaborated by Abraham and Torok. Within the context under discussion, their delineation of a "vital contradiction" in the Wolf Man would seem to lend an unsuspected raison d'être to "the convergence of two narrative logics that do not give rise to a synthesis" (Culler, *Pursuit of Signs*, p. 183) in Freud's text. The "effect of self-deconstruction" (Culler, p. 183), that is, the process of invalidation performed by the ambivalent status of Freud's narrative, could now be perceived as an undetected clue or symptom of the Wolf Man's own dilemma. According to Abraham and Torok, the Wolf Man cannot state whether the event or the action he witnessed was real or imagined. For while still a child, he was summoned to be the sole witness for the prosecution and was *at the same time* disqualified as such by the defense. The Wolf Man's life, as it is interpreted, is neither a sequence flowing from a reconstructed originary event nor a progression positing a fictional event for its own coherence. Rather, his life is an impossibility or evasion of narrative in both senses.

In a section entitled "The Contradiction Implied in the Fact of 'Witnessing' " (chapter 8), Abraham and Torok explain how some thirty years after the initial scene of testimony, the Wolf Man continues to be frozen in a double and contradictory hypnosis: compelled to testify *for and against* the reality of an alleged misdeed. The Wolf Man's creation consists of elaborating an oeuvre (explicitly verbal as well as somatic) that refers to the words used to describe the alleged event without, however, conferring any truth value on them. This procedure, called variously *crypt*, *cryptonymy*, or the *broken symbol*, resolves the following dilemma: how to live without having to say yes or no to reality or fiction while continuing to refer to both.

The procedure itself is a manipulation of verbal entities and is entirely poetic in that it suspends by definition the question of truth and falsehood, reality and fiction. To use Paul de Man's terminology (in *The Epistemology of Metaphor* among other works), no insight can occur apart from understanding the process itself. Cryptonymy and the broken symbol work actively against the process of cognition, whether it is defined positively as the institution of knowledge, or negatively as its deposition. Cryptonymy (coined from the Greek prefix *crypto* for "hiding" and an analogy with rhetorical terms such as meto*nymy*) is a verbal procedure leading to the creation of a text (in the Wolf Man's case understood as coextensive with life) whose sole purpose is to hide words that are hypothesized as having to remain beyond reach. In fine, words are manipulated by cryptonymy as dried flowers in a herbarium. Divested of metaphorical reach and the power to institute or depose an extralinguistic event or action, cryptonyms create a collection of words, a verbarium, with no apparent aim to carry any form of knowledge or conviction.

In order to arrive at their discovery of cryptonymic procedures, Abraham and

Torok have had to establish that the Wolf Man could not acquire an identity, be it sexual or psychological, unless he found some device for the suspension of the positional properties of language, that is, of its capacity to distinguish true from false and determine value. What prompts the authors to hypothesize a verbal mechanism that obstructs comprehension is their initial realization that the Wolf Man's material is unreadable. They do not in fact undertake to interpret isolated symptoms or dreams at first, but to transform the Wolf Man's unreadability itself into his foremost symptom. Once it is demonstrated that the Wolf Man is himself only when he creates himself as enigma, the question arises as to what situation necessitates the systematic evasion of the significant or telling aspects of language. The fundamental query is in short: What leads a person to make himself unintelligible?

> The only pertinent answer seemed as follows: It is not a situation *comprising* words that becomes repressed; the words are not dragged into repression by a situation. Rather, *the words themselves, expressing desire, are deemed to be generators of a situation that must be avoided and voided retroactively.* In this case, and only in this case, can we understand that repression may be carried out on the word. . . . For this to occur, a catastrophic situation has to have been created precisely by words.

Carrying out repression on the word implies that cryptonymy inhibits the process of definition or meaning by concealing a segment of the associative path that normally allows one to move freely from one element to another in a verbal chain. Such is the case, for example, when a chain becomes established among the synonymous elements "to operate, perform, run" and is extended by various grammatical devices to "operator, performer, runner," while the fact is concealed that the entire chain owes its existence to the verb "to go" in the sense of "to pass away." The free proliferation of the verb "to go" in the initial sense of "to function" effectively bars it from being associated with another of its (variant) meanings: to die.

A brief discussion of the Wolf Man's anal symptoms will elucidate the import of this procedure's discovery. In sketching out a survey of his patient's sexual development, Freud stressed the Wolf Man's anal eroticism and repressed homosexuality, tracing them to the child's identification with his mother in the scene of coition he supposedly observed. According to Freud, childhood theories of sexuality convinced the Wolf Man that the intercourse was performed through the anus, while his identification with the so-called passive partner, the mother, led him to recognize the reality of her being castrated and to adopt the anal zone as the organ by which his passive homosexual attitude toward his father could be expressed. In Freud's interpretation, the associative chain moves along the path of "castration, feminine attitude, homosexuality, passivity, and cloacal theory of intercourse," all of which are offered as a definition of "anal," that is, as explanations for the persistence of the Wolf Man's intestinal symptoms. Using their hypothesis of repression carried out on the word itself, Abraham and Torok were able to interpret the Wolf Man's anal symptoms and their associative proliferation in Freud's study as an effect of the obstruction put up against the association of anal with the name of the Wolf Man's sister Anna. Though not stated in these terms, the freeing of the passage leading from anal to Anna is what permits the authors to reverse the tide of Freud's understanding of the Wolf Man, as based on the vicissitudes of sexual instincts, and to elaborate another interpretation concerned with the question: How does one make the unreadable readable?

A further distinction between Jacques Lacan's conception of the signifying chain and the concept of cryptonymy may be of interest here. Lacan's understanding of the individual as subject to an indelible lack in being is formulated in linguistic terms as the irreducible separation or barrier between a progressive chain of interlocking signifiers and stable meanings (i.e., signifieds). While cryptonymic analysis acknowledges the mobility of the signifying chain, it operates by studying the nature of the barrier that serves to separate the chain of signifiers from a potential signified. The signifying chain initiated by "anal" in the preceding example thus need not appear as founded on a lack (castration) if the obstruction or the bar itself, placed between "anal" and "Anna," becomes a subject of inquiry. Cryptonymy treats the barrier between signifier and signified as a specific obstacle to understanding or reading, created for reasons that are themselves subject to analysis. Furthermore, what is being obstructed in cryptonymy is not a meaning, but a situation (both intersubjective and intralinguistic) whose interpretation consists precisely in evaluating its resistance to meaning.

4. The Literary Uses of Cryptonymy: *The Red and the Black*, Author of *STENDHAL*

The Guillotine and the Unreadable Ending

To most readers a discussion of Stendhal will seem surprising if not inappropriate in an introduction to *The Wolf Man's Magic Word*. Yet such a discussion of *The Red and the Black* suggests itself here since it can serve as a specific demonstration of the general value and impact of *The Wolf Man's Magic Word* as a critical tool. *The Red and the Black* has enjoyed universal acclaim, yet its critics have consistently viewed it as fundamentally defective. Readers have called the novel's ending incomprehensible and have faulted the author for failing to justify the execution of its hero. With *The Wolf Man's Magic Word*, it is now possible to explain the discomfort of Stendhal's critics caught in the paradoxical situation of having to proclaim the novel a masterpiece while at the same time affixing blame either to the author or the novel itself for its defect. Cryptonymic analysis provides Stendhal's readers with the tool for recognizing that there is no need to affix blame precisely because there is no defect in the novel, no need to reconcile an "unjustifiable" ending to what precedes it. Abraham and Torok's work on the Wolf Man can reveal by implication that a concealed principle of cohesiveness links the beginning of the book to its end, that the guillotine, far from being a foreign body in the novel, constitutes the essential key to its interpretation.

The interpretive possibilities offered by *The Wolf Man's Magic Word* lead us to make the guillotine into the central concern of the novel from its very beginning. That is, the obstruction *The Red and the Black* puts up to its own comprehensive analysis can now become an object of inquiry in its own right. Cryptonymy allows us to convert the disruption or intrusion represented by the guillotine into an apparent discontinuity and to hypothesize that this blatant rupture owes its existence to some underlying opacity or enigma in the text. Equipped with the critical option of hiding, rather than cutting, the guillotine may be linked to other apparently extraneous elements in the novel that also conceal their pervasive pull on the text. Such an element may be the first word of the book, the pseudonym of the author, Stendhal.

The Pseudonym: A Word that Lies

It should be clear that the following sketch does not pretend to give an exhaustive account of *The Red and the Black*. Its function is simply to suggest one way in which cryptonymic analysis can reverse the orientation of a critical tradition and reveal the so-called weak spot of a literary work as its hidden force. Elaborations of deception and fraud have been the mainstay of the numerous psychological commentaries on all of Stendhal's works including *The Red and the Black*. Though there is valuable work on the psychological aspects of the disguise afforded by Stendhal's various pseudonyms (see Jean Starobinski's essay "Stendhal pseudonyme" in *L'Oeil vivant*. Paris: Gâllimard, 1961), no textual investigation examines the pseudonym Stendhal in the context of *The Red and the Black*. Abraham and Torok's procedure of interpreting proper names as significant entities in a text inspires us to take Stendhal *pseudonym* literally and to hear in it the sense of a "word that lies." *Stendhal* may thus be a deceitful word not only because it tricks the reader about the identity of its (and the novel's) author, but also because it conceals its verbal significance and the way in which it belongs to the text. Stendhal, a pseudonym, may also be understood as Stendhal *cryptonym*, a word that conceals a possible connection between the body of the novel and its conclusion, the guillotine.

Deception and fraud appear in the form of textual opacity when the pseudonym Stendhal is considered alongside the misleading use of the roughly seventy epigraphs and place names in *The Red and the Black*. Editors of the novel throw up their hands before confused attributions and the meaning of as many as half of Stendhal's quotations. An epigraph attributed to Hobbes and quoted in English – "Put thousands together / Less bad, / But the cage less gay" – generates editorial comment suggesting baffling problems ahead. "Frequently to stimulate his reader [Stendhal] surprises him, puzzling him with riddles: the text heading the first chapter is among the most disconcerting and it is very doubtful whether Hobbes is its author" (G. Castex in Stendhal, *Le rouge et le noir*. Paris: Garnier, 1973, pp. 515–16). Further on, why would Stendhal attribute untraceable lines to a certain Madame Goethe (Book II, chapter 40), ascribe dubious quotations to fictitious authors (Book II, chapter 6), and lend Schiller's name to a quotation from Shakespeare's *Julius Caesar* (Book II, chapter 15)? This fanciful play of hide-and-seek, shared by Stendhal and the most earnest of his commentators, becomes particularly acute when the initial setting of the novel, "the little town of Verrières," has to be located on the map.

> There are in the Franche-Comté two *Verrières*: Verrières-de-Joux and Verrières-du-Grosbois. . . . It does not appear that Stendhal went to these localities during his travels in that region; in any case, he draws on none of their characteristics. He must have known another Verrières quite near Troyes, in a region where he did stay at his friend's Crozet. . . . The site of this Verrières in no way corresponds to the one described in the novel. . . . Who will ever know, anyway, what mechanism worked in Stendhal's mind as he put a name to his "petite ville." (Castex, in Stendhal, *Le rouge et le noir*, pp. 515–16)

There are, of course, other enigmas posed by the novel, elements that now appear to be the splinters or the disjointed paths of a hitherto undiscovered textual labyrinth. In the light of *The Wolf Man's Magic Word*, the object of inquiry becomes: What hidden principle of coherence is being denied the reader by which he might tie together the pseudonymous attribution of spurious epigraphs, the pseudonym Stendhal, the choice of the name Verrières, and – last but not least – the presence of the guillotine?

The Hidden Rhymes of Verrières

The last chapter of the novel, in which the blade of the guillotine falls, ends with a footnote by Stendhal curiously omitted from most popular editions. In the first edition of the book, the author's footnote is appended to the word "End." Its effect (on this reader) is to topple, literally to upend, the progression of the novel by sending the guillotine back to Verrières in the first chapter.

> The disadvantage of the reign of public opinion is that, though it procures *freedom*, it meddles in things it has nothing to do with; for ex-

ample: personal life [*la vie privée*]. Hence the sadness of both America and England. To avoid tampering with personal matters, the author invented a little town, *Verrières*, and when he needed a bishop, a jury, and a trial court he placed all that in Besançon where he had never gone. (Stendhal, *Le rouge et le noir*, p. 489)

Stendhal's underscoring of *Verrières* (as opposed to Besançon) does more than call attention to the verbal aspects of his invention. By framing his fictitious Verrières in references to England and America, Stendhal replaces the town in the context of the first chapter, "A Little Town," where its description begins under the aegis of a spurious quotation from Hobbes in English and ends with another judgment on public opinion in the United States. "The tyranny of public opinion . . . governs every bit as *foolishly* in the small towns of France as in the United States" (p. 6). These diverse elements suggest that *Verrières* is every bit as spurious as the sham English-language quotation that heads the chapter. Considered alongside Verrières, the "author's" intention "to avoid tampering with personal matters" now appears enigmatic. Why indeed should the "author's" aversion to "the reign of public opinion" lead him to invent a "little town"? There is no reason, unless the underscored name of the small town were to shield him from "the tyranny of public opinion." In that case, it would appear that the "author" of *The Red and the Black* invented a "little town" to conceal his own privacy—his identity. Let us suggest that *Verrières* itself is merely a counterfeit pseudonym of this so far unseen "little town." To add mystery to enigma, the question may be raised, though not yet resolved: In what way is Verrières related to its pseudonym and, at the same time, to the guillotine?

It is not generally remembered today that Marie Henri Beyle chose his principal pseudonym after Stendal, the little German town where Johann Joachim Winckelmann was born in 1717. (The famous critic's essays on allegory, symbol, and the plastic arts of Greco-Roman antiquity influenced such major figures in the eighteenth century as Goethe and Herder.) Perhaps to commemorate the anniversary of Winckelmann's birth one hundred years earlier and the discoveries he made during his travels in Italy, Beyle first used the pseudonym Stendhal for the publication of *Rome, Naples, and Florence in 1817*. The list of three towns here is followed by a fourth, namely, Stendhal. If the "little town" invented by the "author" of *The Red and the Black* is Verrières and, as the information just revealed suggests, may also be Stendhal, then we must read through "Verrières" to reach "Stendhal." A first approach could be to take (the counterfeit pseudonym) Verrières at its word and hear in it its meaning in French: "window," "glass," or "stained glass." Are we to see, through Verrières, a paradoxical "window" somehow hiding Stendhal?

As we have observed in the case of the spurious attribution of epigraphs, the taboo of the proper name is repeatedly broken in *The Red and the Black*. In addition, the name *Verrières* has been confirmed a pseudonym (a deceitful word) that lies, along with Stendhal, about its function in the text. "Stendhal" lies by suggesting that it masks the identity of the author's real name, whereas it actually masks a "little town," and as such, an allusion to Verrières. The lie of "Verrières," in turn, is to appear a "little town," while its function in the text is to provide an alternative pseudonym to "Stendhal." Once we are willing to entertain the idea that a proper name may deceive, this same word and others surrounding it will acquire new significance. Thus when we read in the first chapter of *The Red and the Black* the sentence, "High above Verrières rise the broken peaks of Verra" (p. 3), we may wonder whether the proper name of the mountain Verra might not itself be make-believe, whether Verra might not be a "broken" fragment of Verrières. *Verra*, the third-person future of the verb *voir* (to see), imperceptibly ushers the reader into "seeing" some broken pieces of *Verrières* (stained glass) throughout the chapter. To cite one among several, the epigraph placed directly below the title of *Book I* reads: *La vérité, l'âpre vérité* (Truth, harsh truth). Whatever the "truth" of this quotation may be (attributed to Danton with no apparent foundation), the initial fragment of the word *vérité* has in common with *Verrières* the sound *vers*, meaning "verse" in French.

There is no reason, however, to privilege any one meaning of the sound sequence "ver," which among others can also signify the French noun "glass" (*verre*) out of which a "glass window," *Verrières*, is made. "Verse" simply serves to state the form of concealment at work in the text. As in the case of the Wolf Man's concealed vocabulary, hidden "rhymes" thus coalesce into a collection of words, that is, a verbarium, of the word (and not of the proper name) *verrières*. Yet, though a hidden poem has been found in the "little town of Verrières," its link to the guillotine is still missing.

To conclude this all too brief consideration, let us return to the question of the guillotine. Already in prison and awaiting his execution, Julien Sorel quotes some reflections (attributed to Danton by one of the characters in the novel) on "to guillotine" as a defective verb.

> "It is curious, the verb '*to guillotine*' cannot be conjugated in all its tenses; one can say: I will be guillotined, you will be guillotined, but one does not say: I have been guillotined." (Stendhal, *Le rouge et le noir*, p. 466)

In this passage, the action of the guillotine can be understood not merely as an instrument of physical severance but as a sign of some verbal defect in the novel. Julien's musings on the guillotine may be further interpreted as a clue suggesting that certain words in the novel are uncompleted. The lethal action of the guillotine is thus only apparently devastating to a coherent interpretation of the novel. For, paradoxically, the obstacle to interpretation, the cutting edge of the guillotine, may itself function as a key to uncovering the hidden coherence of the novel.

This coherence cannot be recovered without considering the specific verbal obstacle to comprehension the guillotine signals within the language of the text. Once this obstacle is identified, the blade of the guillotine will lose its cutting edge and, instead, reconcile the reader of the novel and its "defect." As was stated earlier about *The Wolf Man's Magic Word*, the characteristic aim of cryptonymy is to make the unreadable readable. Should "Stendhal," "Verrières," and the "guillotine" prove interrelated through some clipped verbal operation, the novel itself may ultimately prove to contain a response to the critical tradition that has seen it as a defective masterpiece.

To return from the ending to the beginning, to close the gap between the guillotine and Verrières, an obstruction between the two has to be annulled. This obstruction consists in a forbidding bar placed between "the little town of Verrières" and the lunette of a guillotine. The obstruction will endure as long as "Verrières" is understood as a geographic site and the guillotine a cutting instrument. The blade of the guillotine is "lifted," however, once we read a concealed poem in the French word *Verrières* and attempt to uncover a verbal link between it and the guillotine. An associative path between Verrières and the guillotine becomes established when "lunette" (a semicircular window in a vaulted roof) is understood as a synonym of *verrière* (a glass window), and their lexical relationship to a hidden meaning of lunette (i.e., the opening of the guillotine that encircles the head of the convict) is revealed. As soon as "lunette" opens to view, "Verrières" shifts from being considered an uncertain geographic site to a cryptonym, a word that hides within itself, from the outset, the pervasive presence of the guillotine.

The suggestion of a cryptonymic link, in *The Red and the Black*, between "the little town of Verrières" and the guillotine is not meant to be taken on faith. It is offered as a possibility of listening hitherto unavailable to Stendhal's novel. Neither should it appear that the foregoing interpretive sketch is advanced as the end point of an analysis. On the contrary, the hypothesis of cryptonymy initiates a process of reading that implies a whole new sequence of questions. A study of *The Red and the Black* wishing to take into account its cryptonymic procedures would ask, What kind of novel is one whose beginning anticipates, cryptically and in secret, its own ending? Furthermore, the resolutely verbal nature of the cryptonymic operation should not blind us to the obvious fact that Stendhal's work describes the loves and career of Julien Sorel. Our psychological understanding of the development, or *Bildung*, of the hero and his demise can be expanded by this new perspective. For we can ask what intersubjective configuration of the characters justifies a life scenario in which the hero is condemned to death *in petto* at the very moment he is given fictional birth. These questions cannot be divorced from the finding that the "author" of *The Red and the Black* chose *Verrières*, by the evidence of his final footnote, as a cover or screen for his "real" pseudonym *Stendhal*. Another step in the cryptonymic interpretation of the novel might address the problem: Can *The Red and the Black*—the novel that between its covers spans the space from the guillotine to Verrières *sotto voce*—explicate the secret of *Stendhal*?

This brief analysis of *The Red and the Black* is intended as exemplary of the kind of contribution cryptonymy can make to the study of literature. Cryptonymic analysis proceeds by investigating the ways in which certain elements in a text, which appear to obstruct interpretation, may be converted into readable entities. As the example of *The Red and the Black* shows, an obstacle to interpretation can be rendered readable if it is reinstated in the specific verbal situation it hides and from which it had been excluded. Cryptonymy is a critical instrument that permits us to pinpoint areas of silence in works of literature as well as in the oeuvre of a human life, and grant them the potential of expression, that is, the possibility of untying their tongue. By making the tongue-tied speak (whether it is a human life or a work of art), cryptonymy opens an area and a method of inquiry equally useful to clinical psychoanalysis, literary analysis, and the historical study of psychoanalytic theories and movements. The convergence of these fields and the new approach to interpretation their encounter implies will gain deeper significance as the reader is led through the realm of *The Wolf Man's Magic Word*.

5. Deconstructing and Decrypting: Jacques Derrida and *The Wolf Man's Magic Word*

The Wolf Man's Magic Word begins with a long study of Abraham and Torok's works (elaborated between 1948 and 1975) by Jacques Derrida. The juxtaposition of Derrida's essay with Abraham and Torok's text represents an encounter between two distinct critical trends. The usefulness of this encounter, for the academic reader in particular, resides in the fact that two separate theories of reading come together without excluding each other. The book can thus be said to have a strategic function in contemporary discussions of literary theory since it outlines a style of criticism that is neither for nor against deconstruction. The authors offer a neutral and nonpolemical vantage point for evaluating the contribution of deconstruction to literary studies while, at the same time, Derrida's essay brings into sharper focus the nature of Abraham and Torok's project.

Jacques Derrida's Scenarios of Textual Controversy

In the United States, the name Derrida is synonymous with deconstruction. Whether it is in connection with Kant, Rousseau, Foucault, or Heidegger, we are accustomed to seeing Jacques Derrida dismantle their systems of truths. In the self-confidence and self-sufficiency of texts, he instills a principle of disorder called *différance*. His brand of reading delivers a text(ure) whose fibers are radically reoriented and whose weave stands in counterpoint to itself. Derrida's program of analysis (developed from 1962 onward) could be tersely grasped as both historical and textual. On a first critical level, his readings create a compendium of philosophical concepts he seems to root in a universal need for integrity. The history of philosophy, as he sees it, consists of conferring names and constructions upon this need. Supposing that the aim of all philosophy is completeness, Derrida is led to pinpoint the coherence and interdependence of all philosophical principles. It is in this sense that he can talk in shorthand about the "system of Western metaphysics" and establish a sort of relay mechanism among concepts, according to which any one concept (e.g., essence) has the power to place all the others (God, identity, origin, telos, proper name, presence, light, logos, truth, etc.) on call.

Against this backdrop, the novelty of Derrida's approach to the history of philosophy is distinct. While supposing a need for integrity, he also surmises an activity of disintegration. The two tendencies are seen as simultaneously flowing crosscurrents. Derrida's aim is to rehabilitate (or reinstate) the fact of disintegration in the face of its subjugation by the need for integrity. He thus creates a counterhistory of antiphilosophical concepts (or deconstructions) on which he confers names (e.g., writing, spacing, remainder, *différance*, dissemination, *écart, envois*).

The counterhistory of disintegration is discovered, studied, and played out in specific texts. Derrida uses the semantic diversity as well as the phonetic and anagrammatic ambiguity of words (that is, age-old poetic devices) in order to demonstrate that (philosophical) texts are at cross-purposes with themselves. His readings often yield one or more words whose transparent meanings in the text are treated as indications of the need for integrity whereas their less obvious lexical, phonetic, syntactic, and typographical aspects are revealed as the text's own insidious hints of disintegration. Every analysis thus leads to new names for and new procedures of disintegration. The difficulty and originality of Derrida's work lie in its multifaceted linguistic creations; he assumes that language activates contrary modes of expression at the same time. To take a very brief example, he can demonstrate that the French word for "step" (*pas*), ostensibly used in a text to suggest progression or regression, is, at the same time, stayed or canceled out by homophony since *pas* can also mean "no." This word and the many others like it (*supplément, éperons, glas, retrait, différance, pharmakon, fors*, etc.) are meant as scenarios of textual controversy. Their potential proliferation notwithstanding, they could be placed alongside the names used by Derrida for designating antiphilosophical concepts and procedures. The verbal scenarios of textual controversy thus form a network of disjoining practices that correspond, as so many countermoves, to the anthology of traditional philosophical concepts.

Derrida's interpretations characteristically move back and forth between highly systematized notions of unity and seemingly arbitrary instances of verbal disintegration. Furthermore, Derrida's essays can be easily distinguished by the relative absence of argumentative discourse (characteristic of most philosophical and literary commentary), coupled with an attempt to situate the reader concurrently on the level of a particular text's explicit statements, its incompatible and proliferative verbal tendencies, as well as the interpreter's technical commentary on his own linguistic discoveries and procedures.

Fors, the foreword Derrida wrote to *The Wolf Man's Magic Word* (1976), is at once an introduction to and an interpretation of Abraham and Torok's work. Derrida's initial outline of their project suggests an encounter with his own modes of research. This book "no longer conforms to any law and order—certainly not to philosophical order; which thus finds itself moved to the point of no return." The first section of Derrida's essay delineates the topographical features of Abraham and Torok's notion of "crypt" and arrives at a pithy formulation of the "displacement," or shift in position, he has announced: " . . . the walled surfaces of the crypt create an innermost heart of hearts . . . which is an excluded outsider inside" (translation mine). The paradoxical aspects of this spatial disposition are epitomized, in typical Derridean fashion, by a semantically double-edged word, *for*, potentially meaning (when modified with the appropriate adjectives) the "innermost heart" or "conscience" (*le for intérieur*) and the "temporal" or "outward" jurisdiction of the church (*le for extérieur*). Derrida's use of the plural (*fors*) might indicate an amalgamation, but actually refers to another, prepositional meaning (namely, "save," except for," "outside of") that is intended to underscore what Derrida perceives to be the principal contribution of the notion of crypt: its deposition of the time-honored distinction between inside and outside. "The inner safe . . . has placed itself outside . . . or, if one prefers, has constituted" within itself "the crypt as an outer safe. One might go on indefinitely switching the place names around in this dizzying topology (the inside as the outside of the outside, or of the inside; the outside as the inside of the inside, or of the outside, etc.) but total con-fusion is not possible." Derrida's interpretation of Abraham and Torok's concept of crypt consists of describing a contradictory "topography of inside outside" (*topique des fors*). Considered in this light, Abraham and Torok's discovery could easily join the ranks of Derrida's own antiphilosophical concepts and deconstructive procedures. Furthermore, the contrary modes of expression the word *fors* willfully capitalizes on create a scenario of controversy within language. "This is no mere wordplay or syntax twisting, not a gratuitous contamination of meanings; only the constraints of this strange topography. This topography has already produced the *necessity* of this kind of language . . . ." On this first level of convergence between *The Wolf Man's Magic Word* and Derrida's own project, the "crypt" and the verbal manipulations it leads to in *Fors* appear to be an allegory of deconstruction.

Nicolas Abraham's Theory of Symbol: Healing the Trace's Illness

The processes of integrity and simultaneous disintegration Derrida has outlined historically and practiced in his readings over the past twenty years can be interpreted in turn through the premises of *The Wolf Man's Magic Word* to which *Fors* refers the reader.

> There is an extraordinary line of continuity, a striking coherence between the 1961 program and all the *anasemic* research of the later work. From the very first page of the 1961 manuscript, in the first paragraph ("The Text of the Symbol") of the first chapter ("Psychoanalysis and Transphenomenology of the Symbol"), one recognizes *The Magic Word*'s milieu.

In his essay *On Symbol*, Nicolas Abraham outlines a theory of disaster or obstacle whose initial premise is the danger of disintegration. Understood as an "impossibility to be," disintegration does not counteract the notion of or the fact of integrity. Disintegration is the opaque beyond or far side of apparent integrity inasmuch as integrity (Being) is nothing but the potentially telling and allusive account of why and how something could not be. With this definition of what is, in relation to something beyond that could not be, *On Symbol* allows us to situate Derridean deconstruction retroactively as the systematic exploration of fictitious verbal scenarios that articulate obstacles to being.

Abraham and Torok's project is different. From the start, they pinpoint and explore specific obstacles to being and search for ways to surmount them through reading. The discovery of cryptonymy is the final stage in a line of research concerned with elaborating language as a system of expressive traces. Trace, for Abraham and Torok, is a concealed and potentially telling reference to an absent and already surmounted obstacle to being (trauma). They treat language as a telltale medium and their discovery of cryptonymy is the discovery of an obstacle to the expressiveness of this medium itself. At the same time, the method of reading devised in connection with cryptonymy (also called decrypting) represents a potential for the recovery of the telltale aspects of language. *The Wolf Man's Magic Word* thus offers an inquiry into and an eloquent "cure" for one particular pathology: the impossibility for trace to speak.

Introduction:
Five Years with the Wolf Man

Five years . . . the average length of an analysis. We have spent them in the company of the Wolf Man. During this entire period, his presence was mediated by Freud, Ruth Mack Brunswick, Muriel Gardiner, and, finally, his own works. He was with us, not in person, like a patient on the couch, but through an immutable collection of documents filling a single volume. This "material," limited in its extent and all of it readily available (except for the memoirs we discovered in midcourse: Muriel Gardiner, *The Wolf-Man by the Wolf-Man.* New York: Basic Books, 1971), required, however, many reworkings, a genuine process of maturation on our part, before we could reach the effective close of our work. There is in this something of an experimental proof that the analytic process is not solely the making of the patient: It involves a double evolution—parallel yet complementary—of two partners at the same time. In our unique experiment, the prolonged repetition of sessions was replaced by numerous rereadings, renewed returns to the same documents.

As for the patient, he was not part of the process; only the analyst "worked."

Translator's note. For the purposes of the American edition, aimed at the student of literature rather than the clinician, the following changes have been introduced. Relevant passages from Freud's case study of the Wolf Man are quoted in full. Whenever deemed necessary, German and Russian phrases or words have been more fully explicated. In chapter 7, sections 5, 6, and 7, the German and English text of the dreams is not quoted a second time for a line-by-line interpretation. Most footnotes have been incorporated in the text. All these changes and other modifications were made with the kind permission of Maria Torok.

In order to attune ourselves to this concrete yet fictitious patient, we needed five years of repeated listening.

Nearly two years ago came the beginning of the end. The "Open Sesame" seemed to fall from the sky. In fact, it had been there from the start. But it revealed itself only after many failures at listening in particular to the dreams. The discovery was that English had been the Wolf Man's childhood language. Freud had taken seventeen years to realize this and to draw his decisive yet succinct conclusions (see chapter 3).

We only had to think of it to locate the valuable reference in Freud. Why precisely at that moment, not later or earlier or . . . never? Why us and not someone else? "Chance" or a "lucky find"? Only a third ear, listening to our listening, could provide an answer. As for us, we have to admit that the subject controlled us more than we controlled it. Insight always came after tense moments and vain fumbling, in moments of grace when suddenly riddles came unraveled, disparity acquired order, absurdity took on sense. The discovery of English as the cryptic language was a crucial step: It allowed us to identify the active and hidden words. But this was in no way sufficient as an instrument of interpretation. All of the source words were known, all the *archeonyms*, or almost, yet there was nothing to weld them into a coherent whole. Until the day when another revelation came: The archeonyms were arranged in the form of a dialogue. From there we took the final step in the construction of a hypothesis: a precocious traumatic scene, removed, sent to a crypt, encrypted. We had the interpretation of the nightmare of the wolves. Better yet, all the dreams and symptoms gradually became accessible. Were we to rest on our laurels?

There followed nearly two years of delight over this "raw material" that had rendered its secrets.

We had to finish it at long last. But could we be happy with a catalogue of deciphered hieroglyphics, however plausible in its coherence, however exhaustive in its breadth? The appeal to the metapsychological "witch" was still needed. This was the last stage, but not the least rich in discoveries. We knew which words had spoken and how. We had also constructed the trauma that had stripped them of their power to convey and degraded them into powerless and ungraspable words. But we still had to restore value to the words, reason to their rhymes, truth to their speech. Yes, the effectiveness of metapsychology was lacking: Place, Force, Benefit. We were bewildered. The Place was not the Unconscious, the Force was not repression, and the Benefit . . . we could still take a crack at it. In the final analysis, could the Wolf Man's "ills" consist precisely of this: that he eludes metapsychology? But nobody can escape the "witch," her rule is absolute. For she herself has the final authority to evaluate whatever might deviate from her.

A false Unconscious: the crypt in the Ego—a false "return of the repressed," the action in the Ego of hidden thoughts from the crypt. In sum, a skewed balance emerges if we compare the amplitude of the manifold repetitions of the traumatic scene with its pleasurable counterpart: A simple word becomes the Thing of the Unconscious. All this appeared to us with increasing clarity. But then how could the "witch" be lured into action?

The "Speech of the Word or the Rhymes and the Thing," part IV of this work, answers this question. With a new broom, the "witch" sweeps away the obstacle and unambiguously exposes the complex workings of a doubly cleft topography.

Let us note the following concerning this new "broom." Our guiding question has been, What new conceptual apparatus has to fill out Freudian metapsychology in order to widen its scope of analytic effectiveness, and at the same time, how can we push the limits of what is considered to lie "beyond analysis" or as falling into the category of "interminable"? The Wolf Man's case is exemplary in this regard and has already been treated in a number of our essays dealing with *cryptophoria*. From the point of view of diagnostic symptomatology, not central to our purpose here, cryptophoria effectively subsumes certain types of "fetishism," "hypochondria," "fixed ideas," "manic-depressive psychosis," "pathological mourning," and the like. Following our study on symbol construed as an *operation* (1961), our reflections on the *anasemic* character of psychoanalytic concepts, and our considerations on the notion of *introjection* (1968), our clinical and theoretical research focused on cases (of cryptophoria) where the symbolic operation is blocked, where introjection is lacking, and where the libido's encounter with the tools of its own symbolic development is wanting.[1]

One more word to emphasize the following: In contrast to the analytic work done between two people—a dialogue that creates new realities—theoretical construction based on documents is merely a translation. It is the translation of an established text into an *invented* text (in both meanings at the same time, "bringing to light" and "creating"). The translator is twice over a traitor: He betrays the other and himself. This would normally void all results. The translator's work is nevertheless tied to an original that, even if tinged with fiction, remains asymptotically the place of convergence for all possible translations and betrayals.

May our "betrayal" have been close enough to our text!

And may readers be endowed with the patience to follow the outlines of our path, so that they may share our hardships and rewards.

I. The Magic Word:
Incorporation, Internal Hysteria, Cryptonymy

The "Break"

The History of an Infantile Neurosis *is one of the most intriguing works by the inventor of psychoanalysis. Polemical in its explicit purpose, it also reflects another debate, that of the author with himself. Throughout this stirring account and within the meanderings of the theoretical discussion, attentive readers will sense a doubt—it is Freud's doubt regarding his own statements. Whether he deals with the unique process that plays a part in this treatment, or with the application to this case of established insights, Freud's exposition is marred by an insidious incredulity. These unconscious doubts are certainly not foreign to the new turn in Freudian theory taking place about this time. It is not accidental, as Strachey points out, that while working on this case Freud was also involved in another seemingly remote field of research. Soon afterward some new views emerged, and by the end of 1914, they had become the first draft of* Mourning and Melancholia. *No doubt Freud, the genius of the Unconscious, sought a path that, for the moment, the polemicist could not follow. Thus originated a certain malaise that has haunted psychoanalytic theory ever since. The first or second topography—the early or the later Freud? This frequently invoked alternative suggests a break. It marks instead a moment of isolation. We shall attempt to link the theories, the two eras, by going back to what we consider to be the very moment of the "break": the analysis of the Wolf Man. We shall steep ourselves in the documents of the past, at a distance of two generations and with our present means, in order to revive in us—even if only as a fiction—the history of this "infantile neurosis" that had the power, to our way of thinking, to sow the seeds of doubt in Freud's first views. We are confident that from this imaginary voyage we will bring back a more unified view of psychoanalysis and, perhaps, along the way, a few harmonies to be used in our daily listening.*

Chapter 1
The Wolf Man and His Internal World

1. Wolf Man, Who Are You?
First Hypotheses and Constructions: Who He Is Not

In *The History of an Infantile Neurosis*, Freud departed from his habit of show-ing, revealing, and rendering manifest. This time his aim was to convince. But who would fail to notice the incoherence here, the unlikelihood there, and the overzealous proofs just about everywhere? We felt an urgent duty to overcome such a malaise. Hence this work. In the beginning we had only a vague intuition that gradually grew more specific. It took on an explicit form that we expressed in these terms: The person in despair who, rendered helpless by depression, con-sulted Freud in 1910 was not quite the same as the one who lay on his couch a few days later. They appeared to be two separate people in one, without either of them representing the basic identity of the Wolf Man. Although often having the same desires as he, they remained nevertheless distinct from him. As a re-sult, a paradox emerged in which the sexual license loudly claimed by one would only reinforce repression in the other. We suspected the existence of a cohabita-tion, at the core of the same person, involving his elder sister's image and his own. Two people in a third one: Freud's listening may have perceived this only unconsciously. Before *Mourning and Melancholia*, this was clearly sufficient to baffle psychoanalytic understanding.

Such was our first idea. It demanded clarification, in particular concerning the genesis of such an internal constellation. How, indeed, could the initial real-ity of two children living together in the same home become transformed into

3

an intrapsychic companionship? How could the particular topography implied by such a state of affairs come into being?

Freud devoted a whole chapter to the so-called seduction by the sister and returned to it repeatedly throughout his account. He placed so much emphasis on it, rather more because he sensed the crucial importance of the seduction by the sister on its own terms than because the ideas supported his own theories (Primal Scene, display of passive desire): These theories did not need this elaboration. As for the concrete content of the "seduction," nothing that filtered through was worthy of this name yet Freud seemed to cling to this label. Rather than branding it a misuse of language, we preferred to see in it the sign of a reliable clinical intuition. There remained to be constructed, despite the absence of all information, the entire scene of this seduction. To suggest a version of it, we had to do a lot of guesswork, as when one has to compute two unknown quantities on the basis of a single equation. Only the clinical study of incorporation was of some help in guiding our steps through unknown terrain (see part I, chapter 2). After eliminating quite a few other possibilities, this is how we were able to summarize what was likely to have happened between the two children: First, the sister claimed to repeat with her younger brother a sexual scene that probably took place earlier between her and the father; second, she attached to the resulting pleasure (in the brother) the meaning of castration. Such a situation, however mythical it may appear, illustrates, if nothing else, the starting point and the contradiction inscribed within the libidinal attitude of the Wolf Man. Its contributions are, on the one hand, a reference to the father and, on the other, the castrating jealousy of the young seductress: two unknowns we must assume in order to justify how, at the time of the seduction, *the Stranger could settle in the core of the Ego.* (We understand Ego as the sum total of its introjections and define introjection as the libido's encounter with a potentially infinite number of instruments for its own symbolic expression.) Such an incorporation of the sister is thus understood as the only possible means of combining within her two incompatible roles: that of Ego Ideal and that of Love Object. It was the only means of loving her in order not to annihilate her, and of annihilating her in order not to love her. Thanks to incorporation, the insoluble conflict between aggressivity and the libido could leave the Object and transfer itself into the core of the Ego. And the Wolf Man had to carry its indelible mark in the very structure of his Ego, that is, in the sum of his introjections. An immediate consequence: Seduced by the sister, as she supposedly had seduced the father, he could not escape a second incorporation, that of the father, and thus his child's penis no longer ceased to coincide in secret with Father's. Hence a double and contradictory exigency: Father's penis must neither perish nor enjoy. Otherwise he, the Wolf Man, would be annihilated. It is conceivable that such an internal situation could have remained unraveled throughout a lifetime.

Our intention here is to retrace the flow of this life, fantastic and pathetic, mediocre and replete with enigmas, along the paths of the Unconscious. After a long trip backward, we hope to retrieve at the end a hypothetical base point: the moment that must have imprinted on the Wolf Man's life its irresolvable and perpetual contradiction, and that must have initiated his unremitting struggle to safeguard a last refuge for his self.

Yes, picturing the Wolf Man with his incorporations, we begin to understand. What a situation indeed! Whether his desire coincided with that of his "Guest" or whether it is contrary to it, the result would remain identical: the impossibility of ever reaching himself. When he wanted to be "castrated," did he do so in concert with his jealous sister or in order to imitate her with Father? Did he desire Father's love for himself or for the sister inhabiting him? The image he fell in love with later, did it feed on his own libido or a libido belonging to Father? Whichever way he turned, he found himself face to face with the same impossibility of being himself. He was, as it were, trapped. He was barred from others and—incapable of assimilating them—he could only put them inside himself, as he had done with his sister. He populated his internal world with both benign and malignant characters; these included Father, Mother, Nania, the German tutor, the Doctor, and, finally, the Psychoanalyst as Therapist. The first incorporation attracted others as a magnet draws up iron filings. The Wolf Man identified, conversed, and schemed with each character in turn. His life was made up of maneuverings to avoid hapless meetings and indiscretions. They were all there in him in order to maintain a fundamental repression of a contradiction within the desire itself: that of a death-dealing pleasure. This repression appeared only in two images, each incomplete in its manifest state: first the erogenous image of a woman in the position of a scrubwoman, then the second one, a complement to the first, of a phobia-producing erect wolf. We understand now that the Wolf Man could expose only his various modes of not being himself to analysis. It was the only way he could reveal—without ever being able to use his own name—who in fact he was.

This is our explicit hypothesis of incorporation. It will help us "speak" the unconscious of the case and perhaps the induced unconscious of its analysts as well. It will also guide us in reading between the lines the following biographical notes based on the publications of Muriel Gardiner.

2. The Wolf Man's Old Age: Some Later Effects of Incorporation

If the Wolf Man is still alive, he must be past the terminal age (eighty-three years and four months) of the person who—after their first encounter nearly sixty years ago—made the second revelation of his life, this time concerning the realm of the Unconscious. The Wolf Man seemed to have preserved the image of his initiator to psychoanalysis just as faithfully as the image of all the other characters he had harbored since childhood, above all that of his very young initiator to love. His own Freud seemed to combine the role of the therapist with that of the father who had been taken away from him for good through the effect of the "seduction." Snatched away as an object of love, snatched away as an ideal image. In the grayness of old age, he mused regretfully that it had not been his lot to accomplish the one thing he felt would have given meaning to a life such as his own: to help others as analysts do. He had resigned himself to remaining Freud's famous case, the one who had given such invaluable service to the cause of science and had been the subject of publications and commentaries. In 1957 he published a recollection of his first meeting with Freud. He signed it: *The Wolf Man*. About the same time, congratulating the young daughter of an analyst friend on her success in the natural sciences, he wrote with black humor in a letter he allowed to be published: "In my youth, I too was interested in animals, they were wolves." Thus, whatever his regrets, he could not do otherwise; he gave himself to Freud as his elder sister had given herself to the father.

It will not be surprising to learn that he remained prone to severe depressions. He was, nevertheless, able to overcome them every time, apparently with no outside help. As for his enigmatic desire for an image, he continued to sublimate himself, with more or less success, by painting landscapes. He would fall in love with some of them at first sight, just as he had done with women scrubbing floors. But there again—as for any other personal accomplishment—who knows what internal devil gave him writer's cramp or ruined his colors? Whenever he engaged in intellectual activities, bringing him closer to his father (for example, after his early retirement when he had free time), his evil spirit would strike at his head, inflicting continuous migraines. Only with his mother could he maintain—in nearly complete social isolation—a harmonious relationship. Were they not in the same shoes as far as the father-daughter couple was concerned?

In their old age, mother and son merged in one narcissistic love, free of all conflict. Looking at her in her coffin at age eighty-nine: "I found it hard to believe," he wrote, "that death could make a human face so beautiful. Never had I seen my mother bathed in such sublime tranquillity, such peacefulness, really she appeared altogether a classical beauty" (Gardiner, *The Wolf-Man by the Wolf-Man*, p. 340).

Many things from the distant past were recalled and discussed between them, among others the marital problems of the parents. In any case, it is clear that his companion in misfortune could hardly become an Oedipal object for him. His desire carried him toward his housekeeper, a substitute for one of the functions filled by his wife—herself a successor to his beloved and hated sister. If it was true that he would never be aware of his hatred, this was not the case for his feelings of love: The model for his choice of objects had always been his sister—he was pleased to state at age sixty-six.

Beloved and hated. When his wife ended her life in 1938, the unexpected suicide put the Wolf Man in a conflictual situation unlike—as we have seen—the later loss of his mother. He suffered an attack of depressive agitation worse than any he had ever experienced. Having lost all touch with reality — he went so far as to ignore the annexation of Austria by the Nazis — he roamed the streets frenzied and repeated forlornly the stereotypical question: "Why, tell me why, did she do this to me?" This would be the same outcry of despair as that of Father, shattered by the suicide of his preferred object.

The identification with the mourning of the internal Father protected him from a grave danger. It prevented him from making a link between his erotic desire for his sister and her suicide, as well as with the subsequent death of the real father. What to do? Return to the couch of R. M. Brunswick as Muriel Gardiner had suggested? Would he find a remedy to his ills at the side of his sister's double, his second analyst? Six weeks of daily meetings with her (in desperation he had followed her in her exile from Paris to London) could not, apart from providing some consolation, alleviate his state. He needed the supportive presence of a male doctor, representing the internal father, in order to reassure him bit by bit: Their common penis would survive this test. Bimonthly chess games with Dr. Albin, a Viennese therapist, and perhaps the hardships of wartime, finally resolved the matter. The Wolf Man became, alongside his mother, once again a man "endowed with acute powers of observation due to his deep understanding of human nature, of art, and psychoanalysis," as he had been known to be before this tragic event (Gardiner). In 1940 he announced that his balance seemed reestablished, his former hypochondria much tempered. The event had been cathartic. Unfortunately, its meaning could not cross the threshold of consciousness and was to remain inaccessible, as we have just seen, to the end of his days.

3. The Symptom of the Nose and the "Group Dynamics" of the Internal Characters

If, following the tragic episode of his wife's suicide, the Wolf Man did not exhibit serious and lasting disorders, as he had twelve to fifteen years earlier upon learning about Freud's illness, and if he was able to recover almost spontaneously, credit must be given to his good analytic relationship with R. M. Brunswick, his former analyst. Unfortunately, the apparently decisive phase of this often interrupted treatment is known to us only through a laconic remark of the analyst alluding, for the first time, to the crucial role of the sister.

"This period of the analysis," she noted, "revealed new material of great import, hitherto forgotten memories, all relating to the complicated attachment of the preschizophrenic girl to her small brother" ("A Supplement to Freud's *History of an Infantile Neurosis* [1928]" in Gardiner, *The Wolf-Man by the Wolf-Man*, p. 263).

Here again, as often elsewhere, Brunswick's formulation bears witness to deep intuition and says more by its form than by its content: "preschizophrenic girl" and "small brother" state clearly that she sensed the presence of these characters in the Wolf Man. It is obvious by now how much we agree with the direction of such an intuition. A good deal of our work aims to expound and illustrate it. We will go quite far on this road and will not hesitate to hypostasize the internal characters by endowing them, for the sake of this presentation, with proper names. These will be the sign of their alien and parasitic nature and will avoid confusion with a self become clandestine. Thus, Brother and Sister have been baptized, respectively, Stanko and Tierka; the other characters will keep the name of their function, emphasized by capitals: Father, Mother, Therapist.

Equipped with this tool, let us once more retrace our steps. The Wolf Man's first encounter with Brunswick was in 1926, that is, twelve years after the termination of his analysis with Freud. It took place, as we know, in rather special circumstances. The Russian ex-nabob, now an ordinary wage earner in Vienna, profited from the collective charity of analysts who enhanced his meager income; these sums were given to him every spring from 1919 on by Freud himself. Initially, these donations were intended to pay hospital bills for the Wolf Man's wife. Such an intention had all the ingredients to be beneficial for his internal world. Setting up Stanko as relay between Father and Tierka, it created new and harmonious relationships among the characters. It recognized implicitly the mutual belonging of the children, as well as Father's love for his son—this motivated the gifts. But an external event modified this beneficent state of affairs. The Wolf Man recovered some family jewels (1922) and, on his wife's advice, said nothing to Freud about the existence of this supposed treasure. He did not know that this lie by omission would become the source of unresolvable torture. What had happened within him? The answer is simple: Stanko and Tierka again shared a secret. There followed—seen from the outside—a genuine alteration of his character. A man until then unconcerned with material advantage and scrupulously honest suddenly became greedy about his savings, a spendthrift (he lost his money in speculations), and in the end doubly secretive, both with his benefactor, whom he kept unaware of his (supposed) wealth, and with his wife, whom he left in the dark about his extravagance.

Seen from the inside, all these changes are comprehensible once it is appreciated that the introduction of the first secret compromised the *modus vivendi* of the internal characters. It revived by induction a host of other secrets and tended to reestablish the occlusion among the characters that, earlier, analysis had tempered. What was the effect of the new connivance with Tierka? It meant, as regards Father (represented outwardly by Freud), first of all that his place was being usurped (he must not find out at any price), and second, that he had been betrayed by Tierka (he would die of sorrow and the son along with him, *ipso facto*), and that, consequently, the unlivable contradiction of the starting point would revive for both Father and Son. Then again, by using the money received from Father for his own purposes, he surreptitiously put himself in the place of Tierka, the favorite. Were she to learn about this, her jealousy would be boundless, and she would be forever lost as Object. There again secrecy was vital. As for Stanko, he had to remain innocent in the face of death wishes entertained by the Wolf Man concerning Father and Sister because of their relationship. Were they not, both, the privileged objects of his desire?

His dissimulation helped to maintain, surely at the cost of internal dislocation, a precarious balance. But when he learned about the seriousness of Freud's illness in the fall of 1923, the Wolf Man's struggle against his aggressive wishes proved ineffectual. For fear that Father might take their common penis into the grave, it became urgently necessary to denounce the very cause of this situation and thereby liberate his own virility. On the other hand, it was inconceivable that he could deal such a blow to someone being struck by fate, someone who was moreover the brace of his internal world.

His only recourse was to rescue Father by rescuing Tierka from suicide. It was for the purpose of finding a compromise between two opposite wishes—make Father die and revive him—that he invented a symptom: *the language of the nose*, the language of his deep and secret desire. He discovered the vocabulary of this symptom in the guise of a wandering wart on his mother's nose. He endowed his own nose, however, with an undecipherable sign. The child's nose is the place, is it not, where adults can read a lie like an open book? A pimple suddenly discovered in the middle of his nose will have to bear witness to the alteration of his identity: that he is no longer Stanko, but Tierka, worse yet, the Tierka who, ill before her suicide, blamed the pimples on her face for her misfortune. Her loss would bring with it Father's . . . . What would be left then to S. P. [Sergei Pankeiev]? Fortunately, since his analysis with Freud, he was not altogether without recourse in such misery. He had placed within himself an additional character: the Therapist. He would reveal the lie to him, and he would cure his sister. Then everything would be as before. But, for the moment, this wish was expressed only in his nasal symptom. He carried his lying nose with Tierka's pimple on it from one doctor to the next. Treatment, scar. A new treatment, a new scar. Would Tierka ever recover? "No, never! Tierka will be marked forever," someone told him. Then the utmost despair seized him. Could it be he who had pushed her into suicide? Dare he appear before the ill Father with such a conjecture? Could he bear it if Father died of sorrow?

On June 15, 1926, anxiety overcame him. The next day he had to go to Freud for the allowance. But to Father he would say not a word of his symptom. He had better conceal from the ill man this forerunner of a disaster. As for Tierka, her confidence in Stanko-Therapist remained limited. For a long time she had wanted his suggestions checked by a second therapist. But now feeling pushed to suicide, she had had enough. She announced plainly to Stanko the ill will, be it conscious or unconscious, of Dr. X. And for S. P. all escape was blocked.

4. The Dramaturgy of the Unconscious
on Ruth Mack Brunswick's Couch

So it was that in 1926, on Professor Freud's counsel, consulted *in extremis*, the Wolf Man proceeded to lay Tierka on R. M. Brunswick's couch. He was reassured seeing her in the hands of a female therapist, safe from any form of seduction or fraternal rivalry. His hope of rescuing Tierka revived. When the Wolf Man would let Stanko speak, Stanko showed himself to be a good little boy and accorded the therapist a showy confidence. During this time, the symptomatic nose was not an issue. It was out of the question for the Wolf Man to let himself be recognized as himself with his persistent anxiety, or to allow this to attract attention to the true reason for the psychoanalytic treatment that concerned his "nose." For the moment, much more important things had to be handled, he would say. It was, no doubt, more helpful to return to his happy relationship with Freud and to lavishly produce lots of wolf dreams, a token of his valuable contribution to psychoanalysis.

Reassured bit by bit, he finally revealed, in retelling a dream, the lie about the jewels. And certainly this revelation carried with it a measure of aggressivity toward the image of the Sister, an image broken by the dreamer's breaking the mirror. But this image, was it not also the portrait depicted by his first analyst in his famous monograph? And this breaking, was it not in the end the "breach" of his own sex exploding in lust against the bulwarks?

Stanko's nose spoke, Tierka's had been destroyed. And there was immediately a dynamic change. The Sister's retort was ready. Up to then S. P. had let Stanko speak. Now the lines were given to the injured Sister. The Wolf Man's new speech — Brunswick reported — slid into ideas of "megalomania" about his friendship with Freud and into clearly manic ones concerning his lack of scruples in accepting money. His ideas relative to the alleged maneuvers of his first analyst to strip him of his fortune were paranoid:

Yes, it's really his fault that I lost everything. Of course, he did not mean any harm, but he preferred to keep me beside him.

These are Tierka's words to Stanko, to be understood thus:

First of all, Stanko, you will never be as intimate with Father as I! It's me he loves and you accuse me of having seduced you only because I myself was seduced by Father's love. His money is my due for the pleasure I lavished on him to satisfy his love. I was loved too much; that's what I suffer from.

On the same level and in the same breath, Stanko reiterated relentlessly his own response:

Now you're going to be cured, Tierka. You're in good hands. Your present therapist has no need to love you excessively or subordinate you as Father and Freud did. She will not mutilate your face like X., that charlatan!

We do not know how this dialogue between Brother and Sister would have ended. One thing is certain: Following as it did the disclosure of one secret, it was meant to serve as a diversion in order to conceal another. Which one? The analyst did not know yet. If she got wind of any of it later, it could only have been after the analysis while reading the Wolf Man's account on the prodromal tribulations of his nose. There is no reason to believe that she could see the slightest connection between his concealment and a certain detail of the report. It happened precisely in Professor X.'s office. In his zeal to cure Tierka, the Wolf Man was again consulting a doctor. Professor X. pressed the pimple on the nose. Blood spurted out "under the doctor's hand," and the Wolf Man experienced what he later called *ecstasy*! Tierka miraculously saved from suicide! Of course. But also, and no less miraculously, was not the Wolf Man now the impromptu owner of an orgasm? But that, that had to remain his secret and his alone.

The analyst had no idea why the treatment became engulfed in panegyrics sung to her qualities and in charges against Professor X. She felt only one thing: It was high time for transference to take place. With chance playing into her hands, she had recourse to a rather unconventional ruse. Having received advanced knowledge of the news, she abruptly announced Professor X.'s death. Stanko sprang from the couch and exclaimed with an air of melodrama:

My God! Now I can't kill him any more! I wanted to do it because death is all he deserves for the injury he made me suffer.

But this time the analyst was not fooled, nor did she allow the internal Tierka to reply. From her chair, she began to play the aggressive and rival sister. With relentless comments she attacked like a machine gun:

You accuse Freud, you accuse Father! I know why: because it's me they love. You claim you're his favorite? He doesn't even invite you to his home. I alone have the privilege of his intimacy. You? The Wolf Man, his famous case? He's written on quite a few others. Others have stayed longer on his couch than you.

Result: Tierka passed to the exterior in the relational transference. She led the troika of the analysis. The new movement took the form of rebuttals. A series of dreams bore witness to it:

You attack me, you resent me! You're just great to see with your boots and trousers. You, a poet? You, Father's nightingale? But you don't even know Russian. I'll tell you what you are: an old liar of a gypsy woman spreading false rumors.

But Stanko's attempted rejoinder was futile. He convinced neither Tierka nor the Wolf Man. The next dream took him back to the incorporated Father and to his function, within the internal world, as an inadmissible model.

The Father . . . resembling a wondering musician . . . sits at a table . . . and warns the others present not to talk about financial matters in front of the patient because of his tendency to speculate. His father's nose is long and hooked. (Gardiner, *The Wolf-Man by the Wolf-Man*, p. 286; translation of quoted material has been modified throughout in accordance with the French version—Trans.)

In this dream Father and Son merged in the hypocrisy of the nose, in their deceit, in their "gypsy lifestyle." They both had a secret connected to "money" and "speculation," a secret of undue pleasure. Thus, Tierka-analyst would learn nothing about the orgasm in Professor X.'s office. Yet, the Wolf Man's desire for Tierka, the analyst, grew. Along with it grew the sense of the impossibility to *tell*. And this would be the first nightmare. On the couch of the Harem, the vision of the star in the half-moon remains untranslatable. No! No way here to reveal by what desire and by what detour the Wolf Man wanted to become Father to Tierka. Was the image before his eyes not the hallucination of a "madman"? Would that the analyst stop urging him to say the unutterable. He begged her and threw himself at her feet. What special favor would he like to obtain?

The Wolf Man's desire must remain silent. The following nightmare explains this characteristic:

> In a wide street is a wall with a closed door. To the left of the door is a large, empty wardrobe . . . Near the other end of the wall stands a large, heavy-set woman . . . But behind the wall is a pack of gray wolves, crowding toward the door and pacing impatiently back and forth. Their eyes gleam . . . I am terrified, fearing that they will succeed in breaking through the wall. (*Ibid.*, p. 288)

Here is the paradox: The "wardrobe," if it is emptied, is emptied—according to the Wolf Man's associations to the dream—by the "Bolsheviks"; it stands to the "left." By which we understand: Were S. P. to unburden himself by telling, he would commit an illegitimate act. On the other hand, if he keeps the lie (the scar on his nose), then he stands on the right, he is on the right side. Unable to state his unutterable desire, represented here by the rushing back and forth of the wolves, the Wolf Man takes a backseat to his Guests. The "wolves" of his desire, however, crowd to his lips (like a diarrhea that comes "wolfing" out); the words are ready to cross the limiting wall. They gleam at what the eyes had seen, they throng in a rush to break the obstacle, the anal hymen that can hardly contain them. To say all would be orgasm: Tierka consenting, a "wolf" in hand! This is a nightmare of the end of the world.

No, neither lust nor cataclysm will break out this time. But in the Wolf Man, backed up against his desire, not knowing which way to turn, rage rankles. He would kill them all—Father, Tierka, Therapist—and this time it is not just melodrama. The director has fired the actors. He himself acts. A persecutor-persecuted. He exacts, threatens. He would do anything, and seriously . . .

rather than . . . *tell*! After a long period of disorderly agitation a solution finally emerges: the Mother. He dreams:

> My mother takes the icons down and throws them on the floor. The pictures fall and break into pieces. I am astonished that my pious mother should do such a thing. (*Ibid.*, p. 291)

Thus he makes the Mother accomplish the gesture required by his own wrath, his own desire. She, not he, removes the saints of the family. She, not Tierka, will take hold of, break up—shine—his penis. An ingenious subterfuge to achieve climax while avoiding telling. Incest for incest. And this thought will have the virtue of putting everything back in order. His system of contradictions and insulations will be not broached but, for a while, buried. At most, according to the next day's dream, the mommy-hand of the masturbator joins with the gaze of the warm Sun he has become, to contemplate in aesthetic admiration the gambols of Father and Daughter (not of the parents as Brunswick claims). His lust, altogether aesthetic, dapples the meadow with lovely spots. "Stones of a strange mauve" placed here and there retain their secret, however, and like the Rosetta stone, await their Champollion. Such an idyll can only be, alas, the wish of a dream. Tomorrow, the violent desire to betray, along with its impasse, will revive.

The next dream already—a nightmare again—shows him cornered with his erection.

> I am with you in a skyscraper where the only way out is a window . . . , he awakens in great anxiety, looking desperately for an escape route. (*Ibid.*, p. 292)

The escape of telling would be too dangerous. Another must be found at all costs. What would it mean to tell? A second dream of the same night makes this explicit: It would mean accusing Freud of child molesting for having used him in an undue account of his case. Let Freud forbid him such an accusation (the dream about penal law); that would protect S. P. from the temptation to betray. Moreover, this recent secret would cover up the old one and the new "seducer" would reinforce the order of silence of long ago. The analyst conforms to this wish under the cover of a denial. She says: Such a prohibition coming from Freud is inconceivable. The money Freud gave him was certainly not hush money. This suggestion was not apt to open the window of telling. It nonetheless brought something like a recovery to the internal Father, as well as to his Tierka-penis.

With the Father thus restored to his potency, a pseudo-Oedipal triangle begins to take shape, though in a strange fashion. Father on the couch, Tierka in the chair, and finally Stanko, projected to the outside in Freud, being eliminated. In fact, this final sequence is meant to restore the idyllic union between Father and Daughter by casting out Stanko. Yes, the next dream will say, Tierka holds the remedy, let her reserve it for Father. For by himself, he could not treat the headache of the "young" (the old) Austrian (Freud as Stanko). "No, not really, – he continues in other dreams – I wouldn't give even ten shillings for Freud's old music." "I accepted his 'colored postcards' because I had not the courage to refuse them, but the *pages* that you will write about me I will be able to take on my knees as the true penis you are for me" (for me, meaning Father, of course). We do not know, far from it, what was said between analyst and patient, and Brunswick's account does contain many regrettable, though understandable, gaps. What we know for sure is that Freud's image as a seducer was broken down along with the idea of complicity between the first and second analysts. Henceforth, S. P. can again close his eyes to the secrets living on in his momentarily pacified internal world. The Therapist is reinstated in his function, the "gonorrhea" cured for good, and the final dream of this new treatment expresses the wish – never articulated much less attained – that Freud should recognize what analyst and patient have already admitted to each other, namely, that there had been a mistake and that the famous "Wolf Man" refers to someone else's case, not to S. P.'s: "No, no, it is not this man but another" are the words he attributes in his last dream to the dermatologist who lives on the same street as Freud.

For the Wolf Man this meant a turning point. For years he had been unable to enjoy novels, formerly his favorite pastime. He stated that he could not identify himself with either the heroes arbitrarily created by the authors or the authors themselves. Now he was certain the pages his new analyst planned to write about him, with his collaboration, would not fall into the same category. Thus he recovered his old passion for literature, "became once more a keen, scrupulous, and attractive personality endowed with a variety of interests and talents, and with a depth of analytic understanding that made his company a constant source of pleasure."

S. P.'s veil was not torn loose any more than in his analysis with Freud. Yet, as we have seen, behind the veil there reigned something quite different from mere calm. There were some oppressive moments, some storms, and some lovely clearings. But the secret had not come through; the secret of something a child had experienced and had transformed into an erect *wolf* with a grandmother's bonnet on its head and big rocks in its stomach. Officially we were supposed to remain ignorant of the fact that he might have had dealings with this wolf other than being afraid of it under certain circumstances.

The analytic transformations we have just experienced, which allowed the Wolf Man to recover a precarious balance, unfold like a drama in three acts.

The first act shows a protracted confrontation with the pathetic impossibility of killing Father's Tierka without harming Father and thus himself. On a more superficial level, this represents the impossibility of destroying the false image of himself that Freud's mirror seems to hold without implicating Freud.

The mirror is shattered only in a dream; but the second act opens with an unexpected turn: the psychodramatic personification of Tierka by the analyst. A drama about the persecution of cornered desire, of the struggle against rage. But once again the solution is whisked away. At the crucial moment, the action breaks off. Again, icons are shattered in a dream rather than the secret unveiled in words. For imagining the murder of the Father-Daughter union will not suppress in him the foreign body that the union constitutes. To achieve that the union would have to be denounced. At the height of conflict, the impulse to do so becomes a source of terror in several nightmares, and the second act aborts in turn.

The third and final act of the analysis shows definite progress. Freud-Father is denounced at last. But to whom exactly? To his own accomplice, Tierka. Short-circuit. The Father-Daughter union is only apparently broken. In fact, a redistribution of roles appears preferable. Such is the pseudo-denouement. The Wolf Man will take on Father's role. He can therefore eliminate Stanko, the enemy and lover, represented by the now undesirable Freud. The curtain falls on a manic Oedipus.

For at least two years, the "wolf" will lie dormant. When the analysis is taken up again in 1929 precisely because of a symptom of impotence, Father will have ample opportunity to talk about his son Stanko again, and add many new details. Will Father be rehabilitated or eliminated? We do not know. It is likely, however, that S. P.'s desire for the "Sister" as well as for the "erect wolf," her instrument, will remain—to the very end—outside the circuit of speech.

Chapter 2
Behind the Inner World

The Wolf Man's drama remains incomplete for its hero. But once set in motion, its action cannot be stopped; it must proceed in us inevitably to its final outcome. And here our dissatisfaction, spurred on by a providential *deus ex machina*, expounds, imagines, dreams. An irresistible force pulls us: to save the analysis of the Wolf-Man, to save ourselves. With time the fourth act opens within us, stretches before us, and in us comes to fulfillment, bringing salvation.

1. An Impromptu Walk Through a Verbarium: Cryptonyms and What They Hide

The authors arrived at this very juncture in the process of their writing, and planned to take up Freud's text again with their point of view – incorporation – in mind, when it occurred to them to consult a Russian dictionary. This gesture, performed out of conscientiousness, brought an extra load of unforeseen work, but also a host of altogether unexpected insights. First, it enabled the authors to refine their hypotheses about the genesis and working of incorporation in general and about the specific incorporation of which the Wolf Man was both actor and victim. But even more, it brought home the fact that someone could be driven to take on the same attitude toward words as toward things, namely, objects of love, and that such word-objects could upset a topography to the point where incorporation would seem a self-therapeutic measure.

Initially, the authors had wanted to be certain there was no hidden ambiguity behind the repeated retraction of the number that first appeared in the principal dream. The original number given is six, immediately corrected to seven, whereas on the well-known drawing the number is reduced to five. Six in Russian, SHIEST, also means perch, mast, and probably genitals, at least symbolically. This could have satisfied an ill-formed psychoanalytic mind. Fortunately, the authors' eyes fell on the neighboring words: SHIESTIERO and SHIESTORKA, meaning six or a lot of six people. Contaminated by the German *Schwester* (sister), they could not help checking the word sister as well, and there they discovered, to their amusement and confirming their suspicion, the words SIESTRA and its diminutive SIESTORKA. It became clear that the "pack of six wolves" did not contain the idea of multiplicity, but of the sister instead. Were we not justified from then on to look for the same association of ideas elsewhere? It was likely, in fact, that in the nightmares and the Wolf Man's phobic moments, wolf and sister would occur together. We simply had to survey the Russian vocabulary of the dreams and phobias and, where needed, fill in the gaps with his second language, German.

Here is a brief review of what we found. The nightmare about the "wolves" analyzed in the preceding chapter enabled us to establish rather easily that the "pack of wolves" crowding behind the door in the wall corresponded, insofar as it was a "pack," to a "pack of six," to a "sixter" of wolves so to speak, though the number is not stated this time. We nevertheless potentially have SIESTORKA-BUKA (siswolf). In the dream of the celestial bodies we find ZVIEZDA-LUNA (star moon), the same arrangement of vowels with a slight phonetic distortion. The nightmare of the skyscraper gave us more trouble. NIEBOSKREB (skyscraper in Russian) did not seem to have anything to do with either wolf or sister. Conversely, the German word for skyscraper (*Wolkenkratzer*)—we had to think of it—does indeed contain the "wolf" we were seeking; the other Russian name for wolf, BUKA, being precisely VOLK. As for the "sister," we could only find disagreeable words in the places we had expected her: SKREB, the root of SKREBOK = scraper; SKROÏT = to sharpen,; SKRIP = scraping sound, and here we came close to giving up Russian altogether. But by tinkering with these words, we gained some new terms for our vocabulary: scrape, scratch, cut, bruise, scar, and, through German, cancer (*skreb* = *Krebs*)—all meanings we will encounter again, under various guises, in the clinical material.

Then we ventured a final hypothesis, and this turned out to be our lifesaver. If all these words—we advanced—in some way allude to the sister, this time they do so otherwise than through a veiled evocation of the word: sister. Why restrict our attention to the nightmares and phobias when the hypochondriac fears concerning the nose speak explicitly about scratch, scar, and cancer? Obviously, behind this was lurking the association, undoubtedly left nonverbalized, of a *lupus*, namely a *lupus seborrheus*. The hypochondriac ideas would appear to rest on the same verbal support as the nightmare of the "skyscraper." The same support, no doubt, but what on earth was it? We pursued our inquiry. What was striking—we used to tell each other—was a certain unity of meaning among all these rather different-sounding words whose list could be lengthened at will by a whole series of analogies. This profusion of terms, carrying the idea of *wound* and stated in such diverse forms, did it really refer to the idea of castration? On the basis of the two word couples just reconstituted, *siestorka-buka* and *zviezda-luna*, we had no reason to stick with such a hypothesis. Why deviate here from our initial line of thought and not admit—even at the cost of extrapolation—that all these locutions simply cover up another word, this one signaling sexual pleasure and alluding to the so-called seduction scene? Given the abundance of synonyms, we also understood that there was no mere phonetic or paronymic displacement at work here as in *zviezda-luna*, but that, in order to reach the sought-after key word, we had to move across the signifieds and search for semantic displacements. The key word, no doubt unutterable for some reason, and unknown for the moment, would have to be polysemic, expressing multiple meanings through a single phonetic structure. One of these would remain shrouded, but the other, or several other meanings now equivalent, would be stated through distinct phonetic structures, that is, through synonyms. To make our conversations about this easier, we would call them *cryptonyms* (words that hide) because of their allusion to a foreign and arcane meaning. We also wanted to set them apart from simple metonymic displacement.

Spurred on by these considerations, we turned to the privileged libidinal moment, Grusha, the floor scrubber with her bucket and broom. A rather problematic scene as to its historical truth but nonetheless significant—we thought—for its erogenous value. How to link it to the seduction by the sister? Would she have touched him in a way that the child could have called "polish" as one also says "polish" a wooden floor? What an incongruous idea! Let's check it out anyway! The French-Russian dictionary gives TIERET, NATIERET. Let's go to the Russian-French dictionary; it will tell us whether the meaning "polish" coexists with others like scratch, scrape, and so forth, a necessary condition for the cryptonymic displacement just conjectured. Conscious of our duty, but not very hopeful, we then turned to the word *tieret* and read: (1) to rub; (2) to grind, to crunch; (3) to wound; (4) to polish. The second word *natieret*, of the same root, did not disappoint us either. It exhibits a comparable semantic variety, going from (1) to rub down, rub; through (2) to rub, scrub, wax; to finally (3) to scrape or wound oneself. We could not have asked for more! Finally we understood the rebus of the skyscraper! With all the necessary substitutions, the solution is simple: It concerns the association of the wolf with sexual pleasure obtained by rubbing.

By the same token, a whole area of the Wolf Man's enigmatic material was opened to our understanding. Lingering for the moment on the nose symptom, it became precise and concrete. The symptom had been produced, it was clear now, through the association of two words: one omitted and the other transformed into a cryptonym. The first pointed to the object of the hypochondriac fear, *lupus* (wolf); the second, scar, referred to the name of the action through which the dreaded pleasure would be accomplished: *tieret, natieret*. The hypochondriac *lupus*, coupled with the cryptonym "scar", did nothing more than show/hide the desire of a pleasurable rubbing applied to the "wolf" in order to make it stand up. "Sis, come and rub my penis." This was the key sentence. These were the unsayable words that he posted in the form of a rebus, making sure to add at the bottom: "You will never guess." It became obvious that this hidden sentence would be found everywhere in the Wolf Man's material.

We could fill pages and pages drawing up the catalog of its various guises. We could also, in light of this new approach, take up again, point by point, our earlier psychodramatic reinterpretation of Brunswick's text. In many places we could simplify or even rectify it. If we have left this up to our readers, by printing our initial version intact, we did so wanting to include them all the more in our fumbling around. They will much better appreciate the ground covered.

Among the applications of our discovery concerning the use of cryptonyms, we found most striking our realization that certain words suffered an extraordinary exclusion and that this same exclusion seemed to confer on them a genuinely magic power. The verbs *tieret* and *natieret* had to be entirely banished from the active vocabulary and not only in the sense of rubbing, but also in the sense of waxing or scraping. What if these parallel meanings, these allosemes, had to be stated? Each time they were, by means of synonyms, they obviously implied a constant reference, even if a negative one, to the *taboo word*. It was, we thought, because a given word was unutterable that the obligation arose to introduce synonyms even for its lateral meanings, and that the synonyms acquired the status of substitutes. Thus they became *cryptonyms*, apparently not having any phonetic or semantic relationship to the prohibited word. *tzarapat* (scratch, scrape) bears no apparent relation to *tieret* (to rub). In sum, no simple metonymic displacement is at work here, referring to one element of a concrete situation instead of another element actually intended (as when we say pen to mean style or writer), but a displacement on a second level: The word itself as a lexical entity constitutes the global situation from which one particular meaning is sectioned out of the sum total of meanings. This characteristic could be expressed by saying that what is at stake here is not a *metonymy of things* but a *metonymy of words*. The contiguity that presides over this procedure is by nature not a representation of things, not even a representation of words, but arises from the lexical contiguity of the various meanings of the same words, that is, from the *allosemes*, as they are catalogued in a dictionary. For TZARAPINA (scar), to evoke *tieret* (to rub), a form of lexical contiguity has to be inserted. Having understood the real originality of this procedure, which lies in replacing a word by the synonym of its alloseme, we felt the need of applying to it a distinctive name, *cryptonymy*.

2. Behind the Scenes: Internal Hysteria—
Setting Up and Working a Machinery

With this added clarification and the necessary verification done in the material, the question emerged of how one is led to invent such a procedure considering that it does not provide, either phonetically or semantically, the hallucinatory satisfaction we might reasonably expect. The only pertinent answer seemed as follows: It is not a situation *including* words that becomes repressed; the words are not dragged into repression by a situation. Rather, *the words themselves, expressing desire, are deemed to be generators of a situation that must be avoided and voided retroactively*. In this case, and only in this case, can we understand that repression may be carried out on the word, as if it were the representation of a thing, and that the return of the repressed cannot have at its disposal even the tortuous paths of metonymic displacement. For this to occur, a catastrophic situation must have been created precisely by words. We understand then why they would be excluded, responsible as they are for a situation; why they would be repressed from the Preconscious, dragging with them their lateral and allo-semic meanings. In short: It is the idea that words can be excluded from the Preconscious—thus also from the dream texts—and replaced, in the name and capacity of the return of the repressed, by cryptonyms or their visual representation that is required for a general preliminary conclusion to our inquiry.

Let us now try to fill this formal frame with more concrete content. For such a construction, two elements have to be taken into account: First, the words in question must signify an erotic pleasure received from the sister; and second, they are responsible, because stated inauspiciously, for the castration, that is, the demolition of the father. Based on this double hypothesis, various possibilities can be imagined, and among them we settled on the idea that the traumatic catastrophy could not have taken place at one definite moment, but would have unfolded in four stages.

1. *The "seduction" of the younger brother by the older sister*. The term "seduction" might seem somewhat excessive to describe, as Freud did, sexual play among little children. For such games to take on the magnitude we know they can, an adult must be implicated. That is why we have suggested from the very beginning a stage—

2. *The alleged seduction of the daughter by the father*. The sister would have boasted about the privilege she had over her little brother, and in the process would have threatened him with castration at the moment of pleasure. Now, in light of the cryptonymic procedure, we abandon the idea stated at the beginning of this work of such a threat of castration. We now in fact know that the terms that in the material seemed to evoke castration are simply the cryptonyms of repressed pleasure-words. Nevertheless, the hypothesis of two further stages forces itself on us, stage—

3. *The boy's verification with adults of the allegations made by his sister*, at first perhaps with Nania or the English governess, then with his mother back from a trip, finally with his father—then stage

4. *The outbreak of a scandal*, with an investigation as regards the meaning of the words *tieret, natieret* indicting the father.

This fourth stage is postulated as having the mark of a real experience and can in no way be merged with fantasy. This is what explains, to our mind, the uniqueness of the Wolf Man's case: the radical exclusion of the words of desire. The excluded *words* work as if they were representations of repressed *things*. They seem to have migrated from the Preconscious to the Unconscious. They have taken with them the very possibility of remembering the trauma. Their absence in the Preconscious signifies: The trauma never took place. What distinguishes a verbal exclusion of this kind from neurotic repression is precisely the fact that it renders verbalization impossible. The return of the deeply repressed, if it happens at all, cannot come about within a relation, in the form of symptoms or symbols. It will occur within the psychic apparatus through a kind of *internal hysteria* and will be directed toward the internal Objects incorporated for this purpose. Settled within the Ego with their complete topography—as it had been experienced at zero hour—these Objects remain the invisible yet omnipresent partners of the excluded desire concerning them. They will be oppressed by their own Superegos as in melancholy, or they will be satisfied by fulfilling *their* unconscious desire as in mania. The Ego proper, whose function is to be Hand for the Libido, Hand for Sex, will have become Sex for *another* Hand, Hand for *another* Sex. Its own activity will consist in satisfying or counteracting the desires lent to its Guests, or to their respective Ego Ideals, and of thus maintaining them within itself. The return of the deeply repressed can come about only in relation to this internal world. On the outside, it will merely appear in the form of failure, somatization, or delirium. The *incorporated* guests—hence the term—lodge in the *corporeal* Ego. The internal hysteria of the Ego proper reaches them there. The cryptonymic procedure manages somehow to pass over their heads and address external Objects. The work of the only authentic area remaining in an alienated Ego, it deserves, its strangeness notwithstanding, the respect due any attempt at *being* in spite of everything.

For the Wolf-Man—we understand why—a return of the repressed in the waking state through symbolization, for example, is out of the question. The single exception concerns the expression of *the very act of the retention of telling*, well expressed hysterically by tenacious constipation. But whatever might be the *object* of telling is so deeply buried behind words never to be uttered that its emergence, when it does take place, occurs not in the form of a symbol or a symptom but of a delirium such as that of the nose or later of the cut finger, and finally of the erogenous fantasy itself. In this last instance, the appearances seem safe: What would be delirious about imagining a coitus performed a tergo and the suitable position of the partners (a tiergo the analyst would say with well-taken mischief). Apparently nothing, were it not for its incredible verbal origin: *tieret* visualized into a floor scrubber. We see here a genuine dream process in full wakefulness. In order to tell himself his desire, he has to have recourse to dream distortion. The erogenous fantasy, Grusha the floor scrubber, the washerwoman at the fountain as well as the parents' supposed coitus a tergo, were nothing but a word, translated into an image. The face, the person of the woman are of no importance, provided she illustrates, she embodies the taboo word. It is in this sense that we are going to call this erogenous image, this good-luck-charm fantasy, this magical taboo dodger: *a fetish*. Beneath the fetish, the occult love for a word-object remains concealed, beneath this love, the taboo-forming experience of a catastrophe, and finally beneath the catastrophe, the perennial memory of a hoarded pleasure with the ineducable wish that one day it shall return.

The Wolf Man's hope was deposited in the word whose secret lover he was. This word, his Object, he kept in his possession for an entire lifetime. Initially and by vocation, the word was addressed to someone. As an Object of love, it had to be removed from everyone's reach so that it would not be lost. Saying it without saying it. To show/hide. Walk around with a rebus and pretend it is undecipherable. Repeat tirelessly to one and all, especially to his analyst: "Here is nothing, hold it tight." Inaccessible, wending his way alongside the unattainable. To love without knowing, to love desperately, to love loving the analyst endlessly.

3. The Fourth Act: On Freud's Couch—The Wolf Man as unto Himself

It was—we now know—for never having been able to utter certain words that, sixteen years earlier, the Wolf Man went to consult the famous Professor Freud. Following a bout of gonorrhea (curbed, however, by rather drastic means five years earlier), he remained in a state of near-total impotence. He dragged himself from doctors to health care centers without finding a remedy for what ailed him. The Professor was his last resort. Freud did not consider him a "maniac" for his loves at first sight as psychiatrists had done. He listened, he tried to understand, he requested his collaboration. Together they would find the cause of so much suffering. The Professor inspired confidence in particular by his subdued style of dressing, and the furniture of his office suggested praiseworthy occupations. The austere and sympathetic man of science was perfectly suitable. S. P. was more than reassured. What got into him then when, hardly having lowered himself on to the couch, he requested from his respectable therapist the favor of performing anal coitus and invited him to defecate while standing on his head?[1] Had he been the Tierka he knew at four years of age, he could not have done better. Without a doubt, his "wolf" was surfacing. The same one that had been so cruelly treated at the time of his gonorrhea. Since then, almost five years earlier, his depression had not left him. This was evidence that one does not make "wolf" without risking one's tail, even if it was only a father's tail. Could he ever recover his *buka* standing up, could he finally protect it from danger? He placed all his hopes in the Professor. He would tell him everything. Everything, yes, except . . . one thing: the unsayable. They would launch their investigation together, they would study the facts, their chronology. Together they would draw conclusions about the causes and the consequences. He could sleep with peace of mind, nothing will escape the sagacity of the Professor. Yet, hardly reclined on the couch, this strange thing happens. What a *coup de théâtre* for the analyst! And for him! Has anyone seen a well-bred young man, not suspected of homosexuality, make such a request of an eminent specialist of fifty? No, really, he was no longer himself.

But who, in fact, was he? Before and now? Freud in truth could never establish it. Are we, at the end of this study, in a position to put forth a hypothesis on this score? It seems fairly certain that no affective recollection took place during the transference and that nothing occurred that could have identified him: "Yes, here he is, this is definitely S. P., seduced at three years of age by his sister, desiring his father at five, his mother at eight." S. P. in person was not present. His official identity only served to cover up the other characters he clandestinely sheltered within himself: his father, his sister. A depressed and castrated father for having rubbed up against Tierka, Matrona, that is who he was during his depression. But once on the couch everything changed: The man in the chair was now named Father and the man on the couch automatically took on the complementary role, Tierka's role. This was the unexpected but inescapable effect of the analytic situation. His depression vanished, and with his extravagant request began a flirtation between Father and Sister that was to last four and a half years. This unusual first session was simply Tierka dallying with Papa. As the years went by, the coquetry took on forms more suited to the norms of the analytic dialogue and to the widely publicized desiderata of the father of psychoanalysis. Throughout more than one thousand sessions, Tierka unflinchingly recounted Stanko's memories, dreams, nightmares. She added some of her own invention. Father and Daughter could live happily.

As for Freud, he must have been thrilled and disconcerted all at the same time. Soon he thought he could identify the "wolf" in the nightmare, the "wolf" in the infantile phobia: It represented some terrifying image in relation to the father. It must have been the father himself. He still needed to understand how this kind and loving father could have instilled fright in the child when all the memories of "castration" were linked to female images. Should one incriminate a phrase such as the unfortunate one used to tease children: "I'm going to eat you," or should one appeal to the phylogenetic fear of being castrated by the father? Such answers hardly convinced anyone, including their author. Freud was just as baffled when faced with the allegation of a Primal Scene supposedly observed at the age of eighteen months. Still, the parents' coitus a tergo seen at this tender age could—theoretically—have caused a neurosis and subsequent sexual behavior. The case seemed too good not to be used in the polemic against Jung. Let us admit though that, removed from its context of heated controversy, such an example was altogether untenable. Moreover, Freud needed no such arguments to defend his ideas. In any case, this matter remains a prime example of theoretical and clinical errors occasioned by a heated controversy.

The Wolf Man himself felt reassured. Tierka and Father united, they spoke of Stanko, and for all of them everything turned out for the best. Of course the "wolf" was Father, of course Father had to castrate Stanko, of course Stanko feared him with good reason. So long as Father is not castrated again, never ever, through inopportune words, through the explosion of outraged anger. To void what had taken place once upon a time, the catastrophic words had to be contained at all costs: Squeeze the sphincter tighter and tighter! Constipate the fatal word! And above all, the "window" must never open by itself! Otherwise there would be the horrifying nightmare of the wolves of long ago: a fossilized phrase in a fossilized picture. "*Siestorka* makes *buka* to Father." "Sis, come and make Stanko's "wolf" stand up." No! Such words will forever remain in his throat. Let the two of them be happy and S. P. can live!

Yes, S. P. is entirely a gift of himself in the strictest sense. Did he keep to himself some desire that he had not offered? This will remain unknown to all including himself. No one on earth must know who he is. No one on earth must know that one day he *became* his father or that he carried him within himself along with his castrated desire. This father has to be restored, such is his most fervent desire; otherwise he, Stanko, could never pronounce, in his own name, the sentence of his own desire, say it to Tierka without disaster: "Come Sis, rub me, do Buka to me!" Alas, these words, these diabolical words, he will never give voice to them, for they—yes, we have to admit it—castrated the father, castrated the son. They are the ones that threw the mother into despondency. They are the ones that, through their belated effects, led to the sister's suicide, to the father's premature death. A few innocent words, and all of a sudden the whole family is destroyed.

This sentence, however, always the same one, the Wolf Man will never tire of repeating in riddles. Tieret, to rub, wax, wash. Sissy, "get on all fours" to "brush," Grusha, to "wax," Matrona, yes, do *tronut*, do touch, touch me! I'll go crazy ("become touched"). Oh, Matrona! Matrona, a cherished word: Russian doll, you hold my Jack-in-the-box, *vanka, vstanka*, let's put it on its head, you'll see how it *makes out*! It was enough for me to *act* a word: "scrape," "cut" into a tree and I was already in heaven, I had my little finger "cut." Come, Professor, do these words to me. "Cut," oh! "cut me," "pull me," "rip me," oh, confounded words, unsayable words, oh! yes, rub, rub my genitals for me so they stand up on two paws like a wolf disguised as a grandmother with a white bonnet on its head. Oh, yes "rip off (*tierebit*) the wings of this wasp, of this S. P." (*Wespe*), rub, rub it for he cannot stand it—but . . . .

All this, S. P. does not say clearly. But fast, very fast, in hardly three months, since that was the nonnegotiable deadline Freud had set in order to finish it off, he laid it out in cryptonyms and cryptomyths.

And with his time up, the Wolf Man left, relieved, for his native Russia. He felt relieved since he had spoken and invented disguises for his desire. Relieved also not to have to speak it in disaster words, relieved finally, since he could take back the memory of a new kind of father, of a father whose seductive practices were restricted to harmless words, rather amusing by the way, like the word "castration," so often on the lips of the Professor, and which happily joined the list of cryptonyms.

And in all likelihood everything would have been fine for him after that had the incidents of the Revolution not forced him into exile five years later. In 1919, upon his arrival in Vienna, Freud's famous case study had just been published. He was so happy reading it! The illustrious father had become involved with his case, and more than that, he released his appreciative judgment to the public: " . . . pleasant and likeable personality"; he had spoken of his "sharp intelligence" and of "his refinement of thought."

Yet, deep down in the Wolf Man, there was disappointment and revolt. He went to see the Master once more. He let him know that he had not been cured, and especially not of this constipation that Freud so proudly claimed to have alleviated. Moreover, being financially ruined as he was, he could not afford another analysis. That should not stand in the way! the Professor said with sympathy. And then came free analysis, donations. Wages for not being himself. For the Wolf Man, the apparently happy situation revived a latent despair: Stanko misunderstood, castrated, disposed of. Father giving money to Tierka . . . . When in October 1923, the seriousness of Freud's illness became common knowledge, the horizon blackened even more. If Father disappeared, who would ever free S. P.'s desire? We know the rest.

Forever he will keep his love in his own possession, his Objects which are words. Unable to convert these word-objects into words for the object, his life remains, for himself and for us all, an enigma. Yet, in all this life, unfurling the flag of enigma, the Wolf Man has never left us. He remains with us analysts, to quicken our desire to know. Whether he appears to us as a living support for our projections and resistances or as an ever-renewing source of inspiration, we owe him a character: The Wolf Man, an intuition: Mourning and Melancholia, an anthropology: the second topography. Ever bent on offering a new element in order to clear up his mystery, he further obscures it. Our companion of misfortune in no-knowledge, he has become the symbol of a mirage—haunting every analyst—the mirage of understanding. After so many others, we too have succumbed to it.

Let him be thanked for it!

And let us be forgiven for it!

September 27, 1970

Postscript. It should be clear that the preceding considerations relate to the Wolf Man only as a mythical person. Their wholly fictitious—though not gratuitous—nature illustrates an approach that can be of clinical use. What we termed *internal hysteria*, and considered as the consequence of *incorporation*, often implies unconscious procedures motivated by a particular topographical structure involving the *cryptonymic displacement of a taboo word*. Rightly or wrongly, we discovered such a taboo word in the Wolf Man: *tieret* and its derivatives. The reader may be interested in some additional information that has come to us through the kind generosity of Muriel Gardiner. We refer here to the Wolf Man's *Memoirs*, which began appearing in serial form in 1961 in the *Bulletin of the Philadelphia Association for Psycho-analysis*. These memoirs are of great psychoanalytic interest and deserve an extended study. We mention only two details because they relate directly to our findings. The first is this: Following the suicide of his sister Anna (this was her real name), who ingested a bottle of mercury during a trip to the Caucasus, the Wolf Man went on a trip to these same mountains, without realizing, however, that there might be a geographic connection between these facts. On close reading of his recollections it becomes apparent that the unconscious goal of this trip was to climb to the head of a mountain stream named Tierek. Upon arriving after a long and anxious ascent, he could not keep from taking out his paintbox and brushes to "paint" (*tieret*) a view of the landscape. He also recalls that he was served *trout* caught in the *Tierek* River. The second point we want to make concerns the love at first sight he conceived for his future wife, a pretty nurse in a Kraepelin clinic (in Munich) where he had come to stay in the throes of a depression. He did not exchange a word with her, but an elderly Russian lady, also a resident there, furnished, with the appropriate Russian accent no doubt, one crucial piece of information: the name of the young woman. Her name was Sister Theresa (homophone of the Russian verb TIRETSIA, to rub oneself) and the diminutive was Terka, pronounced in Russian fashion: Tierka. We might have guessed it. In any case, our choice of the same name to designate the incorporated sister predates this information and—though inspired by the verb *tieret*—must be considered the work of some lucky coincidence.

II. The Nightmare of the Wolves: Contribution to the Analysis of Dreams, Slips, and Phobias

Chapter 3
The Nightmare of the Wolves

1. The Request for Truth

When we pick up our work three years later, Sergei Wolf Man is in his eighty-seventh year.[1] He has been speaking to analysts since his twenty-fourth year. For a long time to Freud, then some fifteen years later to Ruth Mack Brunswick. Many others followed, and to this day he continues his psychoanalytic sessions. During this half century he has led his life, so to speak, concurrently: his marriage with Theresa, the loss of his enormous family fortune, exile, financial aid from analysts, his job as insurance agent, a stormy sexual life, his wife's suicide at the time of the *Anschluss*, his subsequent breakdown and the helpful assistance of Muriel Gardiner, another analyst; the war, its hardships, the loss of his mother at age eighty-nine, the last member of his close family; work with paint brushes, much work with brushes to paint with bold "brush-strokes" certain landscapes he finds fascinating, just as he once found fascinating the image of white wolves sitting on a tree; then his years of retirement, leaving him plenty of time to engage in his favorite pastime; his correspondence with Muriel Gardiner; and, finally, prompted by her request, the writing of his well-known memoirs, recently published in English, then in German, and soon to appear in French. A best-selling author at age eighty-four, he is the owner of a small fortune won thanks to people's interest in his words by way of Freud and psychoanalysis. According to the latest news (summer 1974), he is in excellent health for his age.

This man, who is at once strange and average, has always lived under the guise of a double identity and has never lacked the resourcefulness needed to preserve it. His friends do not know that for analysts his name is Wolf Man and, as for analysts, they do not know, save for a few, what his real name is. It is as if he has had to maintain two separate worlds that cannot, must not communicate with each other.

Freud remarks with profound intuition in *The History of an Infantile Neurosis* (1918), right after having commented on the nightmare of the wolves: "The whale and the polar bear, it has been said, cannot wage war on each other; that is, since each is confined to his own element, they cannot meet" (*Standard Edition*, vol. 17, p. 48). Indeed, there are elements in the Wolf Man's psyche that must never meet. But should one believe that Sergei Wolf Man keeps speaking endlessly to analysts in order not to be heard? Ever since the release of his memoirs he does not simply have *one* analyst, but thousands, yes thousands, of ears to listen to him. Could it be that his purpose is to have his readers confirm the split in his personality that Freud, thinking precisely of the Wolf Man, touched on in his very last piece (*The Split in the Ego*)? The shrug of many a disillusioned or frustrated reader at having been denied some great revelation is not an adequate response to the question.

Between the lines, the Wolf Man is always in search of truth, of a truth he cannot state himself. The apparent literary banality and moral conventionalism of his autobiographical account may also be interpreted as truly symptomatic, as a caricature of the conventional "truths" of the self-righteous. Once this is understood, his work acquires the tragic dimension of a very human oeuvre. In every line he writes, and in all that he chooses not to write, one hears the cry: You don't really want to know anything about what I am!

And yet! . . . how can he overlook the fact that the oeuvre of his life is woven into his analyses and that the writings of Freud, Ruth Mack Brunswick, Muriel Gardiner, and finally his own, make up one great and single testimony, a single poem with several voices, which we will continue to comment on for a long, long time?

2. And Language as Truth Guard

From time to time, made confident by a long-standing friendship, he suggests — albeit incidentally — some tricks for opening our ears. A letter he sent in 1959 to Muriel Gardiner, who lost no time in relaying it to the authors of *The Wolf-Man's Magic Word* when she heard about their article (1970), bears witness to this. One passage, the last paragraph of the letter, is worth quoting. The lines are increasingly squeezed together: Everything must be said before the space runs out. The beginning of the message, written in a big hand is quite insignificant. He writes:

> Despite these misfortunes, I obviously try to keep up my interest in reading. As a matter of fact, I recently read Felix Dahn's book about Germanic gods; until now this had been a totally unknown topic to me. I am interested in this book . . . especially as regards — how shall I put it? — comparative linguistics, for I was able to find the Germanic roots of some Russian words. For example the first name *Trude* comes from the Germanic *Trud*, which means "force." This old Germanic word is very likely the root of the Russian *trud*, since in Russian *trud* designates the "effort" one needs in order to work. The Russian word *molnia* for saying *Blitz*, lightning in German, must be derived from *miôlnir*. Indeed, this word names the hammer of the Germanic god "Thor-Donnar" which, according to popular lore, produced the lightning (*Blitz*). Lightning is supposed to be the wedge-shaped tip of the thunder hammer. The Russian name for water, *voda*, is identical to the one standing for the same concept in Sanskrit: *voda*, *veda* = *Wasser*.[2] It is also quite odd that the sagas make the gods die and fall when the Germans are usually so respectful of authority.
>
> Now, liebe Frau Doktor, I wish you all a very pleasant Christmas holiday season and a happy and healthy New Year.

The subject of this letter only seems to be irrelevant. Its author insists that his reader should not only not overlook but in fact understand and even transmit to her colleagues the fact that in order to understand him (a multilingual person), one must look in several languages for the original meaning of what he states in German only.

This (implicit) suggestion became our own guide to rereading, with a renewed ear, the famous nightmare of the wolves reported by Freud and responsible for the enigmatic patient's being named the Wolf Man.

This new orientation in our reading was confirmed by another fact, mentioned by Freud, which had thus far escaped notice: From age four onward the child had an English governess. A discreet yet unmistakable reference is also made in *Fetishism* (1927) to the role played by the Wolf Man's early and forgotten experience of his *English* nursery. The nurse in question was, according to his long-past account to Freud, a rather nasty person who did nothing but tease him: "Look at my little tail," she would say. She said strange and disagreeable things, even made Nania (his sister Anna) "go out of the room," spread all kinds of rumors, and was finally let go for reasons that remain obscure. This is supposedly the time when the family suddenly moved to a different estate and when, coincidentally, little Sergei underwent his "change in character," becoming choleric and phobic. The development of what Freud called an "infantile neurosis" (and whose explanation is contained in the nightmare of the wolves, according to him) would thus be linked to the presence of the nurse.

Freud's intuition indeed seems irreproachable; the construction he provided of the nightmare remained, however, far too general for being too theoretical. For good reason. The essential material he should have had came to light only in snippets during the next fifty years, and in particular during the Wolf Man's analysis with Ruth Mack Brunswick from October 1926 to February 1927.

Capitalizing on these new developments, Freud jotted down some reflections in *Fetishism* about his ex-patient's use of the English language, thereby paving the way for the approach presented here. He writes:

> In the last few years I have had an opportunity to study analytically a number of men whose object-choice was dominated by a fetish. . . . For obvious reasons the details of these cases must be withheld from publication; I cannot therefore show in what way accidental circumstances have contributed to the choice of fetish. The most extraordinary case seemed to me to be one in which a young man had exalted a certain sort of "shine on the nose" into a fetishistic precondition. The surprising explanation of this was that the patient had been brought up in an English nursery but had later come to Germany, where he forgot his mother-tongue almost completely. The fetish, which originated from his earliest childhood, had to be understood in *English*, not German [our emphasis]. The "shine on the nose"(in German, *Glanz auf der Nase*) was in reality a "glance at the nose" [*Blick auf die Nase, Blick* = glance: *Glanz*]. The nose was thus the fetish, which, incidentally, he endowed at will with the luminous shine which was not perceptible to others. (*Standard Edition*, vol. 21, p. 152)[3]

Who could fail to recognize the Wolf Man's case here, despite the obligatory disguise, with his nasal symptom and his words? We will return later to these words, most certainly taken from the Wolf Man's material, but not coinciding, "for understandable reasons," with the words of the fetish itself. The impression nevertheless prevails that Freud grasped the verbal mechanism of the fetish as well as a princpal aspect of its metapsychological import in this particular case: "The Mother has no phallus." We would say that the penis the mother does not have is the father's, for he deprived her of it by diverting his desire elsewhere. This caused a scandal.

But let us not anticipate. We are fully conscious that what we are proposing here is of the utmost daring. We have to pluck up all our courage to impart to you the unexpected results of our listening. The immediate task before us, for which we ask your indulgence, is an attempt at a new textual translation of the Wolf Man's principal dream, the nightmare of the wolves.

3. The Interpretation of the Nightmare of the Wolves

Let us first recall the dream in its entirety:

> *I dreamed that it was night and that I was lying in my bed. (My bed stood with its foot toward the window; in front of the window there was a row of old walnut trees. I know it was winter when I had the dream, and nighttime.) Suddenly the window opened by itself, and I was terrified to see that some white wolves were sitting on the big walnut tree in front of the window. There were six or seven of them. The wolves were quite white, and looked more like foxes or sheepdogs, for they had big tails like foxes and they had their ears pricked up like dogs when they pay attention to something. In great terror, evidently of being eaten up by the wolves, I cried out and* I woke up.

Around the age of four or five, when his "change in character" occurred and when his nurse left in turmoil, our patient must have had at least a basic knowledge of English. This is confirmed in connection with Elizabeth, his subsequent nurse: She would read children's stories to him in English. It was therefore plausible to look for foreign verbal elements in his early dream material. We do not wish to retrace all the steps of association leading to the translation (*one* of the translations!) of the entire text. In fact, this attempt is the result of a long-term study encompassing all of the Wolf Man's dreams, symptoms, and verbal tics. It would be inconceivable to reconstitute, even partially, the work of deciphering (decrypting) accomplished over the years. But it does seem vital to explain in a few words how the expression "I dreamed" becomes, once decrypted, the amazing sentence: "The witness is the son."

The point of departure for a long chain of associations was not "I dreamed" but the word "window," in Russian *okno*, which returns repeatedly in later dreams and can be cross-checked. Going back for the nth time to associations quoted by Freud, it suddenly appeared strange that the Wolf Man should offer an interpretation of it on his own: "Window" had to be understood through the Russian *okno* as "eye," that is, *oko* or *otch*, the root for its inflected forms. Why dream about "window" when it is understood that one wishes to say "eye"? Contaminated by the idea of the English nurse, we take the German word for window (*Fenster*) to be in English. Another English association from the Wolf Man's material emerges: It was on a *Whitsunday* that the "symptom of the nose" returned in 1925, probably also prompted by seeing the film *The White Sister* on the same day. Very close to the anniversary of this date—another *Whitsunday* in 1926—the Wolf Man sent a letter at Freud's request confirming the early age at which the dream we are analyzing occurred. This was a *testimony* of sorts, since Freud was going to use it against Otto Rank, who maintained the dream was produced during the analysis itself through transference (Gardiner, *The Wolf-Man by the Wolf-Man*, p. 277; and this volume, chapter 5, section 6).

We do not know Russian, we can barely sound out the words in the dictionary, but this difficulty is also our good fortune. It permits us to avoid the blinders of language to follow better the avenues of our own listening. Thus, if "window" means "eye" for the Wolf Man, perhaps we must listen to this very word "eye" . . . as it opens . . . But onto what? At the entry *oko* (eye) in the dictionary, we stumble on the compound word: *otchevidietz* (eyewitness) and later *otchevidno* ("clearly," a term that also appears later in the dream). *Otche = window*! Now it is talking! There is "clearly" an *otche* and *window* and there is reason to believe this link is contained within the preceding association, *Whitsunday*, which we now hear as the *day* of the *witness* of the *son*. *Otchevidietz* of the son. *Eyewitness* of the son. The idea overlaps with the numerous occurrences in the Wolf Man's material of the English and German syllables *sun*, *son*, *Son(ne)*, *Sohn* . . . which are nearly always linked to the ideas of seeing and illuminating.

Let us take up the dream once again from the beginning.

a) "I dreamed that it was night and that I was lying in my bed." (*Ich habe geträumt, dass es Nacht ist, und ich in meinem Bett liege.*)[4]

Freud italicizes both the text of the dream and curiously the expression "I dreamed." At the end, however, "I woke up" is printed without italics. This seems to mean that "I dreamed" must be considered an integral part of the dream.

Now "to dream" in Russian is *vidiet son*. *Vidiet* resonates with "Whit" and "witness," *son* with "sun" taken from *Whitsunday*. Incidentally, *vidietz* means "witness" in Russian, and *son* (dream) is a homophone of the English "son." There is thus near homonymy, on the one hand, between *vidiet son* "to dream" or "see a dream" and *vidietz* + *son* and, on the other, the English "witness" and "son." "I dreamed that it was night." "Night," the Russian adverb is *notchiu*. We could not help hearing it in English also: *not you*. We venture the hypothesis: **The witness is the son, not you**.

Absurd! But no measure of unlikelihood or strangeness is going to make us back down. We must not ignore any trail.

The dream continues:

"I was lying in my bed." Note the words "bed" and "lying." This could be illuminating. For the dreamer's ear, bed and but may sound alike whereas "lying," that is, "to be in bed," must seem to a Russian child a bizarre homonym of *he is lying* ("not you, but he is lying"). The whole thing then once again: **The witness is the son, not you, but he is lying**.

Now there is a sentence to dream about! It may well have been *engraved* as is, to be disguised later in the manner we have just seen. Is this expert in legal matters of insurance (the Wolf Man's profession in Vienna) an unwitting "witness"? His testimony—once confirmed—does imply some misdeed. What will the next flip of the dictionary turn up to our bemused surprise? "Misdeed," "crime," "sin" are said with nearly the same Russian word as "walnut tree," the legendary tree of the Wolf Man that supports the famous "white wolves" and whose image has long since become his trademark. In fact, "walnut tree" is *oriekh*, whereas "sin" and "misdeed" are *khriekh* with the stress falling on *-ekh*. Our listening gains clarity.

But let us return to our sentence: "The witness is the son, not you, but he is lying." In whose mouth does this shred of dialogue belong? Certainly not in that of Sergei, the "son," since he is mentioned in the third person. Furthermore, if, as we suspect, there was an accusation in English, it must have come from the English governess. As for the response, the sentence must have been uttered by one of the parents. The father, the accused party, was, as we shall see, absent from the scene. Conclusion: These meaning-laden words, spoken in a mixture of Russian and English, must be attributed to the mother and addressed specifically to the nurse.

Let us go on listening:

A rather lengthy parenthetical statement comes directly after these words. In the Wolf Man's head, exchanges and arguments about the validity of a child's testimony move about in a whirl from the mother to the nurse. Perhaps we should not look for excessive logical coherence here. What is striking is the constant repetition of the same ideas in various types of Anglo-Russian homonyms. It is a veritable babel of tongues. The dreamer apparently requests that the manifest content not be adulterated by the dream's disguised subject and that the analyst not, any more than the previous addressees of the nightmare, introduce any other meanings. Yet, the analyst's ear cannot help but continue to resonate with chords of a dialogue. We, of course, do recognize this request—spoken with such insistence—to stick with the manifest content: When he says he was in bed, it is true; he remembers that this "bed" stood "with its foot toward the window." As for the old "walnut tree" (discussed later), there was a whole row of them in front of his window. He knows absolutely, "it was winter and nighttime."

The analyst, however, cannot help twisting the words toward what they are meant to hide. What does the other ear hear?

b) "My bed stood with its foot toward the window." (*Mein Bett stand mit dem Fussende gegen das Fenster.*)

The obvious meaning of this sentence, or nearly so, suggests the idea of a *dialogue*.

"True, his bed was placed footside in front of the window" (the implication being that it was physically impossible for the child to see what was going on behind him). For once, "bed" and "window" are used literally. But this is hardly satisfactory. *Fuss* (foot) makes us think of *truth*. We shall have occasion to test the validity of this hypothesis later. So we propose the reading: "My bed" (*bed* = *but*) "was standing" (for the little Sergei this means), "not lying." In plain language: **But he is not lying.** "Footside" and "in front of the window": *truth* and *witness* (window = eye[witness]). In short, he is a true witness, or better yet: **But he is a truthful witness.**

The proof is in what follows, probably the nurse's reply:
c) "In front of the window there was a row [a series] of old walnut trees."
(*Vor dem Fenster befand sich eine Reihe alter Nussbäume.*)

In "textual" English: **Before the witness there was a series of the old [one's] "khriekhs,"** (*khriekh* = misdeed, paronym of *oriekh* = walnut tree).

d) "I know it was winter when I had this dream, and nighttime." (*Ich weiss es war Winter, als ich träumte, und Nachtzeit.*)

"I know" in Russian, *Ya znayu*, but this can be heard in English in a sarcastic tone: *'Z'naa . . . you,"* "No, it's not you" (who saw it). "Winter" in Russian, *zimoi*. With the aid of the Anglo-Russian *son* and the Russian *samo saboi* ("by itself") occurring later on, we hear it through the distortion: *t'ziboy* (*it is a boy*); "when I had this dream" = he dreamed (*vidiet son*) and "nighttime" (*Notchu* = not you) = it is not you (the witness).
The entire dialogue:
—**But he is not lying, he is a true witness.**
—**Before the witness there was a series of the old (one's) Khriekhs**
—**Z'Naaa you** (it is not you the witness, but the son). **He is a boy, he dreamed a dream. (The witness) is not you.**

Are we going to find out what misdeed of the "old man's" the son witnessed? What misdeed the mother claims can only be a dream, not a child's eyewitness account? Thereupon the Englishwoman raises her voice.
e) "Suddenly the window opened by itself." (*Plötzlich geht das Fenster von selbst auf.*)

"Suddenly the window opened!" "Suddenly," in Russian, *v'droug*, which imitates the English "th'truth." Thus: "The truth: The witness opened himself to me." "By itself," in Russian, *samo saboi*, imitates the English "somewhat as a boy." The nurse states in sum: **The truth is that the witness confided in me somewhat as a boy.**

The disguise continues:
f) "And I was terrified to see . . . " (*Und ich sehe mit grossem Schrecken . . .*)

In Anglo-Russian: I see the great *khriekh*. I see = I understand. *Schreck* (by homophony) = *khriekh* = misdeed. That is to say: **I understand the great sin.**

What is the great sin? The dream is finally stating it:

g) "that some white wolves were sitting on the big walnut tree in front of the window." (*dass auf dem grossen Nussbaum ein paar weisse Wölfe sitzen.*) No doubt this is the crime. But how can we manage to hear it?

"Some," in Russian, *para* = a pair, a couple. **A couple.** And what is said of them? "White wolves sitting = wolf + (sitt)ing = wolf + ing. Are we on the right track? Cross-checking later dreams, there is a great likelihood that a specific Anglo-Russian homophony is at work here. Wolf + ing (pronounced with a guttural "l") = *goulfik* (Russian) = slit, fly; white = wide: A wide fly or a **fly wide open.**

So, this is Sergei Wolf Man's "wolf," the "wolf" of his nightmare, the "wolf" he later adopts as part of his pseudonym.

But the dream is not over yet. We are going to know the sin. He says that of these "wolves,"

h) "There were six or seven of them." (*Es waren sechs oder sieben Stück.*) As was shown earlier, a "pack of six," a "sixter" = *shiestorka: siestorka*, does not denote a number but simply the sister. In a word: **There was the sister.**

i) "The wolves were quite white." (*Die Wölfe waren ganz weiss.*) explains the rest:

In Anglo-Russian: The *goulfik*, **The fly was opened quite wide.**

The dreamer explains his "wolves":

j)"[They] looked more like foxes or sheepdogs, for they had big tails like foxes and they had their ears pricked up like dogs when they pay attention to something." (*und sahen eher aus wie Füchse oder Schäferhunde, denn sie hatten grosse Schwänze wie Füchse und ihre Ohren waren aufgestellt wie bei den Hunden wenn sie auf etwas passen.*)

This is probably an explanation by the mother in Russian: *lissitsa* = fox and *ovtcharki* = sheepdog or police dog. The sentence can be translated: The Miss is a *lissitsa* and Oven an *ovtcharki*. (According to the Wolf Man's memoirs, the name of this first English governess was Miss Oven.) **The miss is a fox and Oven a police dog.**

"For they had big tails like foxes": (**She is a fox**) **because of her big tales.** "And they had their ears pricked up like dogs when they pay attention": (She is like a police dog) **because of her ears pricked up to pay attention.**

As is apparent, English is less and less useful for understanding this passage, which seems to reproduce — clearly without much distortion — the official version of the events, as reported to the children by the mother in Russian, after the mysterious departure of the nurse.

The mother's version nevertheless seems unsatisfactory to the "witness." The nightmare results from this very conflict. On the one hand, little Sergei suffered from living under the terror brought on the family by the governess's threats to divulge (*cry out*) the deeds she believed to be incriminating. On the other hand, the "witness" cannot be reassured by the official version; he relives the mother's fear that, were he to say the truth he is certain he has seen with his own eyes and with all his desire, the family would come to great harm. Had he not been contaminated by the mother's fear, he would not have allowed himself to be treated like a liar and be made to gag on the truth.

Let us proceed to the end of the dream:

k) "In great terror, evidently of being eaten up by the wolves, I cried out and I woke up." (*Unter grosser Angst, offenbar, von den Wölfen aufgefressen zu werden, schrie ich auf.*) He then wakes up in terror and only Nania's soothing words can calm him.

> Here, English would be of little help except, probably, to lend its meaning to what is experienced in the dream as a cry and which must be an allusion to the governess's unsettling threat to divulge what she thought she knew. To cry out = "divulge" and, in the Wolf Man's family situation, "disparage," "dishonor." An interpretation using Russian will suffice. **Anxious that on account of the eyewitness** (*otch-evidietz*) **"Fly" is going to put in jail** (*sidiat*, in Russian, "they will eat," and *siedat*, "they are sitting in prison") **and dishonored** (cried out . . .). Here the dream ends.

"Anxious that on account of the eyewitness" clearly refers to the mother. In point of fact, the dreamer cannot bear the contradiction of having to agree with the mother's fear and hear what he knows to be true called a "dream" or a "lie" and thereby be forced to renounce his desire to take the sister's place (with the father's fly). He tears himself from his sleep at the precise moment when the idea arises of crying out what the mother's anguish begs him to withhold.

Here we are before the original text of what must have been the train of thought translated and disguised into the nightmare of the wolves.[5]

4. Synopsis of the Nightmare of the Wolves

I dreamed that it was night and that I was lying in my bed. (My bed stood with its foot toward the window. In front of the window there was a row of old walnut trees. I know it was winter when I had the dream, and nighttime.)

The witness is the son, not you, but he is lying. But he is not lying, he is a truthful witness. Before the witness there was a series of the old one's khriekhs. Z'naaa you (the witness) **but the son. He is a boy, he dreamed a dream!** (The witness) **is not you.**

Suddenly the window opened by itself and I was terrified to see that some white wolves were sitting on the big walnut tree in front of the window. There were six or seven of them. The wolves were quite white.

The truth: The witness opened himself to me somewhat as a boy. I see the great khriekh (misdeed), **a couple, a wide goulfik** (fly). **There was the sister. The goulfik** (fly) **was opened quite wide.**

They looked more like foxes or sheepdogs, for they had big tails like foxes and they had their ears pricked up like dogs when they pay attention to something.

The Miss is a lissitsa (a fox) **and Oven an Ovtcharki** (a police dog) **because of her big tales, she is a police dog because of her ears pricked up to pay attention.**

In great terror, evidently of being eaten up by the wolves, I cried out and I woke up.

Fearing (that on account of the) **otchevidietz** (eyewitness), **goulfik** (fly) **siedat** (should go to prison), **cry out** (and be dishonored) . . .[6]

5. From the Nightmare to Phobia

Torn from sleep, yes . . . but to awake to what? Awaking to the same anguish—experienced first in the midst of wakefulness, then transformed into a phobia. Yearning for the nightmare to return while awake mingles with his dread of seeing a *wide-open wolf-book* displayed by his sister, and the mother's fear that the *wide-open goulfik*, the wide-open fly, might be spoken about again.

This is the hypothesis drawn from the Wolf Man's nightmare as regards the genesis of his childhood phobia.

A nightmare . . . only to awake to sleepwalking . . . and phobia! Here is a case that cries out for the analytic couch. Theoretically, the apparatus Freud invented could produce a complete awakening from an anachronistic state of fascination. We now understand, though, why this awakening never quite took place in the Wolf Man's case. Freud's own unconscious is not being questioned: Witness his comparison, mentioned earlier, between the "polar (white) bear" and the "whale," very near his study of the nightmare itself. The comparison shows the unconsciously felt but as yet unstated relationship between "white wolf" ("white bear") and *goulfik* (*Walfisch*, whale) that must—in no way!—meet in the patient's mind.

The special difficulty of the Wolf Man's analysis was due to the fact that his position as "witness for the prosecution" put him in a paradoxical situation: He knew that he was the object of his parents' fears. By espousing their apprehension of him, he must have been, to some extent, afraid of himself, afraid of his own impulse to denounce and make his own the act that occurred between his father and his sister and that, subsequently, served as blackmail for the governess. The sleeper's desire wanted the truth, wherein lay his own sexual ideal, to be "cried out," but also to be *accepted*, not hidden and reviled.

Yet the "cry" is the very thing that awakens. How can he sleep with a "cry" inside? And then to what does he awake if not the same cry that would curdle the parents' blood and heap shame and suffering on them? So he awakes to another sleeping state, to a quasi-hypnotic sleep provoked by the mother's wishes, and leads a libidinal life on the strength of unsaid, unspeakable words by twisting them beyond recognition.

Thus the Wolf Man created a secret magic word that, without betraying anybody, allowed him to achieve real or sublimated sexual gratification. This word was: *tieret*.

He also had other secret treasures: *goulfik*, "fly," the hidden attribute of his father, the true name of his ideal transformed into *wolf*, his cryptic family name. He carries within him yet a third disguised word, the name of his vocation as witness: *vidietz*. We no longer have to wonder at the occupation he chose for himself in his exile. He was an insurance agent, a kind of traveling salesman, who asks his clients upon entering their house: *Wie geht's*, "How are you?" (pronounced "vigetz," it rhymes with *vidietz*), an expression that serves in Austria as the somewhat humorous and colloquial nickname for the profession itself.

These three words, *vidietz* (witness), *goulfik* (fly), and *tieret* (rub) form the three invisible yet solid columns constructed by the Wolf Man on the ground of his impossible desire to occupy one or the other place in the scene he saw, his genuine "primal scene." These three columns have been supporting, for some eighty years, a trapped life, held to this day under the sway of a childhood hypnosis.

III. The Return of the Nightmare:
The Crypt's Permanence

Chapter 4
In Some of Little Sergei's Dreams and Symptoms

1. The Dream of the Lion

One of the first nightmares following the main one and the wolf phobia dates from the eve of the day when the new German tutor was to arrive. The child was seven or eight at the time. "That night he dreamed of this tutor in the shape of a lion that came toward his bed, roaring loudly, and taking the posture of the wolf in the picture with which his sister used to terrify him. Once again he awoke in a state of anxiety."[1] Being aware of the preceding interpretation of the nightmare of the wolves, one should have no difficulty in seeing here a variant of the original nightmare. It suffices to translate the German *Löwe* into the English "lion," obtaining "lying" by homophony, and to hear in *Bett* the English bed = but. In sum: **But he is lying!** It is then just as simple to complete *Bild* (picture) by *Schreckbild* (terrifying picture) and hear homophonically *khriekh* (picture of the sin), and then convert this into the image of the "wolf standing upright in the wide-open book" and into its dreamlike transliteration: **a wide-open goulfik, fly.**[2] As in the main nightmare, we recognize the situation of maternal anxiety that demands he wake up.

2. Slip of the Pen: Filivs-Fils

At times fragments of the initial traumatic dialogue become symptoms instead of being dreamed about. The slip of the pen during a Latin lesson is an example. Sergei rather curiously replaces the word *filivs* by the French *fils* (son) in a piece of Latin translation. He omits the letters *iv*. We hear them in English: "you." By omitting *iu* he states in brief: **The witness is the son** (*filivs*) **not you**: No wonder that as he was being taken to task by the teacher (= the governess) for this strange fault, he must have thought to himself: The teacher probably expects to be given some money to mollify him (like the governess).

3. Acting out at V O'Clock

There is yet another way of interpreting the omission of *iv* that confirms our previous reading. This is a visual representation of the Wolf Man's repudiated desire: V equals "open fly" and I the "erect penis." We must recall here one of the Wolf Man's first sessions with Freud: When the clock's hand (I) is showing five o'clock (V), and as it enters the V of five o'clock, the Wolf Man turns around with a *look* of supplication in his eyes. This *look* means: **I looked and saw.** What? **The open fly** (in V) **with the erection** (in I). For Freud the supplication meant: "You are not going to eat me, are you?" and referred to the primal scene. However, if there is a "primal scene" (that is, a return of the libido), it is the erotic scene of the V of the fly and of the clock hand I that emerges in an erect state. And if there is phobia, it is related to a second scene that has nothing to do with the first one: the scene of the *traumatic condemnation* of the erotic scene observed previously and not at all this first scene. The libidinal desire is linked to the father, whereas the supplication is taken over from the mother: Let words never state what Sergei sees at five o'clock as he turns around. We are thus confirming the singular fact that the Wolf Man's desire is linked to a phobia-inducing incident.

4. The Butterfly's *V*

He was chasing a beautiful big butterfly with yellow stripes and large wings which ended in pointed projections—a swallow-tail, in fact. Suddenly, when the butterfly had settled on a flower, he was seized with a dreadful fear of the creature, and ran away screaming. . . . Many months later, in quite another connection, the patient remarked that the open and shutting of the butterfly's wings while it was settled on the flower had given him an uncanny feeling. It had looked, so he said, like a woman opening her legs, and the legs then made the shape of a Roman *V*, which, as we know, was the hour at which, in his boyhood, and even up to the time of the treatment, he used to fall into a depressed state of mind. (*Standard Edition*, vol. 17, pp. 89, 90)

"To see" is to see again. The same "seeing" as in the episode of the grandfather clock is present in the chase of the swallow-tailed butterfly in V. It is the image of the **wide-open fly** that little Sergei is chasing in the playful and erotic sense of the term, and it is also what he pursues as a proceeding in the judicial sense of this latter term. He dares to "pursue" the butterfly as long as the rapid beating of its wings dissipates the terrifying image. But on seeing it settle on a flower with its wings **wide open**, the child is "suddenly" (*v'droug*, th'truth) "seized with a dreadful fear" (*schreckliche Angst*, terrible anxiety), the same fear as always (the sin, *Schreck: khriekh*), and runs away "screaming." The "cry" is the same as the one in his main nightmare and dramatizes his fear of **crying out the truth** he is doomed to cover up in silence. **Cry out? No! I must swallow it**. This anxiety explains the choice of a swallow-tail in addition to the visual image of the wings in *V*: The swallow-tailed butterfly = **I swallow the tale** (of the tail), **it is better to lie**. What is tragic in this tale is that my desire must be eradicated within myself.[3]

5. Laborer with the Tongue Cut Out, Enema, Pressed Pimple, Espe

I analyzed his ceremonial of breathing out whenever he saw cripples, beggars, and such people. . . . At a very early period, probably before his seduction (at the age of three and a quarter), there had been on the estate an old day-laborer whose business it was to carry the water into the house. He could not speak, ostensibly because his tongue had been cut out. (He was probably a deaf mute.) The little boy was very fond of him and pitied him deeply. When he died, he looked for him in the sky. (*Standard Edition*, vol. 17, p. 87)

He has to hold his tongue! No wonder he feels compassion for the "mute" laborer with the tongue supposedly cut out. He, too, holds his breath as long as he can when he watches the laborer, the breath that would give life to his denunciation. Hold it back! What a relief when, with some outside help, for example the nozzle of an enema, his uncoercible feces can finally come out! And true orgasm comes later when, under the authoritative fingers of Professor X., his infected pimple finally pops! Let a man (Freud) tear the truth out of espe-S.P.!

. . . a particularly ingenious dream, which he himself succeeded in deciphering. "I had a dream," he said, "of a man tearing off the wings of an Espe." "Espe?" I asked, "what do you mean by that?" "You know, that insect with yellow stripes on its body, that stings." I could now put him right: "So what you mean is a *Wespe* (wasp)." "Is it called a *Wespe*? I really thought it was called an Espe." (Like so many other people, he used his difficulties with a foreign language as a screen for symptomatic acts.) "But Espe, why, that's myself: S. P." (which were his initials). [In Austria, "Espe" and "S. P." would be pronounced exactly alike.] The Espe was of course a mutilated *Wespe*. (*Standard Edition*, vol. 17, p. 94)

This is, of course, no more than a nostalgic dream of the true and impossible orgasm. To drag the truth out of him would mean—but could it ever happen—giving his own desire back to him.

6. The Sister's VI

Alas, or perhaps fortunately, no one has succeeded to this day. The game, however, is not over yet. With V and I for example. The *I* in the *V* became the sister's trademark, not only because it evoked both six (*siest*, in Russian, = six; *siestorka* = sister) and "sixter of wolves," but also because of the picture of the wolf (shown to him by his sister) that he first observed with pleasure and then converted into the object of obsessive phobia due to the combination of his desire and the scandal. About his sister, apparently a past mistress of erect penises emerging from flies wide open like a V, a cousin ten years his elder told him she had once sat on his lap and opened his trousers to take hold of his penis. She did the same to her younger brother. Better yet, she told him (and this is the Wolf Man speaking) that Nania, the servant girl, used to do the same with everyone, mostly the gardener. A strange coincidence: The diminutive of Anna, the sister's name, is also Nania. And judging by what we think we know, the "gardener," in turn, would be none other than the father himself.

7. The Word-Thing *Tieret*, Grusha-Matrona

Yes, the sister did have her libidinal moment, although since the scandal, it was reduced in Sergei's mind to a petrified emblem: to roman numerals, V and I. But the Wolf Man, what does he have? What remains of what he both claims and denies, of what he saw with his own eyes and felt at Anna's seductive hands? We have shown elsewhere how a pleasure of this type knows how to defy every prohibition and scandal, and how, taking a detour through a word that *reveals the means*, it achieves its ends. In the Wolf Man's case this word is *tieret*, "to rub." It is a word that operates only from the Unconscious, that is, as a *word-thing*. In conscious life it can be recouped only as a visual image as in a dream once it has been transformed into the synonym of a variant meaning (alloseme), for example, "scrubbing floors." Such an image is Grusha kneeling and *scrubbing* the floor, beside her a pail and a short broom made of a bundle of twigs. A pail of water = make water, peepee for pleasure and twigs for punishment. Freud suggests that this is a memory screen of the coitus a tergo the Wolf Man supposedly witnessed at age one and a half, and that over this memory is superimposed yet another screen, the memory of the hunted butterfly just discussed. What is found in this image, in fact, is nothing more than the verbal elements of the scene between the father and the sister. "Knees" (sitting on his knees), "rub," *tieret* (masturbate), water (to peepee) and, perhaps, the "broom" of "twigs" for punishment in case the child should talk. This "memory screen" thus deserves to be called a dream screen or image screen. The same image, word for word, can also be found in the episode of the peasant girl Matrona, his adolescent "love at first sight," kneeling by a pond and washing clothes in the water.

8. The Dreams of the Caterpillar, The Devil with the Snail, and the Celestial Bodies

We conclude the digression on pleasure and its magic word and return to the nightmare and its subsequent reapparitions. We will consider some dream fragments given by Freud, probably from memory, in reported speech. "Sergei saw himself riding on a horse and pursued by a gigantic caterpillar." Another one: "He saw the Devil dressed in black and in the same upright posture of the wolf and the lion which had terrified him so much in their day. The Devil was pointing with his out-stretched finger at a gigantic snail." This dream image reminds him by association, the Wolf Man recounts, of a picture representing the Demon in a love scene with a girl![4] The "copulating" heavenly bodies are also an image of this sort: the moon with a star (*luna* + *zviezda*). The father probably called his daughter "my star." What are they doing together? They are making a Turkish flag (*Turkish* = *turok* by homophony = *tieret*). These fragmentary reappearances of the main nightmare contain the latter's by now well-known elements. Taking into account some homophonies and associations within the Wolf Man's material, the interpretation is: I see = **I understand**; the sectioning of caterpillars was a favorite pastime of little Sergei and he was severely taken to task for it. It was called a "great sin." Thus "caterpillar" = **the great sin**. The "gigantic snail" (*riesige Schnecke*) is another form of *khriekh*, the sin.[5] Any potential doubt surrounding the suggestion that "caterpillar" refers to the same things as "snails" (i.e., the sin) will be dissipated by the Wolf Man's recollection of "trees" on the estate "that were quite white, spun all over by caterpillars." This recollection was reported to Freud at the same time as the dream and connects "caterpillars" to the main nightmare. The important words are *ganz weiss*, quite white (= **quite wide**); *ganz von Raupen umsponnen*, spun all over by caterpillar webs (= the sin). Whole = the hole (of the fly) and perhaps also the whole affair. **I understand the whole affair**. It is easy to guess who the demon is pointing at the great sin.

9. Hallucination of the Little Finger Cut Through

It is not at all surprising that the contradiction between wanting to communicate and having to deny what he saw should also lead to hallucinations rather than dreams. We quote the well-known one about the "little finger cut through." The words used to relate it, more than the fact itself, deserve our attention.

When I was *five* years old, I was playing in the garden near my nurse, and was carving [*schnitzelte*] with my pocket knife in the bark of one of the walnut trees that come into my dream as well. *Suddenly, I noticed to my unspeakable terror [plötzlich bemerkte ich mit unaussprech-lichem Schrecken] that I had cut through [durchgeschnitten] the little finger of my (right or left?) hand, so that it was only hanging by its skin. I felt no pain, but great fear. I did not venture to say anything to my nurse*, who was only a few paces distant, but I sank down [*sank*] on the nearest seat and sat there [*und blieb da sitzen*] incapable of casting another glance at my finger. At last I calmed down, took a look at the finger, and saw that it was entirely *uninjured*. (*Standard Edition*, vol. 17, p. 85; German quoted from *Gesammelte Werke*, vol. 12, p. 118; our emphasis)

This account is constructed in exactly the same way as the main nightmare. There is the "walnut tree" (= **the misdeed**). "I suddenly noticed" (= **I realized the truth**) and the rest can be easily translated: "To my unspeakable terror," **the misdeed is unspeakable (must not be divulged), so I cut my little guesser** (the "little finger" that suspects) **and do not dare tell the governess about what I saw, about what I** (the son) **am sure I saw, otherwise I** (the father) **am dishon-ored** (*sinken*, "to sink down," is a synonym of *herunterkommen*, "to come down," "to lose status") **and will sit in jail** (*sitzen*, "to sit," is also colloquial for "to be in jail"). That he has said nothing to anyone but himself calms little Sergei, and his waking nightmare is aborted.

10. Sensitivity of the Little Finger . . . on the Foot

Truly, it would have been useless to try to find out what the little finger knew. Freud recounts in 1937 (*Standard Edition*, vol. 23, p. 278) that the "patient," obviously the Wolf Man, has to this day a "nervous sensitivity when the two little toes . . . on his feet are touched." This is proof that his lengthy analytic rela-tionship with R. M. Brunswick left him reticent to the end to state what the "little finger" knew and had to keep silent. To say would have meant "castration" like the "castration" of the monstrous child who, born with six toes, had one of his toes cut off at birth (see the Wolf Man's letter to Freud, chapter 5, section 6, this volume).

Chapter 7 will bring out the true subject and the real motivation of this fear — and this desire — of castration.

Chapter 5
The Crypt Screen: Reinterpretation of the Symptoms and the Dreams Related by Ruth Mack Brunswick

1. Analysis Free of Charge and Gifts of Money

In the course of time the Wolf Man will have said everything.[1] Everything that was in his power. But the man who had been behind him for four years was to remain deprived of that privilege the Wolf Man would so much have liked to grant him: the privilege of "pulling out the truth." S. P.'s truth coincides with the "wasp," his governess. Yet he prefers to side with his parents—but does he really have an alternative?—and, by his continued silence, he manages to cover up the scandal that has buried the little boy's sexual ideal. The dream of the wasp puts a provisional end to an interminable analysis.

Immediately afterward, World War I breaks out, he marries Theresa, lives in a belligerent, then defeated, Russia. During this time, the couple seems happy. There are conflicts with the mother concerning money and his inheritance. The large family fortune he inherited from an uncle, bypassing his mother, is depleted. Was this father's money to pay off Miss Oven for her silence? He has to get rid of it. The October Revolution helps him do the rest, and when he is back in Vienna, in 1919, Freud, who is obviously dissatisfied with his patient's appearance, grants him a few months' analysis free of charge, then decrees its end.

Proof is thus given of the Wolf Man's ability to cope with his unconscious conflicts, lead a married life, and weather courageously—as he himself would say—"the hardest blows of destiny." He could even bear unperturbed the fact of having become the object of collective charity for the entire Viennese Analytical Society.

2. The Concealment of the Jewels

A rather insignificant event must occur for the inner conflict to revive. His mother sends him some family jewels from Russia: a necklace and a pair of earrings. Should he tell Freud about his newfound fortune and risk losing his yearly aid? No. The Wolf Man prefers to create another secret, a *crypt screen*. We are now talking about a period in 1922. He writes down the consequences of this concealment in minute and impartial detail, as if he were talking about someone else. He notices a certain change in his behavior. He becomes greedy with money, wonders how large the next present from Freud will be, acquires a certain amount of dishonesty in financial matters, speculates with the money he receives, yet conceals it from his wife, and, in general, behaves somewhat irresponsibly. He himself is surprised by all this.

3. Father's Remorse

It is under these circumstances that, during a summer vacation in 1922 paid for by the generosity of Viennese analysts, he begins to paint his self-portrait. He used to paint landscapes, "views," but now he himself becomes such a view of the countryside. Long ago he had seen and now he is the one seen in the mirror. In his case we could call this remorse. But from what depths of the unconscious does it reemerge? When calling on Freud in July, he finds the Professor's face emaciated following a first operation. It must be remorse for his dishonesty toward an old man who is also ill—one might think naively. Yet, the remorse gnawing at some contrite Wolf Man is not his own, but belongs to the one who was seen by the little Sergei and suspected by the governess. It is an unconscious identification with the guilt that eats away at Father.

4. A Lying Nose and the Tooth of Truth

He is not alone. His mother arrives a year later with a black wart on the tip of her nose. Another person who goes around with a lying nose. The denied truth brings something else—an aching tooth (tooth = truth)—and ends in two (two = true) dental extractions. A bit later, the famous symptom of the nose (= he knows) begins.

He has always been bothered by his snub nose. It must have been snubbed by pressing down on it. And every child knows in Russia (and in Austria) that a nose that can be pressed flat is a lying nose. But this time he has had enough of lying. Blackheads decorate his olfactory organ; he realizes it suddenly (*v'droug* = *th'truth*). At the same time—such is the power of unconscious communication—his wife develops a wart on her own nose. Whom to tell? Surely not Freud. But there is a famous dermatologist he once recommended. A certain Professor X. He will take care of them. Unfortunately, the mother returns on a visit and the blackheads, rather than erupting, swell into pimples. Truth, like the Wolf-Man, is constipated at this time and "hydrotherapy" is prescribed—no different than if he were Father in Kraepelin's clinic. No, this cannot go on! He himself will press the pimple that keeps betraying him as a liar. But removing the lie comes down to saying the truth, does it not? The scratched-out pimple leaves a hole. Yes, he does know the *whole business about the hole* (the open "fly") and the hiding of the jewels at his wife's "counsel." Then, finally, he consults Professor X. about his blackheads. "Obviously, he says nothing to him about the 'hole,' " he writes in his own account. We hear: Say nothing about the business of the fly (hole) just as you say nothing to Freud about the jewels. But on the eve of his departure to the countryside, where he intends to use his brush to paint (*tieret*) landscapes and "views," "suddenly" (*v'droug* = *th'truth*) he starts to worry about a tooth (truth) that might spoil his much-coveted vacation. He therefore rushes to the dentist and has a tooth (truth) pulled.

5. The Misfortunes of a Silent Witness

He deeply regrets it on the following day and wonders whether it was not the wrong tooth. For the moment it is only a vague suspicion. Be that as it may, a "truth" (tooth), whether true or false, has been "extracted." Afterward, everything goes beautifully, the vacation, fall, and winter. Holes, pimples, and blackheads are forgotten; his sex life flourishes again. Easter has to come around for the "truth" to torment him once again. "Suddenly" (*v'droug* = th'truth), he becomes aware of a painful sensation in his nose and starts to worry about new holes and pimples. He borrows his wife's pocket mirror and looks at himself constantly, "viewing" his organ of truth. On *Whitsunday* (on the day of the witness of the son) he chooses a film, among the many to be seen in Vienna, probably for its title: *The White Sister*, containing two words so rich in associations. He cannot stand it any more. This time, the pimple on his nose truly depresses him. The insurance doctor's verdict is final: Nothing can be done. Then he thinks to himself: "I can't go on living like this." His despair drives him to a last resort: Professor X. As the contents of the pimple squirt out and the expert fingers draw blood, he *cries out*. He has said it all but no one knows anything. He has had a narrow escape . . . from Father's suicide.

This momentary euphoria is the father's, not his own. It is not made to last. A few days later, "He observes with horror" (*er bemerkte zu seinem Entsetzen = ich sah zu meinem grossen Schreck: I see the great khriekh*) equals " I understand the great sin." What is the great sin? A swelling of the nose, in order not to disclose an erection.

This swelling must be squeezed out of him like the truth. It will again be in the form of a pulled tooth. The first tooth was extracted instead of the bad one still in place, he states. It is the start of a generalized infection. Once more the Wolf Man observes "with horror" (*mit grossem Schreck* = the great *khriekh*) that the "great sin" could be betrayed by his swollen nose. His nose is no longer the way it used to be, one half is different from the other. Damned truth! Will it come out of his wife's wart on the tip of her nose? This is a good pretext, in any case, to go see Professor X. with her. His wife is cured instantly by electrolysis. His own ailment would be best treated this way, too; he should think about it and return in a few days. But the Wolf Man no longer has confidence. Professor X., who has since become rather contemptuous toward him, may drag the truth out of him for good. He goes to another dermatologist. Even though this doctor recommends a different treatment, he is full of praise for Professor X. He is no quack! The Wolf Man is completely reassured and decides to return to him to undergo the treatment he had been advised against. Nearly the same process occurs with the dentist, another extractor of truth (*tooth* = *truth*). Crown or no crown? Fillings: two, five, or . . . six? What a pity to spoil such beautiful teeth with so many fillings, says the insurance doctor. The "final truth" is going to be "a group of six" fillings (group of six = *siestorka*), a "sixter" of "holes filled": **a sister, a fly—to be closed**.

6. The False "False Witness" and the Rank Affair

We are approaching the great day: June 16, 1926, the day of his annual call on Freud to receive the sum of collected money.

There is an omission here in Ruth Mack Brunswick's account: A decisive event took place two weeks earlier. Fortunately, Muriel Gardiner reported it some forty-five years later in a footnote of the greatest interest (Gardiner, *The Wolf-Man by the Wolf-Man*, pp. 277–78).

In 1926, Freud had written to the Wolf Man asking him certain questions about the wolf dream. The Wolf Man replied to him on June 6, 1926, stating: "I am completely sure that I dreamed the wolf dream precisely as I narrated it to you at the time." He went on to discuss whether he could possibly have seen the opera *Pique Dame* [*The Queen of Spades*], which contained certain elements which might seem to be related to the dream, before having the dream, and felt that this was unlikely, although *Pique Dame* was the first opera he and his sister had attended. Toward the end of his letter, the Wolf-Man writes: "Without any connection to the dream, two other childhood memories from my earliest days recently occurred to me. One was a conversation with the coachman about the operation that is performed on stallions, and the second was my mother's story about a kinsman born with six toes, one of which was cut off immediately after his birth. Both these memories deal with the subject of castration. . . . I should be very glad if this information is of use to you."

On June 11, 1957, the Wolf Man wrote an interesting letter that referred back to this earlier exchange with Freud, which he had recently reread: "I had quite forgotten about this letter. . . . I am now still of the opinion that I saw *Pique Dame (The Queen of Spades)* after the 'dream.' " He explained that until his family left "the first estate," when or before he was five years of age, he had been in a city where there was an opera only for a short time one summer. "I could have been only three or four years old at the time and I cannot imagine anyone taking a child of that age to the opera. In fact I do not think the opera was open in summer at that time." This letter continued with an acute observation: "It is interesting that my letter to Professor Freud is dated June 6, 1926. In June 1926 the symptoms relating to my nose appeared, supposedly "paranoia," for which Dr. Mack treated me. This must have been not long after the composition of my letter to Professor Freud; for on July 1, 1926, my wife and I went on vacation, and I was already in an indescribably despairing condition. If I had waited a few more days to reply to Professor Freud, I would have been in such a mental state that I could probably not have told him anything he would have found useful. Or, could the outbreak of my "paranoia" have had any connection with Professor Freud's question? . . . What strikes me about my letter to Professor Freud is the extent to which I speak of castration. No wonder, if this letter was written on the "eve of paranoia" (Gardiner, *The Wolf-Man by the Wolf-Man*, pp. 277–78; see also Afterword, this volume).

What an incredible surprise. A letter in Freud's own handwriting and quite a letter at that. He asks nothing less than a truthful testimony. Freud's illustrious life, salvation, and honor depend on the poor words of a modest Wolf Man. Why, this Rank, a disrespectful disciple, is beginning to spread the rumor that his (the Wolf Man's) own childhood nightmare does not come straight from the age of five but is, clearly, an effect of transference. The five wolves of his drawing published by Freud are the latter's five associates disguised. Everyone knew their photos lined the wall facing the couch in Freud's office. This is simply too much. Without wasting a moment, the Wolf Man takes up his best of pens and writes a detailed attestation to Freud on June 6, 1926, corroborating dates and confirming the undoubtedly early occurrence of the dream with proofs about his childhood fear of castration. Thirty-one years later he will be quite stunned to read a copy of it. It had slipped his mind. Maybe he never even mentioned it to Ruth Mack Brunswick. In a letter to Muriel Gardiner in 1957, he wonders whether the dates in connection with his testimony are plausible and whether the outbreak of his "paranoia" (the quotation marks are his) was not in some way related to the contents of his letter to Freud. Finally, he is struck by his insistence on castration. In any case, had he waited a day or two more with his reply, he concludes, the "sudden" (*v'droug* = th'truth) outbreak of his symptoms would have prevented him from writing it.

7. Is It You or Is It Not You?

On June 14, 1926, eight days after his answer to Freud, he is on the brink of despair. His heart beats, beats, and beats. He runs to a doctor. Is it because of the cod liver oil he has been taking for some time? Heart neurosis, says the physician. The next day he knocks on the door of the dermatologist who had been so helpful. "Is the scar ever going to heal?" "There is no scar at all. And, incidentally, it is never going to heal. Have you gone to a quack?" He is in the grip of bottomless despair (*eine bodenlose Verzweiflung*). There is no way out any more, a voice inside keeps repeating, and "the verdict rang incessantly in his ears." *Verzweiflung*: It is more than despair. It seals off the possibility of doubt itself. Doubt what? That the child's witness was truthful. *Kein Ausgang*: No *issue* = no way out. **Is it you** (the witness) **or is it not you—that was the question**. The dermatologist's "never" takes away all hope from the father that he might ever be rid of his stigma. Is proof of this not offered by the testimony— false by definition—that he has given in alms to the famous Professor? He has a tiny little white line (*Strich*) on the nose as a result of "rubbing," *streichen, tieret*. It exacerbates the contradiction within the son's sexual ideal. All that is left to him is the little window (= witness) of the mirror in order to "view" his nose and say to himself that along with the nurse, *he* (she) "understood the whole (*hole*) thing."

"An *idée fixe*," concludes the dermatologist. But now his words no longer work to calm the "patient" who feels they are but alms thrown to a crippled beggar (according to his own description: *verstummelt*, crippled; it rhymes with *verstummen*, remain silent). When calling on Freud the following day, he will "of course" not break the silence about his symptoms. Not yet. He will have to consult a third dermatologist in order to realize that, in reality, there was nothing whatever wrong with his nose, but rather with his obsession with Professor X.: How could he have been guilty of such a gross error (such a "sin") as regards *him*, the Wolf Man, and not his sister, whose enviable and tragic place he thus acquired. Was it "a terrible accident" (*ein schrecklicher Zufall* = *Schreck* = *khriekh*), was it a **sin**, an accident, a letting go or an unconscious intention? The transfer to Professor X. of his feelings of hate and revenge finally allows him to speak about it all to Freud, and the analysis with Ruth Mack Brunswick is decided. Is he going to allow, according to his firmest intentions, the truth to be pulled out?

Chapter 6
Is a Witness Always False?

1. The Dream of the Jewels

"I am standing at the prow of a ship and I am carrying a bag containing jewelry – my wife's earrings and her silver pocket mirror. I lean against the rail, I thereby break the mirror, and I think that now I will have seven years of bad luck." (*Ich stehe am Vorderteil eines Schiffes und ich trage eine Tasche mit Juwelen – die Ohrringe meiner Frau und ihren Taschenspiegel aus Silber. Ich lehne mich an die Reeling, ich zerbreche dabei den Spiegel, und ich denke, dass ich jetzt sieben Jahre Unglück haben werde.*)[1]

a) "I am standing at the prow of a ship," (*Ich stehe am Vorderteil eines Schiffes.*)

> "I am standing," we hear: "I am not lying": This time I am saying the truth. "At the prow": In Russian, the ship's prow is called *nos.* (According to Brunswick's account, the Wolf Man himself says *nos.* As in his analysis with Freud, he again draws attention to the necessity of translating his words into a foreign language. Nevertheless, he leads us astray by providing an incomplete "translation"; he omits English.) We recognize the English homonyms: "nose" and "he knows."
> *Schiff* = ship and also *schief* = crooked, a synonym of *rank* = crooked, twisted, and the name of Freud's disciple, Otto Rank. The sentence is translated: **I am not lying, Rank knows it (as I do).** Or, put more simply: **I am in the foreground of the Rank affair.**

b) "And I am carrying a bag containing jewelry," (*und Ich trage eine Tasche mit Juwelen.*)

Taschengeld, pocket money; *Tasche*, bag or pocket; *Brieftasche*, wallet; *Brief*, letter. *Tasche* thus contains *Brief* and *Geld* (money) at the same time. *Juwelen* (jewels) rhymes with *Jubel*; a synonym of *Freude* (joy) = Freud. In short: **I am carrying a "wallet"** (an allowance) **and a "letter" of Freud's**.

c) "My wife's earrings and her silver pocket mirror" (*die Ohrringe meiner Frau und ihren Taschenspiegel aus Silber.*)

These are the concealed jewels (see chapter 5): Earrings in Russian = *sergei* and necklace = *Halsband* in German, which rhymes with *husband* in English. Here, the necklace in the pair of jewels is replaced by a pocket mirror and, similarly, the sister is replaced by Sergei (earrings). The governess's words may be inferred: **This time it is not the sister but Sergei who is with the husband**.

d) "I lean against the rail, I thereby break the mirror." (*Ich lehne mich an die Reeling, ich zerbreche dabei den Spiegel.*)
The mother's reply is:

I am leaning on the disciple (disciple = *Lehrling*, an anagram of *Reeling* = rail) **and thus break the witness** ("the mirror that sees") **and not the husband**. A characteristic of this dream is that its text could very well, with the appropriate changes, be uttered by the nurse alone. The ambiguity (between the mother and the nurse) is going to persist for some time.

e) "And I think that now I will have seven years of bad luck." (*Und ich denke, dass ich jetzt sieben Jahre Unglück haben werde.*)

"I think": The dream thought transfers the dreamer's "I" to Freud. If the Wolf Man were to denounce him, the Professor would be prosecuted. "Seven years of bad luck;" a condensed allusion to at least two trains of thought: The sister was seven at the time of the events, and seven years separate the additional analysis with Freud in 1919 and the present time (1926). During this time, the Wolf Man has been benefiting from annual gifts of money for, he thinks, his silence and his "false testimony." Also, bad luck = *Unglück* or, colloquially, *Pech*. This refers to the misdeed since *Pech* can be read as *riekh* = *khriekh* (misdeed) in the Russian alphabet. We translate: **Freud thinks he is going to have seven years of bad luck for his misdeed**.

Ruth Mack Brunswick adds: "And it was his wife (*Frau* = Freud) who had seduced him (*verleiten*, seduce, lead astray) into concealing the jewels (*Schmucke*, jewels, a synonym of *Juwelen*, a homophone of *Jubel*, joy, pleasure)." We recognize in this behavior the Father's hidden "misdeed" and the governess's accusations. Brunswick remarks insightfully that the Wolf Man is going through an experience quite similar to the one that had led to his "character change" during his childhood. The patient sees himself as the mirror image of his previous analyst, his secretive Father. The present does indeed recall the traumatic past. This fact notwithstanding, it is the first time he has mentioned the concealed jewels. His show of truth is accompanied by an attack of diarrhea heralding another truth that, being more deeply hidden, cannot come to the surface.

Here is a succinct interpretation of the dream of the jewels:

I am at the fore of the Rank affair. I am not lying (this time I am saying the truth). **Rank knows it** as I do. **I am carrying** (I am tainted by) **a wallet and a letter of Freud's.** The governess: **"Not the sister but Sergei is with the husband this time."** The mother replies: **"I lean on the disciple"** and **thus break the witness and not the husband. I think** (as if I were Freud) **that because of this and his misdeed, he should have seven years of bad luck**.

The well-known psychodrama about Professor X.'s death occurs next. Hearing his analyst's sudden announcement of the latter's death, the Wolf Man leaps from the couch as if acting out a dream, and **starts acting out**, with an air of melodrama, **the word "fly" disguised in "wolf,"** the way it is seen in the *wide-open wolf book*. "My God! I can't kill him any more," he cries out. We hear beneath the cry: "tell the truth . . . " Guilt toward the Father (Freud), taken ill, returns and brings with it an immediate change of roles in the scene: The Wolf Man is once again a phobic child, living on the words that reassure the anguished mother. Improving on the tale, the analyst takes Freud's defense. As for the Wolf Man, he has but mockery for the governess, a past mistress in blackmail. The following dreams testify beautifully to the Wolf Man's newfound loyalty to his mother as opposed to the governess.

2. The Dream of the Sleigh

A woman . . . is standing in a sleigh that she drives in a masterful manner, and declaims verse in excellent Russian.

Here is a succinct interpretation of this first part:

A woman appears declaiming "masterfully" some "verse" about "trousers" and "fly" (sleigh, *Schlitt: Schlitz*, slit, fly) **in excellent English (= Russian).**

3. The Dream of the Gypsy Woman

The banter continues:

The old gypsy woman (= *Zigeunerin*, also *Gaunerin*, a cheat by homophony) **chatters away some false "news" in front of Freud's house; she talks at random but no one listens to her**.

He is not going to attack Father in Rank's and the nurse's name, unless his analyst tells him that Freud is uninterested both in his case and in his person. Next the Wolf Man is going to resume his role as witness for the prosecution, though not without some measure of identification with the defendant. The result is a certain amount of ambiguity.

4. The Dream of the Father with the Hooked Nose

The father or the professor resembles a (mute) **beggar; he is sitting** (in prison and not at a table) **and there is a warning; there is the fact that she presents** (*die Anwesenden*, those present). We hear: **She** (the nurse) **presents the story so she can extort money** (*Geldangelegenheiten*, money matters).

"My father's nose is long and crooked." (*Die Nase meines Vaters ist lang und krumm.*)

We hear: *lang* (long), a paronym of *rank* (hooked, rooked) and the latter's synonym *krumm*. *Nase*, nose: He knows. **Rank** (the Wolf Man) **knows about father's** misdeed.

5. Dream of the Word *Ganz*

"I show Freud a long scratch on my hand. Freud answers something, repeating the word *ganz* [whole] several times." (*Ich zeige Freud eine lange Kratzwunde an der Hand. Freud antwortet etwas wobei er das Wort "ganz" einigemal wiederholt.*)

In this dream, the Wolf Man tries again to denounce what he will call his "false testimony" given in Freud's favor: the long letter he sent at the latter's request in order to whitewash the accusations made by Rank, his student.

I show, *zeige: Zeuge*, witness; a long scratch on my hand, *eine lange Kratzwunde an der Hand: ein langer Handkratz*, a long manuscript (literally; a handscratch); scar, *Wunde: gewunden*, crooked, synonym of *rank*/Rank. **I bear witness to Freud with a long manuscript about Rank**. *Ganz* = the whole (thing), hole, fly. Also, the word "repeating" (*wiederholt*), which occurs earlier in the dream, includes in German the syllable *hol* (*wider-hol-t*). Another tack: *Ganz* rhymes with *glance*, that is, to glance at. The German *-hol-* rhymes with the "whole" affair and "several times" recalls "several walnut trees" (see the analysis of the main nightmare in chapter 3). The word *ganz* thus condenses and repeats the threatening words of the nurse. **He looked several times.** The false testimony has been extorted.

A similar conflict of ambivalence arises even more clearly in the following dream.

6. The Dream of Celestial Bodies

"I am lying on a couch in your office [treatment room]. Suddenly, there appears on the ceiling a brilliant half-moon and a star. I know that this is a hallucination, and in despair, because I feel I am going mad, I throw myself at your feet." (*Ich liege auf einem Ruhebett in Ihrem Behandlungszimmer. Plötzlich erscheint an der Decke des Zimmers ein glänzender Halbmond und ein Stern. Ich weiss, dass es eine Halluzination ist. Aus Verzweiflung, weil ich fühle, dass ich verrückt werde, werfe ich mich Ihnen zu Füssen.*)

The Wolf Man is coming nearer and nearer to the situation of original anxiety. This dream therefore contains some elements of the main nightmare as well as its characteristic dialogue form and progression.

a) "I am lying on a couch in your treatment room." (*Ich liege auf einem Ruhebett in Ihrem Behandlungszimmer.*)

Room, *Zimmer: zimoi* (in Russian = winter) rhymes with *t'z a boy* (see chapter 3, section 3). It is clear that this is the mother talking: **He is lying as children do.** The next sentence is the nurse's reply.

b) "Suddenly, there appears on the ceiling a brilliant half-moon and a star." (*Plötzlich erscheint an der Decke des Zimmers ein glänzender Halbmond und ein Stern.*)

Suddenly = *v'droug* = th'truth appears (*erscheint*), appears to me (*erscheint mir*). See the connecting passage in the main dream (chapter 3, section 3) : "The truth is that . . . I see the great sin." Similarly here: *erscheint mir* = **I see** *an der Decke* (on the ceiling). By homophony we obtain *Decke: Schreck* (terror) and further *khriekh*, **The sin.** *Zimmers* = **the boy**; brilliant, *glänzend*, in English, **glanced.** Half-moon, *Halbmond*: Sigmund; the word "half" (*halb*) replaces its antonym, "whole" (*ganz*). **The child saw everything.** Then: **Sigmund** (from *Mond*) and **the sister** (from star, *zviezda*, vocalic homophone of *siestra*; see the childhood dream of the celestial bodies; chapter 4, section 8 and chapter 2 section 1). The nurse states in summary: **The truth of the sin appears to me** (clearly). **The child saw everything: the father and the sister**. Thereupon the mother replies:

c) "I know that this a hallucination." (*Ich weiss, dass es eine Halluzination ist.*)

I know = no: **No, it is a hallucination**.

d) In despair, because I feel I am going mad . . . " (*Aus Verzweiflung, weil ich fühle, dass ich verrückt werde . . .*)

Let us translate: **In despair, because I sense that I will be betrayed** (going mad, *verrückt werden: es wird mit mir ausgerückt werden*, I am going to be betrayed). One can distinguish the superimposition of two complementary states of mind: the one just attributed to Freud and the Wolf Man's own. We will consider that *verrückt* (mad) may well be a distortion *verdrückt* and the condensation of various Freudian terms for "repressed": *unterdrückt, verdrängt*. Given Brunswick's tactics of defending Freud, the Wolf Man has another reason for despair. He feels he has to repress his wish to betray, just as he had repressed it during his childhood. We surmise that his religious upbringing helped reinforce his repression. The dilemma lies in the alternative "cry out" or "repress." The second version of the same sequence is: **In despair because I feel I have to "repress."**

e) "I throw myself at your feet." (*werfe ich mich Ihnen zu Füssen.*)

This can be understood in the manifest sense: **I throw myself at your feet** (the "I" being the mother) to implore the nurse's silence(= Rank = the Wolf Man). A somewhat contrary meaning can also be heard; thanks to a form of homophony passing through the German *Fuss: foot* evokes *truth*. Thus: **I throw the truth** (in your face).

The translation of the entire dream results in the following dialogue:
Mother. **He is lying like a child**.
Nurse. **The truth is that the sin appears to me clearly. The child saw the whole thing**.
Mother. **No! It's a hallucination**.
Freud. **In despair because I sense that I will be betrayed, I throw myself at the feet of the witness and implore him to lie in my favor**.
The Wolf Man. **In despair because I sense that I must "repress," I throw the truth in your face**.
The following dream of the gray wolves is an even clearer repetition of the main nightmare, but this time it does not wake the dreamer. Ambivalence reigns.

7. The Dream of the Gray Wolves

"In a wide street is a wall with a closed door. To the left of the door is a large, empty wardrobe with some whole and some broken drawers. I stand before the wardrobe, my wife, a shadowy figure, is behind me. Near the other end of the wall stands a large heavyset woman looking as if she wanted to go around (and look) behind the wall. But behind the wall is a pack of gray wolves, crowding toward the door and pacing impatiently back and forth. Their eyes gleam, and it is clear that they want to rush at me, my wife, and the other woman. I am terrified, fearing that they will succeed in breaking through the wall." (*In einer breiten Strasse ist eine Mauer mit einer geschlossenen Tür. Links von der Tür ist ein grosser leerer Kasten, in dem ganze und zerbrochene Laden sind. Ich stehe vor dem Kasten, meine Frau als schattenhafte Gestalt hinter mir. Nahe dem anderen Ende der Mauer steht eine grosse schwerfällige Frau, die so aussieht wie wenn sie gern um die Mauer herum, hinter diese gehen wollte. Aber hinter der Mauer ist ein Rudel grauer Wölfe die sich zur Tür drängen und hin und her laufen. Ihre Augen glänzen und es ist klar, dass sie nur darauf lauern sich auf mich, meine Frau und das andere Weib zu stürzen. Ich bin entsetzt und fürchte dass es ihnen gelingen wird durch die Mauer auszubrechen.*)

a) "In a wide street is a wall . . . " (*In einer breiten Strasse ist eine Mauer . . .*)

Street and wall heard together make up *Wall Street* (see the Wolf Man's financial speculations and the dream of the jewels; chapter 5, section 2); Wall Street = stock market, in German *Börse*, also a synonym of *Brieftasche* (wallet). This last word unites, in German, a twofold allusion to: (1) the letter (*Brief*) of testimony and (2) the gifts of money (*Taschengeld*, pocket money). Both the letters and the money are linked to the Wolf Man's present conflict: **A wide-open wallet**, *Breite* (wide) and "Wall Street" together also refer to wide (open) *goulfik* ("wolves" threatening to "break through the wall"). The last sentence of the dream must be heard lexically, that is, the word "wolf" in "wall"; the result is "wolf street" leading to *goulfik* by homophony. This condenses the childhood conflict: **a wide-open fly**.

b) "containing a closed door." (*mit einer geschlossenen Tür.*)

The dreamer tries to reverse the manifest content of his main dream. There is no "window opening by itself" (**No witness speaking**) but its contrary: "a closed door."

c) "To the left of the door is a large, empty wardrobe . . ." (*Links von der Tür ist ein grosser leerer Kasten . . .*)

The current meaning is: **Rank's testimony against the great teacher is unqualified** (*Tür*, door: window: testimony; empty wardrobe, *leerer: Lehrer* (teacher) + *Kasten* = *Schrank* (wardrobe + rank). The opposite meaning is equally valid: to the right (*rechts*) instead of to the left (*links*); he is right: **Rank's testimony against the great teacher is right**. Historically: *Recht* (disguised in left, *links*) can be pronounced with a guttural "h" in both German and Russian, evoking *khriekh* (the sin). If we recall the words of the main dream ("a row of old walnut trees" and "on the walnut tree"; see this chapter, section 1), we hear in *Schrank* (wardrobe) *Rang*, row and in *Lehrer* the master, that is, the "old man" with his "series of misdeeds." Simplifying the overdetermination and condensation the result is: **No testimony, no series of misdeeds committed by the old man** (this is what I say, but I think that) **it is false**. The current conflict overlaps with the childhood one.

d) "with some whole [complete] and some broken drawers." (*in dem ganze und zerbrochene Laden sind.*)

Ganz, whole and also "glance"; *zerbrochene* (broken) is an antonym of *ganz*; *Laden*, drawer and also business. The translation runs: **He saw the whole business: No, he saw nothing**.

e) "I stand before the wardrobe, my wife, a shadowy figure, is behind me." (*Ich stehe vor dem Kasten, meine Frau als schattenhafte Gestalt hinter mir.*)

I stand = **I am lying** according to the system of reversals already observed in this dream. Before the wardrobe = **before Rank** (*Kasten*: *Schrank*: *Rank*). My wife: **my Freud** (*Frau*: Freud), "a shadowy figure." This is an allusion to Freud's illness and loss of weight; the Wolf Man thinks he is their cause. There is a further allusion to the latter's conviction that Freud is **a shadowy figure behind my analyst**.

f) "Near the other end of the wall stands a large heavyset woman . . ." (*Nahe dem anderen Ende der Mauer steht eine grosse schwerfällige Frau*)

Close to the other end: to the right: "I can't say after all, were I to translate my dream image into words, that **the sin is rightful** (to the right), so I say: **at the other end**. But I really do mean the **sin** (right, *recht: khriekh*, sin). I also want to add: **In this whole business Freud** (Frau) **stands there with his difficult case** (heavy, *schwerfällig*: *schwer*, difficult; *Fall*, case); that is, Freud is stuck with his difficult case."

g) "looking as if she wanted to go around (and look) behind the wall." (*die so aussieht wie wenn sie gern um die Mauer herum, hinter diese gehen wollte.*)

She looks like someone who would like to avoid having to talk about Wall (wolf: *goulfik*, Street **in roundabout ways** (*hinter herum*, roundabout, illegally). This is an allusion to the fact that the Wolf Man has been entrusted to another "Freud" (*Frau*, woman): Ruth Mack Brunswick.

h) "But behind the wall is a pack of gray wolves, crowding toward the door and pacing impatiently back and forth." (*Aber hinter der Mauer ist ein Rudel grauer Wölfe die sich zur Tür drängen und hin und her laufen.*)

Behind this analysis is the fact that little Ruth (= Ruterl = *Rudel* = pack) **is pushing the witness impatiently** (*Tür*, door: window: witness; *hin und her laufen* = show impatience) **to disguise his "white wolves" as gray wolves.**

i) "Their eyes gleam, and it is clear that they want to rush at me, my wife, and the other woman." (*Ihre Augen glänzen und es ist klar, dass sie nur darauf lauern sich auf mich, meine Frau und das andere Weib zu stürzen.*)

I am looking ("Their eyes gleam," *ihre Augen glänzen*, translated into dream English becomes: eye = I, *glänzen* = glance) **and it is clear that Freud and his shadow** (*Frau* and the other woman, Ruth Mack Brunswick) **are looking out for the moment when they can lean on me** (rush at, *sich stürzen*: *sich stützen*, lean on), that is: on my testimony.

It is curious that while analyzing this dream, Ruth Mack Brunswick saw fit, admittedly with good intuition, to ask the Wolf Man a crucial question: Did his wolf dream really occur in early childhood? She thus implied some doubt as regards the credibility of Freud's account. She noted her patient's reaction: He deemed the question not even worthy of a response. Perhaps he simply refused to bear *witness* . . . whatever its truth value might have been. Our analysis of the nightmare (chapter 3) established its early childhood occurrence beyond any doubt. The problem was simply that the Wolf Man faced the paradox that by testifying *to the truth* (i.e., the early occurrence of the dream), he thought he was being confirmed in his status of "false witness," a title conferred on him by Father, Mother, and Freud. In other words, any testimony whatever would have functioned as a lie for him. Ruth Mack Brunswick's question made the Wolf Man confront reality and "resolved" his "present neurosis" in a way somewhat similar to the childhood religious education urged on him by his mother. The new solution differs from the old one in one respect only: This time, instead of the devil, the undeniable truth is being invoked. It is high time. The last sentence of the dream is indeed rather disquieting.

j) "I am terrified, fearing that they will succeed in breaking through the wall."

(Ich bin entsetzt und fürchte dass es ihnen gelingen wird durch die Mauer auszubrechen.)

> The phobia is expressed as follows: **I** (Freud) **am deposed** (= *entsetzt*) **if they succeed in breaking through** (*ausbrechen* = *zerbrechen* = *durchbrechen*) **the analysis** and the perjury **by means of the truth** (through, *durch*: truth).

The complete translationof the dream thus reads: **A wide-open wallet, a talkative witness** (which I do not wish to be. So I say:) **No witness, no series of sins by the old man but** (I think that) **this is false.** (I say also:) **Rank** (myself) **is unqualified to denounce the great teacher** (but I think that) **Rank is right to denounce the great teacher. He has understood the whole business; no, he understood nothing about the business. I am lying** (before = behind) **Rank, Freud is behind my analyst like a shadow.** *Sigmund* Freud's *victorious mouth (Sieg*, victory; *Mund*, mouth: Sigmund) is thus reduced to a half-mouth, (half-moon is also *Halbmond*: *Mund*), an allusion to his emaciated face. **In this second analysis, Freud is going to be (stuck) with his difficult case. He looks to me as if he wanted to accomplish his purpose in roundabout ways** (i.e., having me analyzed by a student of his). **Behind this analysis is the fact that little Ruth is pushing the witness** (me) **impatiently to disguise** (the true significance of) **the "white wolves." It is clear that Freud and Ruth Mack are looking out for one thing**: (the moment when they can) **lean on me against Rank. I** (Freud) **am terrified that I will be deposed if** (Rank and he) **succeed in breaking through the Wolf Man's analysis** (and the perjury) **by means of the truth**.

The present and the past merge. Behind the show of obedience to the mother, a cryptic identification with the policelike nurse (who had raised little Sergei to the rank of witness) continues to be active. In addition to the latent content just brought to light, a revival of the "police dog's" English words is also apparent in the barking sounds of the dream's latter half: the diphthong *au* (pronounced *ow*) returns no less than fifteen times in eight lines. The increasing desire to speak out mobilizes the forces of countercathexis. They hark back to the period when the mother tried to use religious training to calm the temper tantrums of the "broken" witness. The analysis thus opens the way to regression. In fact, Professor X.'s death exacerbates, in the same way Father's death had done earlier, the Wolf Man's feelings of guilt; he thinks that his repressed wish to denounce first the one and then the other was the cause of their death. Result: a growing identification with the defendant.

The prosecution is about to reach its climax.

Chapter 7
The Turning Point: A Truthful Witness

We have seen that, while analyzing the dream of the gray wolves, Ruth Mack Brunswick expressed doubts about Freud in the form of a question and was thereby able to resolve, if not the Wolf Man's childhood neurosis, at least his current neurosis. She played the devil's advocate by adopting through the very question she raised the Wolf Man's latent incredulity toward Freud as defendant. The Wolf Man should feel dismayed. The result is an alleviation of the persecutive tension and a real turning point for the analysis. But at the same time, the Wolf Man's childhood phobia revives.

What has happened? Brunswick questions him about the date of his nightmare, no doubt because she has some doubts. If need be, she may even be willing to side with Rank. A mother to dream about: She would not fear blackmail and would not force little Sergei to lie. On the other hand, were his mother to side with the nurse, the Wolf Man would be alone in assuming the task of defending Father's honor. The muffled accusations he harbors vanish at once. *The present is different from the past: The witness can proclaim the truth without doing any harm, without having to pass himself off as a liar.* Is it not true, really true, that his nightmare dates from his childhood? He has had enough of lies and petty acts of dishonesty! He is not going to turn into a liar just because he is receiving cash from analysts. He can again be scrupulously concerned about right and wrong as he used to be.

His present thus "normalized," he turns from being a defendant back to being a phobic. Soon afterward, he will furnish a new edition of his childhood dream. Of course, it will be brought up to date: He will redo his nightmare in lavish colors and pleasing melodies. First another dream has to confirm the present situation. It shows him in his mother's company. He attempts in vain to reinstate the situation prior to the analyst's transformation of it. "Rutma" (Ruth Mack), who had assumed the role of the mother in reverse ("Muta"), becomes once again: *Mutter* (mother). She is not a true mother, however, but the mother's speech reversed a second time. Two negations do not quite make an affirmation as we will see. Here is the dream:

1. The Dream of the Icons

"My mother and I are together in a room. In one corner the entire wall is covered with holy pictures. My mother takes the pictures down and throws them on the floor. The pictures fall and break into pieces. I am astonished that my pious mother should do such a thing." (*Ich bin mit meiner Mutter in einem Zimmer in dem in einer Ecke, die ganze Wand mit Heiligenbildern bedeckt ist. Die Mutter nimmt die Bilder herunter und wirft sie auf den Boden. Die Bilder zerbrechen in Stücke. Ich bin erstaunt darüber dass meine fromme Mutter so etwas tut.*)

a) "My mother and I are together in a room." (*Ich bin mit meiner Mutter in einem Zimmer.*)

Mutter, "mother," is a distortion of *Rutma* (Ruth Mack). *Zimmer* (room) refers to the Russian *zima*, *zimoi* = winter and translated, as in the main nightmare, into the English phrase: *t'z iboy* = **He is a boy!**

b) "In one corner the entire wall is covered with holy pictures." (*In einer Ecke, die ganze Wand mit Heiligenbildern bedeckt ist.*)

From "holy pictures" in the "corner" we get to *Eckbilder* (corner pictures) and by homophony to *Schreckbilder* (terrifying pictures). *Schreckbilder* leads to a picture of the *khriekh*, the sin. *Wand* equals wall, which evokes *Gewalt* (violence, rape) by homophony; *ganz* (whole) = glanced = "I saw." In this reversal (the holy pictures become terrifying) *khriekh* is reduced to *Eck* (corner).

c) "My mother takes the pictures down and throws them on the floor. The pictures fall and break into pieces." (*Die Mutter nimmt die Bilder herunter und wirft sie auf den Boden. Die Bilder zerbrechen in Stücke.*)

Read backward the restored text is: **Mother takes down and breaks these obscene pictures and converts them into holy pictures.** But what is she doing now? **She throws them on the floor as Onan had done with his semen.**

d) "I am astonished that my pious mother should do such a thing." (*Ich bin erstaunt darüber dass meine fromme Mutter so etwas tut.*)

I am really surprised at this contradiction: If she is so pious, how can she condone my masturbating with the image of the sin in mind? She is clearly my mother in reverse.

The succinct interpretation of the dream of the icons reads: **I am with Ruth Mack, my mother turned inside out, but I want her to be my mother right side out, and I want her to say: "He is a boy!" And the nurse should reply: "There is a sin! A rape no less. I understand the whole business." My mother should call the icons obscenities. Instead of making me into a truthful witness, Ruth Mack should break these pictures so that I can continue to be a false witness.** (Unless this one condition is fulfilled, I cannot perform, with her in mind, the fetish act I desire: coitus a tergo, *tieret*, the equivalent of the primal scene; that is, if I continue to be a false witness, I can throw my semen on the ground with my fetishistic fantasy.) Clearly, what the wish expressed in the dream conceals is the true desire of taking the father's place in the original scene (see chapter 2, section 2). **I am surprised at the contradiction that Ruth Mack should be my pious mother in reverse and that she is willing to give in to my fetishistic act.**

The economic function of keeping alive—at all costs—the traumatic scene of witnessing and its hidden words is finally becoming clear. The words of the scene allow him to preserve another word, endowed with another function and precious above all others. This is the secret and magic word *tieret*. Its being visualized in obscene images and scenes makes orgasm possible.

The Wolf Man feels temporarily relieved at having a mother in reverse for economically contradictory reasons. For he also needs to preserve his former goods, namely, the nurse's accusations, even at the cost of further concealment. That should not stop me, he seems to be saying, let's produce a reversed wolf dream for a "reversed" mother. Why not, if this is what mother wants now? But all of this must not bring about a fundamental shift. He must remain at once a "false witness" and be outraged by this imputation.

We can now proceed with a new exercise: We can turn right side up what has been turned upside down twice over for the sake of expediency. This little trick will suffice to recover the elements of the initial traumatic dialogue.

Here is another "reversed" dream: the clarified (*verklärt*) wolf dream or a wrong-sided (*verkehrt*) wolf dream, as the analyst herself has remarked.

2. The Clarified Wolf Dream

"I stand looking out of my window at a meadow, beyond which rises a wood. The sun shines through the trees, dappling the grass. The stones in the meadow cast a curious mauve shadow. In particular, I gaze at the branches of a certain tree, admiring the way in which they are intertwined. I cannot figure out why I have not yet painted this landscape." *Ich stehe an meinem Fenster und blicke auf eine Wiese, hinter der sich ein Wald erhebt. Die Sonne fällt durch die Bäume so dass das Gras ganz gesprenkelt aussieht; die Steine auf der Wiese werfen einen sonderbaren malvenfarbigen Schatten. Ich schaue besonders die Äste eines Baumes an und bewundere es, wie schön sie miteinander verflochten sind. Ich kann nicht begreifen dass ich diese Landschaft noch nicht gemalt habe.*)

a) "I stand looking out of my window at a meadow . . . " *Ich stehe an meinem Fenster und blicke auf eine Wiese . . .*)

I stand = *I am not lying*; window = testimony. **I am not lying (= I am lying) about my testimony.** *Blicke,* I gaze, I see; I see *not* wolves but a "meadow." *Not* wolves = *goulfik* (= fly) but a "meadow," in Russian, *shir* (great expanse). The word *shir* leads incontrovertibly to another Russian word that derives from it: *shirinka,* a small slit or fly! *Shir* is thus an aggrandizer and indicates a very large slit: **a very big wide-open fly!**

b) "beyond which rises a wood." (*hinter der sich ein Wald erhebt.*)

A meadow behind which rises (not to say "surges") something **enormous**! (*Wald* [wood] = *gewaltig* [enormous]; it recalls the "enormous caterpillar" and "enormous snail" [*riesige Raupe* and *riesige Schnecke*] in chapter 4, section 8.) The guess is right: "Wood" (*Wald*) brings up "rape" (*Gewalt*), which is the legal qualification of the **enormous sin.** "A meadow at the foot of the wooded hill": This is the Wolf Man's description of the place where Lermontov's fatal duel occurred. His visit there dates from the period of his sister Anna's death (Gardiner, *The Wolf-Man by the Wolf-Man,* p. 32). It is understandable that *this* "landscape" should have been engraved in his mind.

c) "The sun shines through the trees, dappling the grass." (*Die Sonne fällt durch die Bäume so dass das Gras ganz gesprenkelt aussieht.*)

But the sun (= son) pierces through the truth (through = truth) of the sin (the trees refer to the "walnut trees" = *khriekh* of the main dream). The grass (elsewhere *Boden,* floor) is dappled ("with semen"). A similar "picture" is used in describing the scene of Anna's funeral. "The sun already low on the horizon sank, its last rays piercing the foliage and flooding over the shining metal casket." (*The Wolf-Man by the Wolf-Man,* p. 24)

d) "The stones in the meadow cast a curious mauve shadow." (*Die Steine auf der Wiese werfen einen sonderbaren malvenfarbigen Schatten.*)

This is another allusion to masturbating with a "picture," an idyllic scene of an obscene image. The whole dream is in fact nothing more than a "picture" or idyllic scene, the sense connoted by this term in both Russian and Austrian German. The "frame" is the "window," that is, the "witness." "The stones which cast a curious mauve shadow" probably allude to his paternal grandmother's family, whose name was Petrov ("of stone"); this is the branch of the family from which the Wolf Man's father inherited both his fortune and his qualities as a businessman. The dreamer means to say that in the whole business of the *goulfik*, the strange, barbaric, and even incestuous practices did not fail to cast their shadow on his father (mauve, *malva* in Russian, which also means "it is rumored"). Clearly, the strange mauve shadow also evokes the sunset casting its rays on Anna's metallic casket.[1]

The description of a "picture" follows; it is impressionistic since its model lingered only for a moment.

e) "In particular, I gaze at the branches of a certain tree, admiring the way in which they are intertwined. I cannot figure out why I have not yet painted this landscape." (*Ich schaue besonders die Äste eines Baumes an und bewundere es, wie schön sie miteinander verflochten sind. Ich kann nicht begreifen dass ich diese Landschaft noch nicht gemalt habe.*)

Instead of describing "white wolves," this picture depicts "stones casting mauve shapes"; and instead of showing the action of the "witness" (*Zeuge*), it speaks about branches intertwined. (*Zweige*, branches; *Zeuge*, witness. Note that the Wolf Man disguises "branches" in its synonym, *Äste*.) Thus, all this is beautiful and encourages masturbation and its substitute: "painting views" ("view" is used in Russian and German as well) by stroking — *tieret* — with a brush. In sum, all of this produces a "view" in a "frame" or "window," a "testimony" of what was seen.

The translation of the "reversed wolf dream" may be stated thus:

I am not lying, I understand; the son pierced the truth: The fly lay wide-open! There was the enormous sin of the rape! But this is a beautiful picture — the great sin of the wide-open fly I am witnessing (when I masturbate with the image of the "scrub woman" or when I "brushstroke" a painting).

A great sin turned "beautiful" and left behind it a discarded false witness. No objection is raised on the condition that he may hold on to his magic word and the libidinal detour that permits its existence. Were this word to fall by the wayside, it would be the eve of a complete libidinal reorganization of the Wolf Man's desire. The analysis with Ruth Mack Brunswick is hardly adequate to accomplish it. The original traumatic contradiction is far from being liquidated; on the contrary, at the moment everything contributes to reinforce it. The Wolf Man is therefore careful not to link his sister's death to this dream, however difficult it might be to avoid that connection. Bringing the two into contact would force him to cross a new barrier. It is best to retain his cryptic identification. A "poetess" is dead; a painter is born. The Wolf Man discovers his vocation as painter while on a trip in the Caucasus mountains immediately after his sister's funeral. He is his father's "painter" (the sister had been his "poetess"). None of this will be said in the analysis. Reacting to his new mother in reverse, he chooses a watered-down version of his old nightmare.

3. The Dream of the Skyscraper

"I am lying at your feet. I am with you in a skyscraper where the only way out is a window. A ladder from this window extends down to uncanny depths. To get out I must go through the window." (*Ich liege zu Ihren Füssen. Ich bin mit Ihnen in einem Wolkenkratzer dessen einziger Ausgang ein Fenster ist. Von diesem Fenster führt eine Leiter in die unheimliche Tiefe. Um aus dem Wolkenkratzer herauszukommen, muss ich* **durchs Fenster** [R. M. Brunswick's emphasis].

a) "I am lying at your feet." (*Ich liege Ihnen zu Füssen.*)

To be at someone's feet means to be at his disposal, at his service. Let us translate: **I am lying according to your wishes**! But also: *foot*, *Fuss*: truth. **I am lying the truth according to your wishes**.

b) "I am with you in a skyscraper where the only way out is a window." (*Ich bin mit Ihnen in einem Wolkenkratzer dessen einziger Ausgang ein Fenster ist.*)

"I am with you in *goulfik-tieret* (*Wolkenkratzer*, skyscraper; the first syllable, *Volk*, when heard in Russian equals "wolf" = *goulfik*, "fly" as in the main nightmare; *kratzen*, scrape = *tieret*), you are the only witness. (*Ausgang*, exit = issue is close in English to "is you"; window = witness.) If you tell me to say the truth ("the witness is you") wholeheartedly, you do not disqualify me as I once was ("the witness is not you"; see chapter 3, section 3). But what will happen to me? I am going to lose my magic word pure and simple. **Fine, there is "flly" and "rubbing," I witnessed it**.

c) "A ladder from this window extends down to uncanny depths." (*Von diesem Fenster führt eine Leiter in die unheimliche Tiefe.*)

Remember, this "witness" (of the current neurosis) was properly led (seduced) by Freud (by the "leader": *Leiter*, ladder and also leader) into writing an unusual letter of testimony (letters, *Briefe*: *Tiefe*, depths). **But the witness was seduced by an unusual letter** (therefore he is a false witness).

d) "To get out I must go through the window." (*Um aus dem Wolkenkratzer herauszukommen, muss ich durchs Fenster.*)

For me to get out of being a false witness as regards *goulfik-tieret*, the nurse must say "through (the) window": **true witness.**

And this would indeed be a nightmare from which one could not help but awake with a desperate need to find some way out other than the pleasures aroused by the magic word.

In sum:

I am lying the truth according to your wishes. Fine, there is "fly" and "rubbing," I witnessed it. But the "witness" was seduced by an unusual letter (he is therefore a false witness). **To be a true witness and say "fly" and "rubbing" is a "true nightmare," believe me.**

4. The Dream about Criminal Law

"Freud, to whom I am telling my ambition to study criminal law, advises against this course and recommends political science." (*Freud dem ich meine Absicht mitteile Strafgesetz zu studieren, rät mich ab und empfiehlt Wirtschaftslehre.*) Freud dissuades me from studying criminal law (for it would compromise him) and suggests I study something insignificant like political economy. This is proof that I must remain a "false witness" and, at the same time, "rebel against this characterization." In short: **I** (Freud) **and my pleasure** (*Freud* = *Freude* = pleasure) **must be guilty and I must pay**.

This is a dream and reality at the same time, states the Wolf Man. Now Brunswick knew full well that such an exchange between Freud and the Wolf Man never took place. It is a pity that she did not wonder about the meaning of this curious countertruth in which dream state and wakefulness seem to be reaching an agreement.

Dreaming a supposed reality signals a very high degree of reactive "resistance." But is it conceivable that one could fight a piece of "evidence" such as *tieret* that results from repeated orgasms since childhood and that finds its confirmation in them? Here is precisely where the analyst can once again enter the discussion, asking whether he himself might not provide some fresh "evidence" by passing through the original words of the traumatic "false testimony."

Still, a process complete with admissions and reversals, a process (a proceeding) did take place on the couch. True, the "childhood neurosis" remained, but it had, to some extent, lost its grip on current events.[2] Only the need to preserve the magic word and its context of "false testimony" persisted. The last three dreams of his analytic experience with R. M. Brunswick show the line of demarcation beyond which the Wolf Man does not wish to go, at least not this time. He is busy confusing the issue, producing dream images likely to reassure the person who, for a few more days, might be in a position to threaten the harmonious workings of his "magic word." Has he not already stated the whole and naked truth? Did he not consider himself guilty of the worst of crimes. It is time to take stock of what has happened. People should leave him alone with his "guilt" (his father's, of course). The following dreams will take care of it.

5. The Dream of the Young Austrian

"A young Austrian, who has lived for many years in Russia and lost all his money, comes to see me. This young Austrian now has a minor position in a bank in Vienna. He complains of a headache and I ask my wife for a powder, not telling her that I need it for my friend for fear of her refusal. To my surprise, she also gives me a piece of cake but it is not big enough for both me and my friend." (*Ein junger Österreicher, der viele Jahre in Russland gelibt hat und dort sein Geld verlor, besucht mich. Dieser junger Österreicher hat eine untergeordnete Stellung in einer Bank in Wien. Er klagt über Kopfschmerzen und ich erbitte von meiner Frau ein Pulver, ohne ihr zu sagen dass ich es für den Freund brauche. Ich fürchte, sie würde es mir dann nicht geben. Zu meinem Erstaunen gibt sie mir auch ein Stück Kuchen, das aber für beide, mir und meinem Freund zu klein ist.*)

> I, a young Russian, have lived for several years in Austria and lost my money there (to Freud); I will pay you a visit. I have a major position in Vienna. Now I complain of mental ills (headaches) and ask Freud (wife, *Frau: Freud*) to give me some money (*Pulver*, powder; money in Austrian slang) without telling him that I need it for my pleasure (friend, *Freund: Freude*, pleasure), my speculations, and my masturbating sessions with prostitutes, though I do have a small fortune thanks to my hidden jewels. I am afraid that Freud (*Frau*, wife) will refuse to give it to me (if I tell him the whole truth about how the money is to be used, and the jewels, that is, my pleasures *Juwel*, jewel: *Jubel*, delight). To my great surprise, he (Freud, *Frau*) gives me a piece of analysis (cake, *Kuchen: Rutchen*, a little *Ruth* Mack Brunswick). But this is not enough for the two of us: for me and my pleasure (*Freud = Freude*), that is, for my present symptoms and my pleasure. I only have enough for the one: my present symptoms.

6. The Double Dream of the Generous Doctor and the Page

"I am in the office of a doctor with a full, round face (like Professor X.). I am afraid that I do not have enough money in my purse to pay the doctor. However, the latter says that his bill is very small, that he will be satisfied with 100,000 kronen. As I leave, the doctor tries to persuade me to take some old music, which I refuse, saying I have no use for it. But at the door the doctor presses on me some colored postcards, which I have not the heart to refuse. Suddenly you appear dressed like a page in a blue velvet outfit with short pants and a three-cornered hat. Despite your attire, which is boyish rather than masculine, you look entirely feminine. I embrace you and put you on my knee." *(Ich bin bei einem Arzt mit einem vollen, runden Gesicht (wie Professor X.) in der Ordination. Ich fürchte dass ich nicht genug Geld in meiner Börse habe, um den Arzt zu bezahlen. Doch sagt dieser die Rechnung is sehr klein, er sei mit 100,000 Kronen zufrieden. Beim Weggehen will der Arzt mich überreden, alte Musiknoten mitzunehmen. Ich lehne aber sie ab weil ich dafür keine Verwendung habe. Aber an der Tür drängt mir der Arzt einige färbige Postkarten auf, die zurückweisen ich nicht getraue. Plötzlich erscheinen Sie wie ein Page gekleidet, in einem blausamten Anzug mit kurzen Hosen und einen Dreispitz. Trotz Ihrer Kleidung die eher knabenhaft als männlich ist, sehen Sie ganz weiblich aus. Ich umarme Sie und setze Sie auf meine Knie.)*

I am in the office of a doctor who died for me (like Professor X.). I am afraid that I do not have enough stories to satisfy him. But he says that the sin (*Rechnung*, bill; the first syllable is *Rech* and evokes *khriekh*, sin) is quite small and that he would be satisfied with some pecadilloes (some old "worthless" sins) and an old disguised "truth" (100,000 kronen; crowns were Austria's old currency, later devalued. At the time of the dream in 1927, 100,000K was worth 10 shillings, according to Ruth Mack Brunswick's account; ten, *zehn*, distorts *Zahn*, tooth: th'truth). Reference is also being made to "devalued jewels"— diminished pleasures. As I am leaving, I want to persuade him to keep my old songs. He refuses, saying he has no use for them. But at the door, I press on him some colored and idyllic "views," like my "reversed wolf dream," which he does not dare refuse. The truth is that you understand the terrible rape and the open fly distorted in *Page* (which in German sounds like *pas je*, French for "not I"; blue velvet outfit = *blausamtenes Gewand*, vocalic homophone of *grausame Gewalt*, terrible rape; three-corner hat = *Dreispitz*, homophone of *freier Schlitz*, open fly). I embrace you like Father and take you on my knees not worrying whether you are a boy or a girl.

Who the "I" is in this dream remains unclear. Whoever he may be, he sails under two flags, that is, he dissembles doubly. He is unaware both of repeating for the nth time the nurse's words and of being an idyllic picture offered to the analyst he is about to leave. The analyst will have found out nothing about the importance he still attached to the "police dog's" threats and to his own revolt against the necessity of repudiating his testimony. No, Ruth Mack Brunswick will know nothing of the magic word he so luckily found as a match to a humiliating situation. Everything holds together tightly: Changing any one part of the machinery would unsettle the entire pleasure-producing apparatus. The crypt-screen (the lie about the jewels) has disintegrated, but merely in order to safeguard all the better the structure hiding below.

A drama was nevertheless played out. And a truth admitted. Still, the world did not fly off its hinges. To a certain extent it was a symbolic play within a play taken to the second power. "No, Sergei did not lie"; "No, Father is not guilty." This was a wholly unexpected conclusion since, for Sergei, these two statements should be mutually exclusive. He had to "have lied" in order to "clear" Father. This was and still is the precondition of any sexual enjoyment. The only difference is that despite doing *tieret*, he can now remain an honest man in his daily life. He keeps, for the sake of gratification only and in the depths of his crypt, the words of the scandal and his status as false witness. From now on, he can say to himself: It was not Freud who committed the sin but another: Father.

7. The Dream of the Two Dermatologists

Here is what the last dream states:

"I am walking on the street with the second dermatologist who, with great interest, is discoursing about venereal disease. I mention the name of the doctor who treated my gonorrhea with too harsh a medication. On hearing his name, the dermatologist says no, no, not he—another." (*Ich gehe mit dem zweiten Dermatologen, der sehr lebhaft über venerische Erkrankungen mit mir debattiert, auf der Strasse. Ich nenne den Namen des Arztes, der meine Gonorrhöe mit einem zu starken Mittel behandelt hatte. Beim Hören des Namens sagt der Dermatologe: nein, nein, nicht dieser, ein anderer.*)

> I finished the analysis. I am on the street but I fall in with (*ich gehe mit*) my second analyst. The subject of the treatment was sexual ills. The discussions we had were lively. I named the doctor whom I supposedly "stiffened," that is, in whom I caused an erection: *mit starken Mittel behandelt* (treat with a harsh medication), *mit Starkenmittel behandeln* (stiffen with starch). (It should be added here that the verb *tieret* is the usual Russian word for a starched collar *rubbing* the skin.) Upon hearing this name, my second analyst tells me: No, no, *tieret* did not happen to Freud; it happened to someone else! No, you weren't lying by bearing witness for Freud; somebody else did *tieret* (the father) and you weren't the one doing it with him. It was your sister.

This moment marks a turning point and the Wolf Man, putting aside his suit against Freud, is cured of his symptoms and recovers his interest in the world he had created around him. He is no longer afraid to "open a book" or—one can only suppose—ashamed of his sex life.

R. M. Brunswick's solution is very like the one favored by his mother years earlier. How long will this precarious balance last? In the following twelve years the Wolf Man will have frequent cause to call on Brunswick's analytic talents to extricate himself briefly from flare-ups of his original conflict.

8. On the Contradiction Implied in the Fact of "Witnessing"

What set off the attack, the apparent division of the Ego in 1926? We can assign responsibility to the revival of the child's unhappy testimony. His testimony in Freud's favor challenged his incorporated status as "broken witness" and also defied the mother's anxiety that required him in the first place to be a broken witness: The manuscript (*Handkratz*, "hand scratch") he sent to Freud contained indeed the reviled act of *tieret* ("to rub," "to scratch"; cf. the dream of the word *Ganz*, chapter 6, section 5).

His letter to Freud communicated two entirely incompatible acts to the mother: the act of *tieret*, the deep-seated meaning of his analysis with Freud, and the act of testifying to this act before the entire psychoanalytic family. He also revealed in it that the gifts of money he received through the charity of analysts bought his silence about *khriekh*, the father's sin, and that he was not unhappy about having unconsciously replaced his sister as the object of his father's sin. But this testimony that opened the crypt and gave up the witness himself had a most unfortunate consequence. It barred the use of the magic orgasm word, no matter how distorted. Hence the frenzy of despair.

The Wolf Man recovered his composure only when R. M. Brunswick sagaciously let become clear to him that he did not testify *against* a crime: He can be as certain of this as he is of having been a child of five or six at the time of his nightmare. The crime par excellence, *tieret* between Freud and Sergei, "was never committed." He can sleep the sleep of the just and gratify himself with his magic word.

The analysis with Ruth Mack Brunswick had as its result the recovery of his status as "broken witness." He no longer had to flaunt his crypt on his nose like some rebus. He could keep it on the inside, along with his magic word, without being at odds with his mother.

9. Can the Wolf Man be Analyzed, and How?

Could Brunswick's analysis have gone further? And how? Long ago in his sessions with Freud, the Wolf Man unconsciously played the part of the sister in the father's scene, though without the slightest trace of transference. He "repeated" nothing of his own. He was simply not himself. He *was* his sister.

If Freud had the impression at times of playing the role of the beloved father, it was Anna's father and not Sergei's. Without knowing it himself and without letting anyone else know it, the Wolf Man was Anna. Why? We now know. There was a scandal stigmatizing the incestuous relationship he had witnessed with his own eyes. He innocently opened himself up to the shady governess who, in her English, turned his ideal of pleasure into sin, his father into a criminal, and himself, the little Sergei, into a court of law raised above his father. From then on this pleasure, jealously kept in his innermost safe, could only be the object of total repudiation. At the same time, the fact of not having been part of the scene aroused in him feelings of aggression. These feelings found a happy companion in his new status as witness for the prosecution. The mother, with her Russian words, and the nurse, with her English words, closed two doors at once: the possibility of a sexual ideal, and also any form of aggression directed at the scene. All this did not keep the ideal from remaining alive within the Unconscious or even from appearing later on Freud's couch. It did not surface through transference, however, unless we choose to call the Wolf Man's states of transference fictitious. Rather the ideal surfaced as an unconscious and half-delirious identification from within the father-sister relationship. To overcome this obstacle to analysis and succeed in making the Wolf Man accept his status as witness without any aggressivity or despair, it would have been necessary, without expecting any form of transference, to challenge the juridical code that permitted the nurse's blackmail in the first place. In other words, *the analytic understanding of the father* would have had to be set in opposition to a repressive judicial system. The analysis would have had to extend to the paternal grandparents and even to the great-grandparents, so that the Wolf Man could be situated within the libidinal lineage from which he was descended. Under such circumstances it is conceivable that the extreme emotional charge of the traumatic scandal would gradually have been diluted by the introjection of the stormy instinctual existence of his forebears.

But this would have been an analysis in quite a different style.

IV. The Speech of the Word or the Rhymes and the Thing

Chapter 8
The Wolf Man's Cryptonymy

1. The Broken Symbol

Psychoanalytic listening consists of a special way of treating language. Whereas normally we are given meanings, the analyst is given symbols. Symbols are data that are missing an as yet undetermined part, but that can, in principle, be determined. The special aim of psychoanalytic listening is to find the symbol's complement, recovering it from indeterminacy. From the beginnings of psychoanalysis to the present, theoretical efforts have been aimed at finding rules that will permit us to find the unknown missing complement, in other words, the fragment that "symbolizes with"—or, we might say, that "cosymbolizes."

It does happen, however, that this type of listening runs up against a form of speech that resists the search for a cosymbol and defeats every attempt at completion. In these cases it is as if the sense of the words were shrouded by an enigma too dense to be deciphered by known forms of listening. Or, at other times it is as if speech did not refer to any enigma at all, as if it needed no cosymbol. Trusting analytic goodwill and the regular attendance of patients endowed with this form of speech, we should abstain from incriminating them, as is all too often the case, and inquire into our own inadequacies. This means not backing down from the search for *cosymbols* no matter how concealed they may be. They cannot be lacking—but their discovery may require breaking the usual rules of listening.

The idea of symbol implies a symbolizable entity and a basic presymbolic unity whose dissolution occasioned the formation of the Unconscious. But what happens if an additional fracture fragments the already incomplete symbolic given and if, as a result, the patient on the couch carries a jigsaw puzzle whose pieces are as largely unknown as is their mode of assembly? Confronted with such an enigma, we would have to reconstitute, one by one, most of the fragments as a first step before being able to put them together. Only then could we join these recovered partial components with their hypothetically missing half, that is, with their cosymbolic complement—which has itself been reconstructed in accordance with known rules.

The jigsaw puzzle is, of course, only an image and therefore deceptive, but it does reflect reasonably well the kind of work we did in the preceding chapters. We set out to retrace the broken symbol's lines of fracture. We called the twists and turns of this intrasymbolic line the "walls of the crypt." The walls were created from the dialogue between the mother and the nurse; they were meant to continue functioning as lines of fracture indefinitely.

2. The Word and Meaning

It will be noted that the lines of fracture within the symbol are analogous to the fracture that separates the symbol from its own cosymbol, situated outside consciousness. The crypt works in the heart of the Ego as a special kind of Unconscious: Each fragment is conscious of itself and unconscious of the realm "outside the crypt." At once conscious and unconscious: This provides the explanation for the peculiarity of the *intra*symbolic and not *co*symbolic relationships of the *word*.

What must have struck the reader is the semantic aspect of these relationships, such as synonyms coupled with variant meanings (allosemes), which implies the presence of some agency reflecting on words and their signification. The split symbol itself must contain a lucid yet concealed and isolated area where *goulfik* can be understood as is, without being disguised as "wolves," since this is a precondition for finding a synonym for it. This is the case, for example, when *shir* (expanse) turns into big *shirinka* (slit, fly; see chapter 7), and when the rebus "IV" (missing from *filivs* and interpreted as "the witness is the son, not you"; see chapter 4) is created, or when *goulfik* is transformed into *Schlitz* (German for "fly"), itself giving rise to further distortions. How can one conceive of transformations of this sort without assuming the work of a lucid and reflective agency inside the crypt? We conclude that the distortions to which *goulfik* submits do not emerge from behind the barrier of the Unconscious but from behind a line of fracture or cleavage located within the Ego. There would be no mystery if "wide-open fly" came from the Unconscious disguised as "white wolves"; it would be attributed to the habitual workings of the Unconscious. But for the word *goulfik* to be manipulated, not simply as something missing but as a *meaning* that is, at the same time, not missing, entirely new concepts are needed: the Crypt, the Fractured Symbol, the Rift in the Ego, or, to use another image, the Tear in the Ego.

3. "Where I Was There Should Be It": The Thing

Without this peculiarity the Wolf Man would not be the Wolf Man but an ordinary patient. No mere sexual repression is at stake here but a duality within a split Ego. It is as if one side of the Ego acted the part of the Unconscious for the other half while saying, *Wo Ich war soll Es werden*: Where there was Ego there should be Id. This could have been stated, surely, but without its ever coming to pass. For the crypt *is already* constructed, and the Ego cannot quit the place where it had once been; it can only withdraw into seclusion and construct a barrier separating it from the other half of the Ego. *Where I was there should be it* is the slogan of a *maneuver whose sole purpose is to preserve this nonplace for sexual gratification inside a place where sexual gratification should no longer take place.* This particular area within the Ego, the place that shuns symbolization and is the site of the death of pleasure, knows the word that says pleasure. The pleasure word *tieret* is buried there with the fallacious fiction that it is no longer living. The place where it hides like a chrysalis in its cocoon, however, is subjected to a *genuine repression*, especially as regards the pleasure word itself. As a result, this word (unlike all the other words) is relegated to the Unconscious and thereby *regains its active vital and dynamic function*.

To keep this word from returning in the natural state, as it would via the return of the repressed, *the line of fracture fragmenting the symbol must extend beyond the symbol to its corresponding and unconscious cosymbol.* This complementary formation within the Unconscious we call the *Thing*. A broken symbol has a severed cosymbol as its counterpart; to a torn Ego corresponds a partitioned Id. This must be assumed since, without it, the word *tieret* would not have to return in the shape of undecipherable symbols. The word *tieret* (despite its being the pleasure word) can cross the partition created within the Unconscious only if it appears on the other side of the fracture as the *Thing* of the cryptic Unconscious, and only if it has already been turned into its variant meanings (allosemes) on the side of consciousness. For it is only the alloseme that can cross the partition located within the Unconscious and be turned into a visual image on the other side of the gratified Ego. *Tieret* has another particularity as well. When conscious, the word can break through the symbol's line of fracture, without passing through the Unconscious, provided it is disguised in the synonym of an alloseme, that is, as a *cryptonym*. The presence of the cryptonym signals the existence of a crypt, a split in the Ego, as well as another feature of the word *tieret*: its fetishization within the Unconscious.

4. Twofold Fantasy Life: Symptoms and Dreams

A clarification has to be added concerning the problem of fantasy. We assume that, whether conscious or unconscious, fantasy functions by helping to maintain the topographical status quo. The Wolf Man's fantasies cannot help being related to the content of his crypt, that is, to preservation and conservation. At the same time, we cannot expect the Wolf Man's fantasies to be unambiguous, given both the duality resulting from the split in his Ego and the assumption that fantasy is produced by the Ego (even if, in this case, this means the unconscious half of the Ego). Each half of the Ego must state *something else* in order to survive. The Ego of the crypt thinks it is a "truthful witness" whereas the other Ego demands that the testimony be perjury. Each fantasy is thus double-edged and self-contradictory. The result is a constant tension within the Wolf Man's fantasy life, which aims to maintain two incompatible halves. The symptom of the nose, which takes shape as an "idée fixe," seems to result from this tension. The Wolf Man expresses two opposing fantasies *to himself* with one idea: "He made me happy, I love him" and "He made me miserable beyond repair, I detest him" (see chapter 5, the story of Professor X., sections 4, 5, and 7).

The same is true of dreams, especially as regards the dream thoughts or their originating fantasies. The "ambivalence" is particularly striking, as we have seen, in the dream of the gray wolves. The opposition between the underlying speech and the words of the dream gives rise to a double fantasy moving back and forth at all times (*"in dem sonstigen Hin und Her"*; *Gesammelte Werke*, vol. 17, p. 62 *Standard Edition*, vol. 23, p. 150). This back-and-forth motion also characterizes the Wolf Man's "psychosis" and, at the height of his agitation, the gray wolves of his dream. Here dreams and symptoms derive from one and the same double fantasy life, a double fantasy life that cannot coalesce into a unity unless it is transformed into an absurd thought and, thereby, turned into something acceptable to both halves of the Ego. Dreams and symptoms thus have a common denominator. Through their speech they refer to unspoken words hidden within the crypt.

5. Rhymes

The "speech" of the "word" has a unique character. It is totally unlike symbols, which can be deciphered with the aid of metaphor and metonymy. The speech of the word is made up of *rhymes*: an unsayable followed closely by its rhyme or, depending on the particular context, a group of rhymes generated by the same word. Everything is there, from perfect rhyme to assonance, from audible and sight rhymes to rhymes by meaning and even rhymes for lack of rhyme like a textbook on poetics. Should we perhaps seek the reason for this privileged form of hiding in rhymes in the Wolf Man's cryptic identification with his older, seductive sister, with the "beloved poetess" of their father? Or is this characteristic typical of the fetishistic crypt?

We include in the Appendix a list of the words (about forty) that reproduce the initial traumatic dialogue. They can be considered first as *fantasy producing*, then as *counterproductive to fantasy*. Expressed after being passed through their rhymes, the words wind up as *symptoms* and *dreams*. What speaks in all this are the *original words*, and they speak a language coessential with delirium. The psychic reality here is the inescapable prerequisite of a fractured Ego. What precipitates on the two sides of the line of fracture is the word and its derivative: its *speech* or *rhyme*. The double fantasy life resulting from the severed parts of the Ego is the secondary manifestation or epiphenomenon of this structure. Our approach remained functional and economical by leaping directly from speech to words, without passing through, as much as was possible, the drama of fantasy life. We reconstructed it only as a second stage and rather rarely at that, in the interpretation of dreams.

6. The Silent Word

The only exception to this was the word *tieret*. It was reconstructed from a visual image (of the floor scrubber), that is, a masturbatory or sublimated fantasy.

This particular *word* did not produce any speech, at least as far as its function as pleasure word was concerned. Though semantically deformed — but what does that matter! — the *word itself* was subjected to visual maneuvering. Whereas the other words spoke and then some, this word must be called a *silent word* since it could only speak (for) itself. "Here I am, love personified." Love disguised and dressed up in a "painting."

We know now which words spoke and how. We also surmise what
robbed the words of their power to tell, what crushed them into
words without grasp, silenced them into words beyond grasp.
These words we grasped them, we restored to them their grasp.
Their rhymes within him, within us.
His laughter: his words brought to light, "cracking words" that
restore life. Word of magic, word of panic, word of iniquity
. . . inseparable companions, they create and recreate the poem of
the tomb deep within. Black, their humor rises, white, their
pain recoils, but for pleasure they are mute. From beyond the
tomb, pleasure . . . nevertheless!
In his place, oh my brother, what would you do?

Afterword:
What Is Occult in Occultism?
Between Sigmund Freud and
Sergei Pankeiev Wolf Man
Maria Torok

The following essay is essentially historical in nature and is therefore an appropriate postscript to the American edition of *The Wolf Man's Magic Word*,
written nearly ten years ago by Nicolas Abraham and myself.[1] For some years,
I have been concerned with the possibility of writing a history of psychoanalysis.
It has become increasingly clear to me that the history of psychoanalysis cannot
successfully borrow its methods of inquiry from any other discipline. Whether
it be sociology, history of ideas, or intellectual and psychological biography, the
approaches employed thus far in the critical literature fail to express the nature
of psychoanalysis. For they all pass over the question that for me has become
unavoidable: What is it that lends therapeutic and theoretical meaning to a particular psychoanalytic notion? What inter- or intrasubjective and metapsychological situation sustains and justifies, from the inside, the introduction, use, and/or
discontinuation of particular concepts in Freud's elaborations? The same question can be asked of other psychoanalytic theories, parallel or subsequent to
Freud's own.

Writing a history of psychoanalysis must be a matter of listening (in the analytic sense of the term) to the prerequisite that gives rise to the adoption or rejec-
tion of clinical and theoretical notions. Such a history stakes out its territory by
considering the conditions *sine qua non* of concepts advanced and withdrawn by
various participants in the psychoanalytic movement from its very beginnings to
its most recent developments.

This approach separates history from the study of sources and influences. It
attempts to retrace the paths of *symbolic genesis*, that is, to go back to a point

that imparts meaning and yet need not be a primary notion. The search for sources other than those suggested by the history and filiation of ideas requires a critical reading of canonical texts. At this stage, one may question the purpose of asking why an author introduced a particular psychoanalytic notion. With this question in mind, I am in a position to state the second aim of my historical research, which is in fact its predominant one. The daily practice of psychoanalysis for the last quarter of a century has left me with some disturbing thoughts about the therapeutic usefulness of various notions bequeathed by the heritage of Freudian psychoanalysis such as castration anxiety, penis envy, frustration construed as a rule, primal scenes, and death as a final verdict.

In collaboration with Nicolas Abraham, my research has provided a number of clinical and theoretical correctives to the theories of Freud and Ferenczi such as *preservative repression, the theory of the phantom*, and the problem of *intrapsychic* inclusion. My interest here turns to the explanation of a contradiction in the practice of psychoanalysis. I have been intrigued by the fact that certain psychoanalytic notions, which appear clinically inadequate, continue to be officially transmitted from one generation of analysts to the next. In order to arrive at anything like a history of psychoanalysis, it is essential to explain why psychoanalytic institutions the world over continue to uphold the universal validity of therapeutic tools despite daily proof of their lack of relevance in a great many individual cases. The problem can be posed in yet another way. What sustains these notions if it is not their contribution to therapy? If the patient does not benefit from them, who does? It is perhaps reasonable to suppose that a particular flaw in a clinical or theoretical construction can derive its attraction from some metapsychological efficacy for the person who creates or uses it. This implies, however, a realm of effectiveness outside the patient "in treatment." Once we are able to assign to certain clinically flawed psychoanalytic notions their source of meaning, we will be in a position to evaluate their inter- or intrasubjective significance for those who advance or maintain them.

The following commentary on selected passages of Freud's *Dreams and Occultism* (lecture XXX of his *New Introductory Lectures on Psychoanalysis, Standard Edition*, vol. 22, pp. 31–56) is an example of how I conceive the possibility of a history of psychoanalysis through the analysis of both patients and analysts. In Freud's essay, the patient remains unidentified and is merely referred to as Mr. P. For reasons that will become clear, the patient seems to me none other than Sergei Pankeiev, called the Wolf Man in Freud's case study of 1918. My analysis of Freud's *Dreams and Occultism*, in which he recounts a series of exchanges between himself and Mr. P. (along with some apparently peripheral information about the general situation of psychoanalysis in 1919), will point to a drama (or trauma) hidden beneath the surface of the text that links Freud and the Wolf Man and that, at the same time, prevents Freud from uncovering the "occult" work of his patient's life. In other words, what is being laid out here is one instance of the evasion or impossibility of listening due to obstacles within the analyst, obstacles that need not, however, resist analysis by a third party. The hitherto unpublished letter by Freud to Ferenczi about the Wolf Man, and the letter of the Wolf Man to Freud and to the psychoanalytic journal in the United States, are startling documents in their own right and deserve serious consideration.

At a colloquium held in England in 1981 at Brunel University on the topic of telepathy, I put forward the idea that *telepathy* was probably the name Freud unwittingly gave to a foreign body within the corpus of psychoanalysis, a foreign body that retains its own individuality, walls, and partitions. At that time I stated hopefully, "One day perhaps the Freud-Ferenczi correspondence, which is being kept in this country in some (outer) safe, will say with precision what the two friends Ferenczi-Freud were looking to read in each other through the *medium* called telepathy. It will then be possible to recognize the words of a secretly kept story, hidden elsewhere and by a beyond, in a hitherto unknown psychic topography and in a hitherto undiscovered dynamics.

Telepathy could thus be seen as the precursor to a type of research that dares the imagination as regards oneself and others, that refuses to be imprisoned in systems, mythologies, and universal symbolic equivalents. Telepathy would be the name of an ongoing and groping research that—at the moment of its emergence and in the area of its relevance—had not yet grasped either the true scope of its own inquiry or the conceptual rigor necessary for its elaboration."

Today I think I am in a better position to begin to expose the contents of this foreign body, this unique formation awaiting analysis: a crypt that threw psychoanalysts, Freud included, into confusion in the 1920s.

The Freud-Ferenczi correspondence—which I hoped would one day emerge from its safe—has now become available to me, and the words of a secret story concerning the case of the Wolf Man are slowly regaining their power in and for speech. [2] They will also come within reach of Freud himself and of Sergei Pankeiev Wolf Man, at the same time explaining the reasons for the mutual incomprehension of the two men. The following analysis will suggest that the textual corpus of psychoanalysis has been (and remains) cut off from its own roots.

Telepathy—pain at a distance—can "tell" of the so-called third case Freud left behind by mistake in Vienna as he went to Gastein, Austria, in 1921 to discuss three distinct cases of telepathy with his friends and colleagues. In his prefatory note to the paper read in Gastein by Freud, entitled *Psychoanalysis and Telepathy*, James Strachey says:

> Freud had intended the paper to give reports of three cases, but when he came to prepare the MS. at Gastein he found that he had left the material for the third case behind in Vienna. . . . The original "third

case" has, however, survived as a separate MS. . . . The case is in
fact that relating to Dr. Forsyth and the Forsyte Saga, which is the
last of those recorded in lecture XXX of the *New Introductory Lectures*. The two versions of the case agree very closely, with scarcely
more than verbal differences. (*Standard Edition*, vol. 18, pp. 175–76)

The case of this "third man"—Forsyth, Forsyte, Foresight, *Vorsicht* (German),
"omitted owing to resistance" from the report at Gastein and to this day not
printed in Freud's *Psychoanalysis and Telepathy*—is surely a fable in which
wolves (not excluding werewolves) prick up their ears.

The case of this Mr. Foresight, which Freud asks us to *listen* to ("Listen
then") in 1932 in his thirtieth new introductory lecture, dates from 1919 and is
considered a failure: "His case did not promise any therapeutic success; I had
long before proposed our stopping the treatment, but he had wished to continue
it" (*Standard Edition*, vol. 22, p. 48). The man was between forty and fifty years
of age (in 1932) and had "erotic relations with women." He mentions a pretty,
piquante, and penniless *Dame*. Incidentally, Mr. P. is rather short on money
himself.

> At that period money played no part; there was too little of it about.
> The sessions which I spent with him were stimulating and . . . ana-
> lytic work was being carried on up to a foreseen time limit. (Ibid.)

Trained to hear, the ear must put side by side a series of apparently unrelated
pieces of information in Freud's text: the name Mr. Foresight (*Vorsicht*), a poly-
glot background, an English library from which to lend Freud books by British
writers such as Galsworthy and Bennett (both notoriously influenced by Russian
literature, notably the writings of Turgenev). Later on in the text Anton von
Freund appears through Mr. P.'s mention of an English professor, Madame
Freud-Ottorego, who teaches in Vienna at the public university (*Volksuniversität*). And finally, we come upon this sentence, attributed by Freud to Mr. P.:
"I am a Forsyth, too." The statement comes after Freud explains how Mr. P.
had acquainted him with the name of Forsyte. "I owe to him an acquaintance
with such authors as Bennett and Galsworthy. . . . One day he lent
me . . . *The Man of Property*, whose scene is laid in the bosom of a family . . . bearing the name 'Forsyte' " (*Standard Edition*, vol. 22, p. 49). Mr.
P. is a Forsyte, the hero of a saga. Such a suggestion by Mr. P. could not be
sustained unless he had indeed been the subject of a saga, written by Freud and
called by him *The History of an Infantile Neurosis*. Clearly, this "infantile neurosis" was to be nothing less than a haunting memory for Freud. Indeed a copy
of the saga was offered to Sergei Pankeiev Wolf Man by its author in April 1919.

Bearing all this information in mind, we turn to the Wolf Man's memoirs and
learn that he returned to Vienna in the spring of 1919, called on Freud, and was

encouraged to undergo a second analysis. He did so from September 1919 to Easter 1920. He lived in a boarding house (*Pension*) in Vienna and had practically no money left from his enormous family fortune. With the help of an economics professor, he was fortunately able to get employment in an insurance agency (*Versicherung*, insurance; cf. foresight, *Vorsicht*). And then he adds that Professor Freud, who had some English-speaking patients, used to lend him some books [*livres*, in French, also "pound sterling"] that came from Britain. We also know from other sources (Ruth Mack Brunswick and Karin Obholzer) that the Wolf Man, though married to Theresa, did not stop seeking adventures.[3]

This man—who in his memoirs quotes Rousseau: "La prévoyance, la prévoyance, voilà la source de toutes mes souffrances" ("Foresight, foresight is the source of all my suffering")—how could he be anybody else but Mr. P., the third man whose case was forgotten at the Gastein meeting in 1921? Definitely, Mr. P. is Pankeiev Wolf Man, a foresightful insurance agent. Besides, how could Freud have treated him for such a brief time (cut even shorter by new arrivals) and without the promise of any therapeutic success, unless his was an already familiar case. All the details fit Mr. Pankeiev, Foresight, Forsyte, Forsyth, *Vorsicht*, alias Mr. P.

For even more certainty on this score, we should recall that Mr. P. is concerned about Madame Ottorego at the *Volksuniversität*, at the WOLF University, if we read the German *Volk* (people) in Russian (*Volk*, wolf). As for the linguistic license implied here, we have only to look to Mr. P. himself who makes Freud's name into Freund.

> And for the first time during our long intercourse, he gave my name the distorted form to which I have indeed become habituated by functionaries, officials and *typesetters*: instead of 'Freud' he said 'Freund.' (*Standard Edition*, vol. 22, p. 50; my emphasis)

With this remark, Freud hints at the possibility of hearing some hidden elements of his own text, but more often than not he lays before us words that are closed upon themselves. I shall attempt to open these words by distorting their spelling and typography.

ESANETOR. This was the game of the "red nose" (ROTE NASE) between Sergei and his sister Anna Pankeiev.

> Something comes to mind, but it had nothing to do with what I said before. My sister put it in her head that she had a red nose (*rote Nase*) even though her nose was never red. We agreed to ask each other the question ESANETOR, which means "red nose" (Rote Nase) if you read the words backward. She would ask me: ESANETOR and I

would look at her and reply: No, no, it isn't, everything is fine. (Obholzer, *Gespräche mit dem Wolfsmann*, p. 110)

This word game probably contains the hidden meaning of the Wolf Man's entire
venture with Freud (see the Wolf-Man's persistent nose fetish and the interpretation; chapter 5, section 4) This game of scrambling letters escaped Freud's notice
and he was unable to reach for it behind the façade of words.

The game of distorting words and names provides a clue for deciphering the
name of Madame OTTOREGO (of the *Volksuniversität*). Her name, we recall,
comes after Mr. P.'s distortion of Freud's own name.

I later told P. that I had in a sense paid him a visit in his house; but I
know definitely that I did not tell him the name of the person I visited
in the *pension*. And now, shortly after mentioning Herr von Vorsicht
(Mr. Foresight), he asked me whether perhaps Madame Freud-
Ottorego, who was giving a course of lectures at the Volksuniversität,
was my daughter. (*Standard Edition*, vol. 22, pp. 49–50)

In Mr. P.'s name, I shall propose a distorted typographical arrangement for
Ottorego. The result is the following fictitious speech to Freud. You are your
daughter Anna's (and my sister's) friend (*Freund*). *You are going to see her in
my house and she excites* you. ("Excites" from OTTOREGO–A TOREGO–A TERGO
[sexual intercourse performed from behind]; another avenue leads to TER, a
fragment of TERET, "to rub" in Russian, and, finally: ERRE*gung*, excitement.)

This speech has to be seen as a fragment symbolizing with an encrypted
drama being played out in a shifting and "multiheaded" transferential exchange.
The people involved are by turns the English teacher (Miss Oven, the Wolf
Man's childhood governess), the sister (Anna), the father (here represented by
Freud), the mother, and the son (the Wolf Man) himself. Freud does not per-
ceive, in *Dreams and Occultism*, the shifting positions of this *internal hysteria*
(see chapter 1, sections 3 and 4, and chapter 2, section 2). He does not hear the
"occult" drama hidden in Mr. P.'s speech and thus "tips the scales" toward a
general principle, occultism: ". . . I have a feeling that here too the scales
weigh in favour of thought-transference . . ." (*Standard Edition*, vol. 22,
p.54). Yet, in the same breath, Freud says: "I had later told P. that I had in a
sense paid him a visit in his house . . ." (ibid.). Here, Freud seems to elicit
a form of transference—without, however, remarking on it—that reminds the
Wolf Man of his own father's visits to his daughter Anna (from whom he obtained excitement, *Erregung*).

Freud's *Dream and Occultism*, the thirtieth of the *New Introductory Lectures*,
written in 1932, refers the reader to 1919 as far as Mr. P.'s case is concerned.

Let us put things in perspective. The discussion of occultism and its uncannily miraculous aspects in *Dreams and Occultism* has an as yet unexplored parallel in the letters exchanged by Freud and Ferenczi in the year 1919. The letters of that year talk about something *demoniac*. For example: "Palos. Etwas Dae-monisches" ("something demoniac"). What is being alluded to is the "uncanny" coincidence of Ferenczi's wedding day (March 1, 1919) with the sudden death of his newlywed wife's ex-husband Palos. Equally strange, I would say, are the vicissitudes of Anton von Freund's last months (a Hungarian, his real name was Toszegi Toni). A great friend and supporter of psychoanalysis, Toni appears in eleven letters as the major topic of discussion between Freud and Ferenczi in 1919. Quite demoniac also, I would say, is Tausk's (a fellow analyst) suicide, "whose etiology is obscure" (letter of July 10, 1919).

Quoting from a letter by Freud to Ferenczi (December 18, 1919): "Nun mor-gen zu Toni" — Tomorrow going to see Toni. Is this visit the same as the one mentioned to Mr. P. in *Dreams and Occultism?* Another excerpt from a letter by Freud to Karl Abraham (December 15, 1919):

> . . . Freund knows everything; he has, for instance directed that the ring he wears [one that Freud gave him as well as some of his other intimate associates] is to be restored to me after his death. . . . I think I have stopped sowing and I will probably never see the harvest.
> (*A Psycho-Analytic Dialogue: The Letters of Sigmund Freud and Karl Abraham 1907–26*. Edited by Hilda C. Abraham and Ernest L. Freud. Translated by Bernard Marsh and Hilda C. Abraham. London: Hogarth Press, 1965, pp. 298–99)

1919. So much pain at long distance . . . tele-pathy. The word *demoniac* returns in *Beyond the Pleasure Principle* (drafted in 1919): It is the unexplained aspect of the death instinct. Inventing a so-called death instinct, is this not one way of theorizing, that is, disposing of — by means of a theory — a feeling of the "demoniac" in life itself? Palos-Tausk-Toni (Freund). Could this be true as well of Freud's attempt to formulate a theory of the occult? On August 18, 1921, Freud writes to Ferenczi: "Okkultis. Referat fertig" (report on occultism ready). In 1921, the meeting on telepathy takes place in Gastein and Freud's report is defective because he has forgotten to bring along the case of the "third man," Mr. P.-Pankeiev. A strange fit of forgetfulness. The Wolf Man's case had up to then and will henceforth continue to haunt Freud's works: *Fetishism*, *The Un-conscious*, *The Split in the Ego*, and others. It is perhaps just as well to forget about him at this time — in 1921 — in this demoniac situation. The situation is ex-acerbated by the unexpected death of Freud's daughter Sophie (1920) — not to mention the collapse of Austria-Hungary — Toni's death (1920), and perhaps also the feeling of melancholy weighing on Ferenczi's marriage due to what he calls "feelings of unconscious mourning" (for the ex-husband Palos).

Freud's letter to Ferenczi on June 13, 1932:

Ich schreibe wieder an ergänzenden Vorlesungen zur Einführung. I am
writing again on the introductory supplementary lectures. And then
Freud adds: . . . *wiederkauen is auch nicht das angenehmste
Geschäft.* To chew over the same material again is not the most pleasant of occupations.

Wiederkauen, kauen, chew or ruminate over something. The question could
be raised whether this word does not suggest some form of remorse. Be that as
it may, apart from Mr. P., the examples in *Dreams and Occultism* constitute an
unabashed advertisement for psychoanalysis. Mr. Foresight's case is different.
Here, Freud proposes occultism as a solution, despite Mr. P.'s indecision on the
matter, by "tipping the scales." It is this odd resolution of an unusual case that
makes me suspect that there is something concealed from view in the word occultism, that there is something "occult" (hidden) in *Dreams and Occultism* for
and in Freud himself.

The "scales" can be perceived tipping in one direction and then the other, in
the form of doubts, in several of Freud's theoretical elaborations. Theories are
being advanced, but are they sustained by real conviction? Should Thanatos, a
so-called death "drive"— with no energy or drive to it— be propelled into the age
of psychoanalysis? It seems to me that Freud's fable of Thanatos becomes justifi-
able only in relation to an internal and unknown area in Freud himself. In other
words, the introduction of a "death instinct" into psychoanalytic theory makes
sense only as a "foreign body" whose presence is also clearly perceptible throughout *Dreams and Occultism.* The word itself occurs at the close of Freud's essay:
". . . the action had forced its way that day into the child's life like a foreign
body" (*Standard Edition*, vol. 22, p. 56). And the reader will be mindful of the
same expression (*Fremdkörper*, foreign body) implied in a later text, *Analysis
Terminable and Interminable* (1937), where Freud writes about the Wolf Man:

. . . pieces of the patient's childhood history . . . now came away—
the comparison is unavoidable—like sutures after an operation, or
small fragments of necrotic bone. I have found the history of this patient's recovery scarcely less interesting than that of his illness. (*Standard Edition*, vol. 23, p. 218)

This time, in 1932, the essay on *Dreams and Occultism* begins with *marmalade*, that is, the "irrational jam hypothesis" about the core of the earth
(*Terra*). The essay goes on to discuss—much less irrationally—*meteorites* =
(*mes theories*) = my theories falling from the heavens. Let me add some more
rock fragments to the marmalade: Let us not overlook the rhyme conjured up
by "marmalade." Marmolada is the highest mountain in the Dolomites in north-

east Italy. It is the place where Carrara marble is quarried. It is also the place where Michelangelo obtained the marble he used for his statues, for example his *Moses*, to which Freud devoted an entire essay. I suspect that this inventor of the magma-marmalade hypothesis about the earth's core is quite an artist himself who knows how to turn out some interlinguistic rhymes. Freud warns the reader to be on the lookout:

> But suppose that someone else comes along and seriously asserts that the core of the earth consists of jam [*Marmelade* in German] . . . instead of starting upon an investigation of whether the core of the earth really consists of marmalade, we shall ask ourselves what sort of person this must be who can arrive at such a notion. (*Standard Edition*, vol. 22, p. 32)

The poet who arrives at such a notion — none other than Freud himself — surprises the reader with some hidden rhymes dispersed throughout the text. When he talks about the "Flood," another mountaintop emerges from silence: Mount *Ararat*. "Marmalade" and "Carrara" also lurk behind the water saturated with *car*bonic acid, the first syllable of the English word "*mare*'s nest," and make an encore appearance, at the end of the essay, in the *carats* of Dorothy Burlingham's "gold coin."

Let us keep the dates straight. We are talking about *Dreams and Occultism*, written in 1932 but referring to "facts" occurring in 1919. It was a "demoniac" year for Freud: "Am I going to sow any more? What else is going to happen to me?" Will there be *foresight, prudence* enough for this rare case, for this Forsyth, Forsyte, Foresight, *Vorsicht?*

In 1926 Otto Rank launches an attack. The Wolf Man's childhood nightmare is a dream he had during his analysis with Freud. The tree with the wolves is the tree in Freud's courtyard. The "five wolves" are the photographs of Freud's five associates. The house of psychoanalysis is in danger. Freud writes to Ferenczi on June 6, 1926.

> I wrote to the patient that he should once again carefully describe everything he knows about his dream. . . . I am quite certain of the outcome even before his reply and I will of course let you know everything the Russian tells me.

Not quite everything. We are going to read Sergei Pankeiev Wolf Man's letter to Freud (1926) as printed in *The Psychoanalytic Quarterly* (vol. 26, no. 4) in 1957. It will be followed by the "patient's" reactions upon rereading this letter to Freud thirty years later (1957). But first of all: What did Freud read in the Wolf Man's letter? Needless to say, Freud read the manuscript version of the letter (written in German) in its entirety. What does he choose to communicate from it to Ferenczi on June 8, 1926? Freud quotes selected passages of the Wolf Man's letter and adds his commentary in parentheses.

Freud's letter to Ferenczi:

Prof. Dr. Freud   6.8.26
                                                               Vienna IX
                                                            Berggasse 19

Lieber Freund,

I don't want to keep you in the dark about Rank's insinuations. The patient (Dr. Pankeiev) wrote to me: "As to points 1 and 2, I am completely sure in my belief that I dreamed the wolf dream precisely as I narrated it to you at the time. (I did not mention to him in my letter that the question arose as to whether this dream was fabricated subsequently. He never had this suspicion.) I have no reason to doubt the correctness of this memory. On the contrary, the dream's brevity and clarity have always seemed to me to be its most characteristic qualities. Also, so far as I know, my memory of this childhood dream never underwent any change. After it, I was afraid of having dreams of this sort, and as a counteracting measure, I used to bring before my eyes, before I went to sleep, such things as frightened me, among them this dream. The wolf dream always appeared to me to be central among childhood dreams, if for no other reason, because the wolf dominated my childhood fantasy. However, when I later on saw a real wolf in the zoo, I was quite disappointed, and I did not recognize in it the wolf of my childhood. The wolves sitting on the tree were in fact not wolves at all but white spitz dogs with pointed ears [in German, *spitzen Ohren*] and bushy tails. As to point 3: I narrated the dream of the wolves to you near the beginning of my analysis, to the best of my recollection within a month or two after the start. (In 1911, that's important for me.) The solution came then, as you state entirely accurately, only at the end of the treatment."

He adds some associative material to the dream which further reinforces the reference to a love scene.

Freud sends to Ferenczi the second and third paragraphs of the Wolf Man's letter verbatim. It is unnecessary to reprint them here. Crucial, however, are the sections printed below that are missing from this "everything" (*alles*) Freud promised Ferenczi. As it was, Ferenczi had no knowledge of Tchaikovsky's opera *The Queen of Spades* (*Pique Dame* in German and *Pikovaia Dama* in Russian) or of the lady Pankeiev calls the old Englishwoman in his letter to Freud. This old Englishwoman has so far remained mute for posterity. In the same way, Mr. P.'s identity, the forgotten "third man" in *Dreams and Occultism*, has never been unveiled. Here now is the remainder of Pankeiev's letter to Freud (*Psy-*

choanalytic Quarterly, vol. 26, no. 4, pp. 449–51), interspersed with my commentary.

Sergei Pankeiev Wolf Man's letter to Freud:

Dear Professor   Vienna, June 6, 1926

I am able to add the following on the subject of the dream. About fourteen days ago, after I was in bed, I recalled the dream again, and I imagined that the window to our room suddenly opened by itself. Then I thought of the Russian opera *Pique Dame*. The opera was written using a story of Pushkin as a text. A young officer named Herman breaks into the bedroom of an old lady called Pique Dame [Queen of Spades] one night and forces from her the secret of three cards by means of which one can win every game. Immediately after his departure, Pique Dame has a stroke. In the next act, Herman is seated all alone in the room facing the window. It is night. All at once the window, just as in my dream, opens by itself, and a dazzlingly lit-up, white figure [the deceased Pique Dame] passes by.

The Pique Dame, passing by a window that opened by itself, is an elderly Englishwoman from whom a Russian-German man forced the secret of *three* cards. All the terms of the wolf dream, which were left undeciphered until the interpretation proposed in *The Wolf Man's Magic Word*, reappear in Mr. Pankeiev's letter, one by one: "window," "suddenly," "by itself," "at night," "the Englishwoman." Later in the letter we find the following sentence about the number "three": "Even the number three that I could not get rid of during my obsessional neurosis could [would like to] find a place here."

Pique Dame was, it should be noted, the first opera that my sister and I attended. At the time, however, the scene with the window made no impression on me whatever, and I retained only the impression of dazzling uniforms. Indeed, next day we played at being Pique Dame and Herman, at home. I was Herman. Later, however, whenever I saw the scene with the window that opened by itself, I had an uncanny feeling. It is difficult for me to answer whether I saw the opera before I had the dream. It seems not to be the case. Yet, on the other hand, the fact that when I first saw the scene with the window it made no impression on me is in favor of the idea. Also, the opening of the window, the breaking into the bedroom, the Pique Dame herself (i.e., the elderly Englishwoman) were all familiar things to us. Another scene in the same opera, in which shepherds and shepherdesses make amorous proposals to each other, could be taken in connection with the spitz dogs, which were surely sheep dogs. The shepherds [N.B. There is a misspelling in the German longhand; Pankeiev writes *Schaffer* for *Schäfer* (shepherds)] and shepherdesses wore large white perukes, which again would remind one of the white dogs, or their white tails. Even the number three that I could not get rid of during my obsessional neurosis could [would like to] find a place here.

Without any connection with the dream, two other childhood memories recently occurred to me, from my earliest days. One was a conversation with the coachman about the operation that is performed on stallions, and the second was my mother's story about a kinsman born with six toes, of which one was chopped off immediately after his birth. Both deal with the subject of castration. A bridge to the opera *Pique Dame* might be glimpsed in the fact that Herman is a German name, and in the Pushkin tale he is expressly stated to be a Russian-German. This characteristic would bring him into connection with the mute water carrier, of whom I told you during my analysis (*Nemetz = Deutscher—der Stumme*). In Russian, mute is *nemoy*, German is *nemetz*, that is, German equals mute. I should be very happy if the above information is of service to you. In accordance with your wish, I shall visit you on the 16th in the morning, and I am extremely delighted that I may see you again.

We both thank you, dear Professor, most sincerely for your kindness; it is a great consolation that you have not forgotten us. My wife and I send you our greetings and our best wishes.

Devotedly and gratefully,
S. Pankeiev

In Freud's account to Ferenczi, the number three and Tchaikovsky's *Pikovaia Dama* (*The Queen of Spades*) are washed over as by floodwaters (and this is no mere figure of speech as we shall see). Yet, the mere homophony between the names *Pikovaia* and *Pankeiev* should make us hear one of the cryptic identities of the Wolf Man: the "Englishwoman" (that is, Miss Oven, his English governess). The Wolf Man is also opening his reader's ears to his persistent symptoms relating to the number three.

What Ferenczi was not in a position to see now stands before our eyes. The Wolf Man states in short: I am Herman, both Russian and German, but am mute (*nemoy*) in German (*nemetz*). Turn to someone else to unlock my secret. The old Englishwoman, Pikovaia, with the *three* cards has it. Me, Pikovaia-Pankeiev, I do know the secret meaning of the number three, left unrevealed during my obsessional neurosis. I run the risk, however, of having to die with my secret untold, though I did provide its multilingual key. (It should be noted here that neither Tchaikovsky's opera nor Pushkin's tale of the same name contains any reference to the nationality of the Queen of Spades. The Wolf Man's statement that she is an "elderly Englishwoman" may be viewed as an explicit clue for understanding the role an Englishwoman and the English language had played in his childhood.)

In reading Freud's sentence about a "love scene," Ferenczi had no way of knowing that the reference was to Tchaikovsky's opera. S. P.'s fable with his supposed primal scene could thus persist undisturbed. Similarly, Ferenczi had no way of comparing "the number three left unclear" with Freud's own letters to him in 1910 in which Freud describes the arrival of his Russian patient and talks about his symptoms relating precisely to the number three.

1957. Sergei Pankeiev comments on his letter of testimony, written on "the eve of a paranoia." Professor Freud is no more. Ferenczi died in 1933. As for the authors of *The Wolf Man's Magic Word*, the relevant issue of *The Psychoanalytic Quarterly* did not reach them. Muriel Gardiner published in *The Wolf-Man by the Wolf-Man* (1971) some sentences of S. P.'s two letters, but failed to state that both letters were available in their entirety. She also continued to keep the Wolf Man's real name a secret. The authors of *The Wolf Man's Magic Word* had by that time guessed its first syllable by transliterating Rank's name into the Cyrillic alphabet: Pank. The rest of Pankeiev's name reached us by mistake.

The Wolf Man's letter to the Freud Archives:

June 11, 1957

. . . Concerning my letter to Professor Freud, which you sent me. . . . First of all, let me affirm that I had forgotten completely all about this letter. I remember now, indeed, that at the time Professor Freud had some question as to the correct account of the Wolf-dream, or perhaps something was not clear and he wished some confirmation of my remembrance of this dream. As my letter to him shows, the chief question was whether I had seen the opera *Pique Dame* before the Wolf-dream. I am at present still of the opinion that I saw *Pique Dame* after the dream. Furthermore: The estate on which I was born was sold by my father when I was five years of age. However, we had moved from there some months previously to the city of N and I have not seen the place J since then. J, now a city of some sixty or seventy thousand inhabitants, lies on the E river, and the journey by ship to N lasted several days, so that we broke it and spent one night in D.

I can vaguely remember that my sister and I made such a journey one summer before this with the English governess. I believe we stayed in N a couple of weeks only. I was perhaps three or four years old and I cannot imagine anyone's taking a child of that age to the opera. Indeed, I do not think the opera was open in summer then. Now it would suit the interpretation of the Wolf-dream much better if the contrary were the case and if I had been to the opera before I had my dream. Unfortunately all of my memories speak against this. And I am convinced that I recounted the Wolf-dream to Professor Freud accurately right away. The dream was brief, clear, unequivocal, and always remained so in my memory, so that I cannot imagine that it could have been different.

It is interesting that my letter to Professor Freud is dated June 6, 1926. In June 1926 the symptoms relating to my nose appeared, ostensibly "paranoia," for which I was treated by Dr. Mack. This must have been some days after the composition of my letter to Professor Freud; for on July first, 1926, my wife and I went on vacation, and I was already in an indescribably confused condition. If I had waited a few more days to answer Professor Freud, I should have been in a mental state in which I should probably not have been able to tell him anything which he would find useful. Or, could the outbreak of the "paranoia" have had any connection with Professor Freud's questions?

It is striking to me that my letter to Professor Freud abounds in orthographic errors. Evidently I was then "orally" a master of the German language but not in writing. Moreover this has psychoanalytic meaning. As you know, my sister and I had any number of tutors and governesses; for example, our teacher of mathematics, head of the N Observatory, was a nice, quiet man, who praised me to my father because of my mathematical gift; so that my father thought I took after his elder brother, who had studied mathematics. The same teacher complained to my father about my sister, who enchanted all the other teachers, because she persistently said, "I don't know." Later, after I had completed my *Matura* examinations, by chance I met this teacher on the street and told him I wished to study law; he was annoyed that I had not chosen mathematics or at least the natural sciences.

A contrast to this teacher was L, who taught us Russian, a great patriot and admirer of the Tsar. He constantly praised my sister, while I was his bête noire. I did well in my lessons with him, except that each dictation ended in an attack of rage on L's part because of the numerous *orthog(ra)phischen* [N.B. This reproduces a corrected misspelling in the letter] mistakes (interesting lapse in writing, here!), which I always made.

Later, when L came to visit us and learned that I was a good student at the Gymnasium, he was astonished and moved. In any case, a result of L's method of teaching is the unhappy fact that I have to use a dictionary even today to find how one spells this or that word.

The editor who received Tolstoy's first manuscript tells us that he had never before seen a manuscript with so many mistakes in spelling, and also that he had never seen one so well and interestingly written. This statement consoled me. Finally, what strikes me about my letter to Professor Freud is the extent to which I speak of castration. No wonder, if this letter was written on the "eve of paranoia." (*Psychoanalytic Quarterly*, vol. 26, no. 4, pp. 458–59)

Pankeiev Wolf Man was given the opportunity in 1957 to study his letter written to Freud on June 6, 1926. He knew that his *Pikovaia Dama* had not had a chance to be heard. Part of his 1957 letter deals with her. One could even say that he draws attention to the homophony between his own name and Pikovaia's by insisting on his and Tolstoy's spelling mistakes. These are, it seems to me, Pankeiev-Pikovaia's clues for reading him, his efforts to open up his own drama, hidden in Pushkin's play. The wolves that are changed into his spitz dogs also begin to "talk" in a most touching manner. This breed of small Pomeranian dogs (as they are also called) tells of the death that befell the participants of the game of "three" (*ter*, three; *teret*, to rub; in Russian: *teret* between Father and Sister witnessed by little Sergei): *pomeret* (in Russian), to die.

Let us establish a link between the sections omitted from the Wolf Man's letter by Freud in his report to Ferenczi and the passages in *Dreams and Occultism* (1932) that refer to events dating from 1919. I shall propose an interpretation of this link based on the following question: In what way do Sergei Pankeiev's words in his letter of 1926 coincide with the driving force behind Freud's statements in *Dreams and Occultism* on Mr. P., Prudence, Foresight, *Vorsicht?*

To begin, we should remember that Mr. P. is interested in a *"piquante Dame."* Something of the *Pique Dame* seems to have lingered in Freud's ears. The (three) cards taken from the Queen of Spades have a parallel in Dr. Forsyth's visiting card shown by Freud to Mr. P. ". . . [the *piquante Dame*] used to call him Mr. Foresight. I was struck by this information; Dr. Forsyth's visiting card lay beside me, I showed it to him" (*Standard Edition*, vol. 22, p. 48). Freud also insists on Mr. P.'s relation to all kinds of things English. (Though not British himself, he had lived in England, had English books, etc.) And Freud managed to make Mr. P. give up his place to some Englishman, richer than he and, above all, better suited to spread psychoanalysis after the calamities of World War I.

Karin Obholzer quotes Pankeiev speaking:

I went there. An elderly lady opened the door and said: You want to stay with my niece *Ter?* Her name was *Ther*esa, too. I said: I'd like to take a look at her first. Out comes the niece, pretty as a picture. Not yet twenty. I used to go there—what can I say—for some time. One day, I am walking down the Kärtnerstrasse and this *Ter* is coming at me. *Aufgedonnert.* Dressed like nothing you have seen—thunderstruck. . . . I never went back. I only tell you all this to show you how *vorsichtig* [cautious, foresightful] I was. (Obholzer, p. 129; emphasis on *Ter* and *Ther* mine)

The Wolf Man's letter on "etymology" (see chapter 3, section 2) makes much of the term *Donner* (thunder; cf. *aufgedonnert* in the preceding passage), the Germanic thunder God Thor (= Donnar), and the feminine name Trude. In the short account to Karin Obholzer, the Wolf Man summarizes his life-long preoccupation with the sounds *three, ter, thor, tru-tur.* Once more we hear the insistence on the number three that accompanied the Wolf Man throughout his "obsessional neurosis" — a number that was never understood, yet never forgotten. Decades later *Ter* reappears in the Wolf Man's mouth, the number three of the *third* case left behind by Freud in 1922, the same number three Freud forgot to include in his account to Ferenczi of the Wolf Man's letter (1926). In 1932, Freud begins his article with a metaphor of the earth (*Terra*). The solution to the problem of occultism also seems to depend on *three* questions. Freud actually raises not three but four questions yet says that there are only three. The interplay of "three" and "four" is, of course, not unknown to the Wolf Man. Freud writes to Ferenczi on February 13, 1910:

> When he saw in the street three heaps of excrement (3 *Dreckhäufchen*), he felt uncomfortable because of the Trinity and he would anxiously look for a fourth one to avert the consonance [*Anklang*, harmony, agreement, concord, unison, rhyme].

As to the spelling mistakes Pankeiev Wolf Man is concerned about in 1957 while rereading his letter of testimony to Freud, consider this quote from *Dreams and Occultism*: "And for the first time during our long period of intercourse, he gave my name the distorted form to which I have indeed become habituated to by . . . typesetters . . . " (*Standard Edition*, vol. 22, p. 50). Without focusing on why his name is being deformed next to Madame Ottorego's, Freud searches for a general meaning to the coincidence between the names Freud-Freund and the series Foresight, *Vorsicht*, Forsyte, Forsyth. The result is a belief, willy-nilly, in occultism. Pankeiev's concerns about spelling thus become to Freud's mind a matter for *Dreams and Occultism*.

What I am describing in this extended and somewhat convoluted commentary of *Dreams and Occultism* is a *metapsychological phantom* and not, as Freud would have it, a simple instance of thought transference (telepathy). Here is an analyst haunted by the effects of a crypt lodged in someone else (his patient). The analyst is like a child whose parents hide a secret, whose parents falsify reality by terming it fiction, and who require the child to accept it as fiction. Witness to a *real* event, the child is told that it was all a dream, illusion, and fiction. With the hypothesis of a metapsychological phantom, we are now perhaps in a position to assign a metapsychological status to what is "occult" (concealed) in Freud's rather self-conscious option for occultism. The working hypothesis of many years of research seems to be reconfirmed here: Freud carries a crypt within him that resonates with the Wolf Man's.[4] Freud's crypt can be described by studying the text of the dialogues between the two men. My preliminary interpretation of *Dreams and Occultism* can be stated in brief: Haunted by the Wolf Man's crypt, Freud gives a card to occultism.

A child turned into a falsely "false witness" at his mother's request — such was Sergei Pankeiev's fate after having participated in a dialogue full of excitement

(*Erregung*) between the slanderous English governess and his Russian mother. The excitement (whose Anglo-Russian fragments the child attempted to grasp) was over his father's honor and its connection to some *teret*, an act of sexual "rubbing" performed by the child's elder sister. The nurse tried to use the child as a witness for the prosecution, while the mother denied everything, saying that the child had simply had a dream.

Freud speaks, in *Dreams and Occultism*, of Mr. P.'s nightmare, that is, of the English word Mr. P. mistakenly substitutes for "nightmare."

> At the end of the same session he told me a dream from which he had woken in a fright—a regular *Alptraum* (nightmare), he said. He added that not long ago he had forgotten the English word for that, and when someone had asked him said that the English for *Alptraum* (nightmare) was a "mare's nest." This was nonsense, of course, he went on; "a mare's nest" meant something incredible, a cock-and-bull story: the translation of *Alptraum* was nightmare. (*Standard Edition*, vol. 22, p. 50)

Before analyzing the significance of the word "mare's nest" for either Freud or the Wolf Man, let us raise a few questions. Is there any kind of link between the Wolf Man's habit of associating God with filth (see Freud's preceding letter to Ferenczi) and his substituting "mare's nest" for "nightmare"? Why is it that Freud is content with the Wolf Man's translation of "mare's nest" as a *Räubergeschichte*, a cock-and-bull story? And finally, in what way is this imprecise translation significant for either Freud or the Wolf Man? The answer to all these questions will come by way of *cryptonymy*.

First of all, let us think about English for a while and the Englishman who arrives in Vienna (1919) and in the text: Ernest Jones, author of a monograph *On the Night-Mare*. Shortly after discussing the associative relationship between the Wolf Man's mistake about "mare's nest" (supposedly meaning "nightmare") and Jones's monograph, Freud muses on the possibility of psychic transference operating in the great insect communities. "It is a familiar fact that we do not know how the common purpose comes about in the great insect communities; possibly it is done by means of a direct psychical transference" (*Standard Edition*, vol. 22, p. 55). Given the manipulation of proper names (Foresight, Forsyth, Forsyte; Freud, Freund) and of common nouns (mare's nest and nightmare) earlier in the text, it is difficult not to think of a "hornet's nest" here, especially since the name of that particular "insect community" resonates with the last syllable of both Er*nest* (Jones) and mare's *nest*. The analogy of "psychical transference" in a *hornet's nest* is further sustained in the present context by the Wolf Man's well-known dream about a wasp (*Wespe*), containing the initials of his own name.

> "I had a dream," he said, "of a man tearing off the wings of an Espe."
> "Espe?" I asked, "what do you mean by that?" "You know, that insect

with yellow stripes on its body, that stings." I could now put him right: "So what you mean is a *Wespe* (wasp)." "Is it called a *Wespe?* I really thought it was called an Espe." (Like so many other people, he used his difficulties with a foreign language as a screen for symptomatic acts.) "But *Espe*, why, that's myself: S. P." (which were his initials). (*Standard Edition*, vol. 17, p. 94)

S. P.'s dream of the wasp and the associative presence of Ernest Jones leads me to imagine the hidden thought in Mr. P.'s mind. "Careful about stings. Have prudence and foresight. Here comes the stinging Briton (hornet's Ernest)."

What about "mare's nest"? To grasp its meaning for the Wolf Man, we have to introduce Russian, not only because he himself is Russian, but also because the encrypted dialogue between his mother and his nurse took place in Anglo-Russian. What I am looking for, in essence, is the Russian word or words that are elided in the Wolf Man's erroneous equation of "mare's nest" with "nightmare". Assuming we find the relevant Russian word, the question as to what dialogue ensues between English and Russian, that is, between the governess (Miss Oven) and the Wolf Man's mother, of course remains open. The Russian dictionary reveals a consistent series of words resembling the English sounds "mare('s)" and "mare's nest." They are *mraz, marat, zamarat, merzest*, meaning "filth," "to dirty," "to sully," and "abomination," respectively.

Here then is the Anglo-Russian dialogue I can reconstruct as having taken place between the mother and the nurse. The dialogue also links "mare's nest" (and its Russian rhymes) to the Wolf Man's symptom of placing a fourth heap next to three heaps of excrement that he feared obsessively because of their resonance (for him) with the Holy Trinity. This reconstructed exchange should also be considered a sequel to the interpretation of the nightmare of the wolves (see chapter 3).

Mother. "You chatter." You *chettir*, you "four," hears the child in Russian. Adding a "fourth" one to three heaps (cf. *teret*, to rub, and *ter*, three) is thus a memorial symptom.

Nurse. "It isn't chatter." The child hears: It is not four (*chettir*). It is "three." The nurse goes on: "It isn't a hoax." The child hears "fox." "It isn't a tale." The child hears "tail."

Nurse. "It isn't chatter. It isn't a hoax. It isn't a tale. Bog. Bug(ger)! 'T is a morass, isn't it! The *Chef* . . . it's a morass, isn't it!" The child hears *Bog*, "God" in Russian. In "morass" he hears *mraz* (filth), then thinks of *zamarat, merzest* (to sully, abomination). As for *Chef* (a customary way of addressing the master of the house in Eastern Europe), the Wolf Man seems to recall him when he makes a mistake in spelling the German word *Schäfer* ("shepard"; pronounced like *Chef*). There is a "mistake" in the master, the spelling error would suggest.

Mother. "It isn't a morass, it's not a bog; it's a nightmare." (In Anglo-Russian: It's not *mraz*, t's bad *vidiet son*.) The child is thus led to invent an Anglo-Russian word *mrazisn't*, combining *mraz* (abomination) and *is not*. The drift of the mother's statement, "It is not an abomination," surfaces in the Wolf Man's substitution of "mare's nest" (i.e., *mrazisn't*) for "nightmare."

The linguistic situation being described here is also similar to the one analyzed earlier in chapter 4, section 2, under the heading "Slip of the Pen":

> At times fragments of the initial traumatic dialogue become symptoms instead of being dreamed about. The slip of the pen during a Latin lesson is an example. Sergei rather curiously replaces the word *Filivs* (son) by the French *fils* (son) in a piece of Latin composition. He omits the letters *iv*. We hear them in English: "you." By omitting *iv*, he states in brief: **The witness is the son** (*filivs*) **Not you** [*fils* and not (*fil*) IV (*us*)].

The omission of "night" from "nightmare" corresponds to the absence of IV, as interpreted in the preceding passage. In fact, "night" (also in the Wolf Man's main nightmare) is *notchiu* in Russian and is pronounced quite like the English "not you." With "mare's nest" (where "night" is missing) the Anglo-Russian series "night-*notchiu*: not you" is erased. It is as if Mr. P. contradicted, just once, his mother's request that he remain a *false* witness. It is as if, by omitting "night," he objected to his mother's having qualified him as an "unreliable child" who had seen nothing at all and had simply had a "nightmare." There is a shift, in *Dreams and Occultism*, in the Wolf Man's relationship to his own childhood testimony. It is as if he said in himself: If there is no choice but to give up his place, that is, his sessions with Freud, to Britons (i.e., the stinging English governess), then his confusion is complete. He thus opens the door to danger, threatening to sully the honor of his family, his father, his sister, and himself. In substituting "mare's nest" for "nightmare," he runs the risk of exposing some "abomination" or "filth" (*merzest*, mare's nest). The risk is increased by the fact that the occurrence of the word "mare's nest" follows Mr. P.'s inquiries about Madame Ottorego's relationship to Freud. Anagrammatic fragments of *teret* (to rub) and *Erregung* (excitement) are thus placed next to "abomination" (*merzest*, mare's nest) at a WOLF university (VOLKS*universität*).

However, the risk is averted just as it is being incurred. "This was nonsense, of course, he went on; 'a mare's nest' meant something incredible . . . the translation of *Alptraum* was "nightmare." Holding on, in the end, to the mother's words—"It is a nightmare, there is no abomination"—Sergei P. reestablishes his status as a false witness.

But we could, of course, also imagine that, in his childhood, he had turned to the English governess with the question: What is a *mrazisn't?* Miss Oven might have replied: You mean a "mare's nest"? A "mare's nest" is a hoax, a fraud. Even more complicated than that. It is a fake, a swindle. And it is, I should add, an extraordinarily complicated situation in which truth is passed off as falsehood. Or the reverse. In any case, it is some kind of hocus-pocus meant to disorient and confuse you. As when you open your eyes to something truly happening before you and then see a figure of supreme authority, a mother for instance, who vetoes reality. She closes the "window": the eye that saw (*otchevidietz*; cf. analysis of the main nightmare, chapter 3) and could testify. She says it was all fantasy, "a cock-and-bull story" (*Räubergeschichte*), an incredible lie. She confuses the meaning of words and strips them of their references to reality.[5]

The "occult" contribution of Freud's *Dreams and Occultism* to the Wolf Man's clinical material is the cryptonym "mare's nest" (hiding the Russian word *merzest*, "abomination," and its relationship to his nightmare of the wolves). Freud placed the Wolf Man's musings on English in his text—perhaps for us to hear some of their secret assonances—but chose not to analyze them. By surrounding his account of Mr. P.'s linguistic distortions with thoughts on telepathy (pain at a distance), Freud suggests an "occult" avenue for explaining his incomprehension of the Wolf Man's case. This avenue of listening is the result of new research and was not yet available to Nicolas Abraham and myself at the time we were writing the major portion of *The Wolf Man's Magic Word*. Today, my working hypothesis consists of establishing a form of *verbal* thought transference between the significance of "mare's nest" for the Wolf Man and for Freud. In the case of *Dreams and Occultism*, this implies a cryptonymic and metapsychological analysis of Freud's words, metaphors, and the secret rhymes embedded in his text. A consequence will be the suggestion already hinted at that Freud himself carries a crypt—a painful reality beyond himself (i.e., an occult telepathy)—that is quite similar in its structure to the Wolf Man's. The uncovering of this crypt (only very discretely touched on here) combats the canonization of Freud's theories or person and holds out the hope of one day rooting psychoanalytic theories in their own (human) sources of meaning.

Certain poetic procedures in the text (the rhymes *mar*malade, *mare*'s nest, and Ernest) have already become apparent. Dr. Forsyth, the hero of the piece, so to speak, is referred to as "a doctor from England . . . , the first dove after the Flood (*die erste Taube nach der Sintflut*)" (*Standard Edition*, vol. 22, p. 53). Dr. Forsyth (whose name is repeatedly distorted) is thus a "dove" on Mount Ararat who brings a message about a deaf spot in the text, since *Taube* means both "dove" and "deaf." Given the many transformations his name has already undergone, Dr. Forsyth can be used as a key to interpretation. Steering close to the cryptonym "mare's nest" and its archeonymic forms in English and Anglo-Russian ("morass, isn't it" and *mrazisn't*), we can discover, thanks to Dr. Forsyth, the deaf spot in the text. To formulate it as a question: What message does the dove (the Englishman) bring about the Flood? What is there in the German *Sintflut* (flood) that is at the same time English and German and as yet unheard or "deaf"? (Let us note in passing that in German the archaic word *sint* is no longer heard independently and is used only in the compound *Sintflut*.) As for the key to English, the ear will open as soon as we let Mr. P.'s and Freud's spelling license take over. *Sint* may then be read as the English ('t) isn't and isn't (it).[6]

We have as yet no way of knowing to what unheard (of) text in Freud the words ('t) isn't and isn't (it) opened our ears. For the moment, we can merely hear the unspoken rhyme brought by the (deaf) dove after the Flood: the Mount *Ararat*. Freud's text resonates with it in "*mar*malade" and "*mare*'s nest" but never states it explicitly. If we assemble all the spoken and unspoken rhymes' of *Dreams and Occultism*, we obtain the following homophonic poem.

ARARAT

Marmalade	Marmolada	Marble
Carrara	Carbonic	Carat
	(Night)mare	
Mare	Mar	Mr
Mare's nest	Ernest	Hornet's nest
Mraz	*Zamarat*	*Merzest*

Now, if "mare's nest" has Ararat for an unspoken companion, this poem of hidden rhymes calls on us to discover yet another deaf spot in "mare's nest," especially since the word is introduced in the text as an error in translation: "He added that not long ago he had forgotten the English word . . . and when someone asked him said that the English for *Alptraum* (nightmare) was a "mare's nest." Though the confusion between "nightmare" and "mare's nest" is set straight, the German translation of "mare's nest" perpetuates an imprecision. It is translated in German as a *Räubergeschichte*, literally a tale told about robbers, which is therefore exciting and incredible. James Strachey in *The Standard Edition* follows Freud's (or Mr. P.'s) *Räubergeschichte* and writes "cock-and-bull story." "This was nonsense, of course, he went on; 'a mare's nest' meant something incredible, a cock-and-bull story" (*Standard Edition*, vol. 22, p. 50). Yet, a "mare's nest" actually means a "hoax" or a "fraud." It is as if the word "robber" (in "tales told about robbers") robbed "mare's nest" of one of its meanings: fraud. The question becomes suddenly urgent: Where is there a (hidden) fraud? Can this place emerge through the typographical scramblings suggested by Freud's text? If we are guided by the sound poem *Ararat*, brought to Freud by Dr. Forsyth from England, we obtain the following transliteration: MARESNEST-MANSESTER. Is there a fraud in Mans(ch)ester, as heard by a child's ear, namely Sigmund Freud's? His half brothers, Philip and Emmanuel (living in Manchester at the time), are they or are they not involved? 'T ISNT! – ISN'T IT? (true). There is here both a negation subsequently put into question ('t isn't! – isn't it?) and, conversely, a question subsequently denied (isn't it? – 'tisn't!).[7]

In relation to some "fraud" in Mans(ch)ester this structure of question/denial represents an oscillation whose motion protects the child from either affirming or denying the existence of a fraud originating in Manchester. The oscillation between a denial that is put into question and a negated question keeps in perpetual motion a balance tipping now to one side, now to the other. The scales (*Waage*) that are said in *Dreams and Occultism* to "tip in favor of" occultism are in fact the image of someone who does not dare (*wagt*) weigh the "reality" of *maresnest*, that is, the "reality" of the fraud in Mans(ch)ester. The two pans of the balance keep alternating continually between a fact and *its* counterfact.

SINT in *Sintflut* (flood) led us in two directions: the anagrammatic transliteration into *'tisn't/isn't it* and the hidden rhymes converging on a silent place, namely Ararat. It would seem that these two directions represent two distinct ways in which *sint* had been made unreadable. (1) Even if we become aware that *sint* carries a hidden question/denial in English (isn't it?/'t isn't!), we would still have no idea about what this question/denial relates to. (2) Should we find the hidden rhymes of the broken symbol "mare's nest," through *Sintflut* (flood), in the assonances of the (silent) "poem" *Ararat* (ar, mar, car, etc.), we would still not know whether they express something specific or whether something is being stated about them. This twofold obscurity in *sint* maintains a double equilibrium. It ensures that *maresnest* will not be translated into a (true) nightmare: that it will never be transliterated into Mansester for Freud and *Mraz, Merzest* (filth, abomination) for the Wolf Man. The oscillation pivoting on "mare's nest" balances the two sides: Freud-Pankeiev. Nevertheless, the arm of the text's balance cannot come to rest on the desired inclination toward occultism. When Freud hands a card, so to speak, for occultism to Mr. P., the latter is not eager to seize it. To Freud the coincidence between Dr. Forsyth's earlier visit and the occurrence of the name Foresight in the session with Mr. P. seems miraculous (*Standard Edition*, vol. 22, p. 52). Yet, "Mr. P did not say, for instance: The name 'Forsyte,' out of the novels you are familiar with, has just occurred to me. He was able, without any conscious relation to that source, to weave the name into his own experiences" (*Standard Edition*, vol. 22, p. 51).

In refusing Freud's card for occultism, P. unmasked the face of a "true" nightmare, both for Freud and in "his own experiences." Pankeiev-Wolf Man is at that moment speaking to the Englishwoman Freud became by handing him a card (see the secret of the three cards and the Englishwoman in the Wolf Man's account of *The Queen of Spades*). P. says, at first in accord with the Englishwoman, that there truly was a "filthy affair" (*merzest*) and a sham nightmare (a "mare's nest"). Subsequently, he states, for his mother, that there had been a mistake and finds the right word in English for "nightmare." He thus obeys his mother's wish to obstruct the path of speaking out about a real "filthy affair." Though refusing the card to occultism, P. gives Freud a word in exchange. Freud takes him up on it, provided that the word "mare's nest" continues to remain associated with the imprecise meaning of a cock-and-bull story. As long as this "fabrication" through translation persists, the impossibility of ever hearing a "fraud in Mans(ch)ester" in the locution "mare's nest" continues to be intact.

In conclusion, "occultism" in Freud's *Dreams and Occultism* can be defined as the vacillating balance between two *calamities* [*fléaux*], making sure that a "mare's nest," the Wolf Man's sham nightmare, reveals nothing whatever about Freud's own true nightmare.

Appendix:
The Wolf Man's Verbarium

For the sake of clarity and orientation in this study (and certainly not without the intent of providing some additional proof for our claims), we have drawn up the following repertory of the Wolf Man's words and their respective speeches. We give this list without regard to any linguistic or taxonomic criteria, lifting it as is directly from notes taken along the way.

The Wolf Man's Verbarium

The Words or Archeonyms	The Rhymes	Translation of the Rhymes	
		German	English
Not you	notchu	Nachtzeit	night
	IV missing from		
	filivs		
	not you		
Is You	issue	Ausgang	exit
It is a boy	zimoi	Winter	winter
	Zimmer	Zimmer	room
Lying	lying	liegen	in bed
	lion	Löwe	
Not lying	standing	stehen	
(he) knows	nose	Nase	
	nos	Vorderteil	prow
		(eines Schiffes)	
Hole	whole	ganz	
	wall	Wand	
	hole	Loch	
Truth	v'droug	plötzlich	suddenly
	tooth	Zahn	
	foot	Fuss	
	through	durch	through
	durchs	durchs	through

The Wolf Man's Verbarium

The Words or Archeonyms	The Rhymes	Translation of the Rhymes	
		German	English
Witness	vidietz (son)	träumen	to dream
	otche (standing for otchevidietz and otchevidno)	Augen	eye
			eyewitness
			obviously
	window	offenbar	
	Whitsunday	Fenster	
	widower	Pfingst Sonntag	
		Witwer	
Sister	siestorka	ein Band von sechs	a lot of six
			a "sixter"
Wide	white	weiss	
Not wide	gray	grau	
	closed	geschlossen	
(I) know	no	nicht	
Son	sun	Sonne	
Swallow the tale	swallow-tailed	Schwalben-schwanz	
It's better to lie	butterfly	Schmetterling	
Water (to)	voda	Wasser	
Somewhat as a boy	samo saboi	von sich selbst	by itself
Glance	ganz		completely
Husband	Halsband		necklace

The Wolf Man's Verbarium

The Words or Archeonyms	The Rhymes	Translation of the Rhymes	
		German	English
Freud	Frau		woman
	Freund		friend
Sigmund	Mond		moon
	Halbmond		half-moon
	Vollmond		full moon
Ruth Mack	Mutter (Muta)		mother
Ruterl	Rudel		pack
Rutchen	Kuchen		cake
Oven (Miss)	ovtcharki	Polizeihund	police dog
Rank (rank)	krumm		hooked
	Schiff		ship
	schief		crooked
	Wunde (gewunden)		wound (crooked)
Sergei (Wolf Man)	sergei	Ohrring	earring
P. (S. P.)	Rank		
Goulfik (slit, fly)	wolves		
	Wolke		clouds
	Wall Street		
	Walfisch		whale
	Lupus (seborrheus)		wolf (skin infection)

The Wolf Man's Verbarium

The Words or Archeonyms	The Rhymes	Translation of the Rhymes	
		German	English
Shir (meadow)	(shir) – inka missing from shirinka = slit, fly	Wiese	meadow, large opening
Schlitz (slit, fly)	Schlitt		sleigh
	Blick		look
	Blitz		lightning
	Dreispitz		three-cornered hat
	(freier Schlitz)		open fly
	Schnitt		cut
	schnitzeln		to cut
Siestorka (sister)	siestorka	ein band von sechs	a lot of six
	zviezda	Stern	star
Khriekh (sin, misdeed)	oriekh	Nussbaum	walnut tree
	Schreck		horror
	Schmecke		snail
	Eck		corner
	Deck (+ related forms)		ceiling
	Pech (pronounced in Russian riekh)		bad luck
Siedat (sit in prison)	sidiat	sie werden auffressen	they will eat up

The Wolf Man's Verbarium

The Words or Archeonyms	The Rhymes	Translation of the Rhymes	
		German	English
Vue	vue	Postkarten	postcards
		Ansicht, Landschaft	picture, landscape
Tieret (tor)	Tierek (the river)		
"What the sister did to Father and Sergei" (not in in the text)	Tür		door
	Thor – Donnar		
	Turok		Turkish
	Tieretsia	Theresia	Theresa
	(Wolken)kratzer		(sky)scraper
		frottieren	brush, scrape
		kratzen	scratch
		glänzen	shine
		malen	paint
		hauen	beat

Notes

Notes

Foreword: *Fors*

1. [*Ana-* indicates: (1) upward, (2) according to, (3) back, (4) backward, reversed, (5) again; *-semic* indicates "pertaining to the sign as a unit of meaning." "Anasemia" is thus a process of problematizing the meaning of signs in an undetermined way. *Anasemias* is to be the general title of Nicolas Abraham's collected works. – Trans.]

2. Nicolas Abraham. "L'écorce et le noyau," *Critique* 249 (1968): 162–81. Available in English as "The Shell and the Kernel," *Diacritics* 9 (1979): 16–31.

3. [In French, this sentence plays on the expression *for intérieur*, whose literal meaning is "tribunal of conscience." – Trans.]

4. Maria Torok, "Maladie du deuil et fantasme du cadavre exquis," *Revue française de psychanalyse* 4 (1968).

5. Nicolas Abraham and Maria Torok, "De la topique réalitaire, Notations sur une métapsychologie du secret," *Revue française de psychanalyse* 5–6 (1971).

6. Ibid. See also Nicolas Abraham and Maria Torok, "Introjector-Incorporer, Deuil *ou* Mélancolie," in *Destins du cannibalisme, Nouvelle Revue de Psychanalyse*, Fall 1972. Available in English as "Introjection – Incorporation: Mourning *or* Melancholy," in S. Lebovici and D. Widlocher, eds., *Psychoanalysis in France* (New York: International Universities Press, 1980). We will encounter this *transphenomenological* motif again, which, along with the *anasemic* rule, has long oriented this research. This motif is obviously involved in the reinterpretation of the notion of fantasy. "To say that the fantasy [here, of incorporation] underlies the process [here, of introjection] would imply a reversal, of no small consequence, of the whole psychoanalytical procedure. To try rather to find out, through the fantasy, what modification of what process it has come to *oppose*, would be to pass from the description of the phenomenon to its working mechanism, its transphenomenal mainspring. This would be equivalent to finding the geometrical point from which the metapsychological origin of each fantasy could be deciphered, all the way back to the 'origin' of the original one itself."

117

7. "De la topique réalitaire."

8. Ibid. The problematics of the Third and of the "Name of the Third" had been sketched out by Nicolas Abraham in a text of 1961, *Le Symbole, De la psychanalyse à la transphenomenologie* (unpublished manuscript, Paris, 1961). The problem can be seen everywhere in Abraham's work.

9. This is not mere wordplay, or syntax twisting, not a gratuitous contamination of meanings; only the constraints of this strange topography. This topography has already produced the *necessity* of this kind of language, even before being described through its bizarre turns of phrase, its syntactical ambiguities, its outward resemblances.

10. Nicolas Abraham and Maria Torok, " 'L'objet perdu – moi,' Notations sur l'identification endocryptique," *Revue française de psychanalyse* 3 (1975). In English, *SubStance* 43.

11. Notably in *Le Symbole*.

12. This is a reversal of Freud's expression "Wo *Es* war soll *Ich* werden": "Where it (Id) was, there shall I (Ego) come to be." Thus the analytic process was already described by Freud in a topographical way. – Trans.

13. "All incorporation has introjection as its nostalgic vocation"; "Introjecter-Incorporer, Deuil *ou* Mélancolie.

14. It is precisely in his *The History of an Infantile Neurosis* that Freud articulates together the problems of "deferred action," reconstruction, the real or fantasmatic character of certain traumatic scenes, and the analytic narration (relation) itself. Let us remind the reader once and for all: *The Magic Word* cannot help presupposing a knowledge of Freud's text (and even the entire body of post-Freudian literature on the Wolf Man), but for obvious reasons it was necessary to avoid redefining at every moment *The Magic Word*'s relation to the Freudian or post-Freudian analyses. With respect to the whole analytic bibliography on the Wolf Man (who has just added, still in several languages, a last contribution), the reader's discernment will determine what is considered definitive, what is abandoned or contradicted, completed or realigned, consolidated or upset. To account for the *unbelievable* as such was the object *The Magic Word*'s authors were seeking. Freud had warned us: The Wolf Man is "incredible." ("But certain details seemed to me so extraordinary and incredible that I feel some hesitation in asking others to believe in them.") The Wolf Man, who gave rise to a whole tradition of the unbelievable, here expands the range of the incredible even further, far beyond the boundaries Freud had determined. Faced with a demonstration of this, the unbeliever can always resort, if he does not end up enjoying the demonstration, to rubbing his eyes.

15. Nicolas Abraham, "Psychoanalysis lithographica" (apropos of Conrad Stein's *L'enfant imaginaire*), *Critique* 319 (1973): 1102–17.

16. Ferenczi, *Thalassa, Psychanalyse des origines de la vie sexuelle*, followed by *Masculin et féminin*, edited, introduced, and annotated by Nicolas Abraham (Paris: Payot, 1962).

17. *Le Symbole*.

18. Cérisy-la-Salle, September, 1959. Nicolas Abraham gave a paper there, "Réflexions phénoménologiques sur les implications structurelles et génétiques de la psychanalyse" (*Genése et Structure* [Paris: Mouton, 1965].

19. Nicolas Abraham, *Le cas Jonas*, a translation and psychoanalytic commentary on *The Book of Jonah*, "The work of a great Hungarian poet, Mihaly Babits (1882–1941) . . . a poem written in the space of a few weeks just after the poet had learned that he was suffering from an incurable, fatal disease. It is a sort of inner autobiography, following quite closely the Biblical story of the prophet Jonah. . . . " Nicolas Abraham completed this work in 1973.

20. Imre Hermann. *L'Instinct filial*, preceded by an "Introduction to Hermann" by Nicolas Abraham (Paris: Denoel, 1972).

21. Although the words "ghost" [*fantôme*] or "haunting" are sometimes unavoidable in designating the inhabitants of the crypt within the Self (the living dead as "foreign bodies in the subject"), one must rigorously distinguish between the foreigner incorporated in the crypt of the Self and the

ghost that comes haunting out of the Unconscious of the other. The ghost *does* have a place in the Unconscious; but he is not an effect of repression "belonging" to the subject he comes to haunt with all kinds of ventriloquism; he is rather "proper" to a parental unconscious. *Coming back to haunt* [*la revenance*] is not a return of the repressed. Whence the strangeness of its analysis, the uselessness or impotence, sometimes, of transference. No ghost effect is pointed out in *The Magic Word*. It nevertheless remains that in spite of their strict difference, *ghost* effects and *crypt* effects (of incorporation) were discovered nearly simultaneously, in the same problematic space and the same conceptual articulations: What is in question in both is a secret, a tomb, and a burial, but the crypt from which the ghost *comes back* belongs to someone else. One could call this a *heterocryptography*. This heterocryptography calls for a completely different way of listening from that appropriate to the cryptic incorporation in the Self, even if it is *also* opposed to introjection and even if the "fantomogenic" words, in their verbal or nonverbal form, *also* follow the paths of allosemes. The heterocryptic "ventriloquist" speaks from a topography foreign to the subject. The metapsychology of the "ghost" effect was dealt with in the following texts: Nicolas Abraham, "Notules sur le fantôme," *Etudes freudiennes* 9–10 (1975); Maria Torok, "Histoire de peur, le symptome phobique: retour du refoulé ou retour du fantôme?", ibid.; "L'objet perdu—moi," especially p. 410, no. 1, and developed in the course of a Seminar on Dual Unity since 1974 (Institut de Psychanalyse).

22. *Hamlet's Ghost or the Fifth Act*, preceded by *Intermission of "Truth"*: "The 'secret' revealed by the 'ghost' of *Hamlet* entailing a command of vengeance can only be a catch. It masks another secret, this time real and genuine, but one which springs from a non-speakable ignominy which, without the son's knowing it, weighed upon the father's conscience." "The enigma of the secular fascination for *Hamlet* must come down to the perennial presence in us of the 'ghost effect' and of our sacrilegious wish to reduce it.

23. Nicolas Abraham, "Le temps, le rythme et l'inconscient, Réflexions pour une esthétique psychanalytique," *Revue française de psychanalyse*, July 1972. This is the complete version of a lecture delivered at Cerisy-la-Salle in September 1962, during a colloquium held there on the theme "Art and Psychoanalysis." That essay relates to all the motifs we are dealing with here. In it a type of psychoanalytic elaboration tests its coherence against a tremendously rich mass of material (Narcissus, Ulysses, Kafka, "what haunted Hamlet," the rhythmic pattern of Goethe's *Sorcerer's Apprentice* or of Poe's *Raven*, etc.) in order to formulate the question of the "fictive" genesis, the "fictive" author, the author "induced by the poem" and the work's unconscious. The measure of a "genuine work," writes Abraham, is its unconscious. That is its price (paid first by its author). Also its law, its rates, and proportions, as we will soon see. In English, *Diacritics*, Fall 1985.

24. "This same image [the image of the ghost, which has just established itself in this case as the name, in the wider sense I mentioned earlier, of the inhabitant of a crypt belonging in the Self—J. D.] also designates, for the patient, the very occasion of his torment, a memory he had buried, *without any legal sepulcher*, the memory of an idyll lived out with a prestigious object, an idyll that for some reason has become unavowable, the memory thenceforth being buried in a safe place, pending its resurrection. Between the idyll and its forgetting, which we called a 'preservative repression,' there occurred the metapsychological trauma of loss, or rather: a 'loss' by the very effect of that trauma. . . . In a recent study we felt obliged, impiously, to violate the 'sepulcher'—itself completely hypothetical, moreover—which the Wolf Man supposedly carried within him, in order to uncover inside it—behind the inexpressible memory of his seduction by his sister—the memory of another seduction, the seduction which the sister was supposed to have undergone on the part of the father." "L'objet perdu—moi."

25. [The French word *fur*, derived from *forum* means "proportion."—Trans.]

26. "Maladie du deuil et fantasme du cadavre exquis."

27. "De la topique réalitaire, Notations sur une métapsychologie du secret."

28. A borrowed position, then. It is not only of a piece of property (or two, if one wishes to

play on the split between the two properties in the beginning of *The History of an Infantile Neurosis* that he is dispossessed, or of which he can dispose only under the conditions of a *mortgage*. The position as guard is itself mortgaged. From out of its place in my scholastic memory, that English word has been haunting me throughout this reading: the word *mortgage* [in French, literally, "death pledge"—Trans.], a linguistic ghost coming back, intact, safe, in all its decomposition.

29. "introjecter-Incorporer."

30. Ibid. On these points (Introjection, magical demetaphorization, etc.) see again the introduction to *Thalassa*.

Chapter 2. Behind the Inner World

1. According to Ernest Jones, *The Life and Works of Sigmund Freud* (New York: Basic Books, 1955 p. 274), who quotes an unpublished letter written by Freud to Ferenczi on 13 February 1910: ". . . he initiated the first hour of treatment with the offer to have rectal intercourse with Freud . . ." This first session is not recounted in Freud's case study. In view of our hypothesis, the Wolf Man must have requested from Freud to stand "on all fours" (rectal = from behind = *a tergo: tieret* = to rub) and to let his "Jack-in-the-box" reach orgasm.

Chapter 3. The Nightmare of the Wolves

1. Following a lecture given before the Paris Psychoanalytic Society on January 15, 1974 to commemorate the 100th anniversary of Ferenczi's birth.

2. The crucial importance of the roots *tr, tor* (*tor*, past tense of the verb *tieret*, to rub) is now corroborated. We shall demonstrate in the following chapters the equally crucial significance of the words "lightning" (*Blitz*), "water" (*voda, Wasser*), and "strength" (*Trud*).

3. Why stop midway and leave untranslated the German word *Nase*, nose = (he) knows. The unexpected result of this restoration will be clear shortly.

4. The German text of the dream is quoted from Sigmund Freud *Gesammelte Werke* (London: Imago, 1947), vol. 12, p. 54.

5. It is worthwhile to note that the rendition of a dream's original text requires more than sheer verbal deciphering. In moving from a manifest to a hidden text the entire metapsychology of the person involved has to be considered both synchronically and diachronically. It is the overlapping of the various hypotheses operating on all levels simultaneously that allows the interpreter to confer rigor on his attempt at "retranslation."

6. The textual restoration of the dream thoughts (to use Freud's terminology) sheds new light on the dream work in general and on nightmare production in particular. This subject warrants elaboration, but let us be content for the moment with the following remarks.

First, in this case, the dream thoughts are comprised of the evocation of the initial traumatic dialogue between the mother and the nurse and of the subsequent conciliatory words of the mother. Finally, the dream states the reason for the mother's anxiety. The dream wish is: Let there be no reason for the parents' anxiety. Only if this wish is fulfilled can Sergei attempt to cut the father out with the sister and vice versa, that is, attempt to carry out a form of triangular introjection.

Second, the nightmare does not merely result, as we have suggested, from the child's identification with his mother's anguish concerning his father but also from his own anxiety that he might lose—in real life and not in fantasy—his love objects who, in any case, were to remain no more than secret models. These remarks also apply to the structure of the Wolf Man's infantile phobia. The phobic moment is a fault in wakefulness; the nightmare bursts into the waking state with all the features of a dream.

Chapter 4. In Some of Little Sergei's Dreams and Symptoms

1. This chapter is based on the dreams and symptoms discussed by Freud in his *History of an Infantile Neurosis*. The following are the page numbers of the relevant passages in *The Standard Edition* (vol. 17) and the *Gesammelte Werke* (vol. 12), abbreviated respectively *S.E.* and *G.W.*, matched with the sections in this chapter. Section 1: *S.E.*, p. 39; *G.W.*, p. 66; section 2: *S.E.*, p. 39; *G.W.*, p. 67; section 3: *S.E.*, p. 40; *G.W.*, p. 67; section 4: *S.E.*, pp. 16, 89–90; *G.W.*, pp. 39, 122–23; section 5: *S.E.*, pp. 87, 100, 94; *G.W.*, pp. 120, 133, 128; section 6: *S.E.*, p. 20; *G.W.*, p. 44; section 7: *S.E.*, pp. 91–92; *G.W.*, pp. 124–25; section 8: *S.E.*, pp. 69–70, 87; *G.W.*, pp. 101, 120; section 9: *S.E.*, p. 85; *G.W.*, pp. 117–18. On the dream of the celestial bodies and the Turkish flag, see Gardiner, *The Wolf-Man by the Wolf-man*, p. 288.

2. These German words are added to the Wolf Man's vocabulary by his new language—which is also the language of his psychoanalysis with Freud. Compare the following passage from *The History of an Infantile Neurosis*: "Thus he could recall how he had suffered from a fear, which his sister exploited for the purpose of tormenting him. There was a particular picture-book, in which a wolf was represented, standing upright and striding along. Whenever he caught sight of this picture he began to scream like a lunatic that he was afraid of the wolf coming and eating him up. His sister, however, always succeeded in arranging so that he was obliged to see this picture and was delighted at his terror" (*Standard Edition*, vol. 17, p. 16). About *Schreckbild* see also the dream of the icons (chapter 7) reported by Ruth Mack Brunswick. We can see the transformation [translation] of a wish word (*goulfik*, fly, slit) into a visual image (*Bild*, image) on account of the misdeed (misdeed, *khriekh*: *Schreck*, terror).

3. See also his mistrust of *tailors* in *The Standard Edition*, vol. 17, p. 87, and *The Wolf-Man by the Wolf-Man*, p. 272.

4. *Weeping on a Poet's Tomb*. This dream might be related to the illustration of a famous poem by Lermontov: *The Demon*. In the poem the demon seduces a young princess before her marriage and kills her with a deadly kiss. When his sister (their father's "dear poetess") died, the Wolf Man went to the Caucasus mountains and wept on the tomb of a great poet, Lermontov, who had been killed in a duel. Clearly he was making a displacement (in Freud's words) in complete identification with his father's grief. In his heart of hearts, he was only too glad to learn of his rival's death just as he must have been to learn of Lermontov's. He did misstate to Freud that she had shot herself, though he knew full well that she had poisoned herself with mercury.

5. *Schnecke* (snail) = *Schreck: khriekh* since the letter *n* is pronounced *P* in Cyrillic longhand and the capitalized letter *P* is pronounced like an *R*.

Chapter 5. The Crypt Screen

1. The complete case history Ruth Mack Brunswick provides is quoted word for word from the Wolf Man's own account that he gave her immediately after the close of his analysis. The Wolf Man's account became chapters II and III of "A Supplement to Freud's *History of an Infantile Neurosis*" in *The Wolf-Man by the Wolf-Man*, pp. 267–78. Our interpretation of the case history refers to these two chapters.

Chapter 6. Is a Witness Always False?

1. [The German text of the dreams is quoted from Ruth Mack Brunswick, "Nachtrag zu Freuds *Aus der Geschichte einer infantilen Neurose*," in *Internationale Zeitschrift für Psychoanalyse*, vol. 15 (1929):16–40. The English translation follows the German original; the reader may also refer to *The Wolf-Man by the Wolf-Man*, pp. 268–97.—Trans.]

Chapter 7. The Turning Point: A Truthful Witness

1. Other reflections on other coffins . . . We read in Barbro Sylwan's article, "A Propos des Memoires de l'Homme aux loups" (*Revue Française de Psychanalyse*, no. 1, [1971]): "The Wolf-Man *takes the trouble* to take a cab so that he can see, under the rain and at a late hour, the funeral procession of the royal couple (i.e., of Franz Ferdinand and his morganatic wife). In the light of "*the flickering torches*" he saw the two hearses" (emphasis ours). This "view" of the "flickerng torches" (*ter-tor*) had to be worth the trouble even in a thunderstorm. And if it is true, as Sylwan suggests, that "the Wolf-Man had had his last analytic session with Freud," the urge to see this "picture" might have allowed him to foresee that the session with Freud the night before would not be the last.

2. There is one exception to this, eleven years later (in 1938) when, following his wife's suicide, he nearly lost his balance. Ruth Mack Brunswick had dislodged his cryptic Ego from its position as witness. And now through a quirk of fate he became a *widower*, not to say, a "window": *otchevidno*, an "eyewitness." His grief over the beloved person is much perturbed. The Wolf Man has to go to Paris and London to recover his position as "widower" through the comforting words of R. M. Brunswick, who had left Vienna. If he receives her token of compassion, then he is not an aggressive and harmful witness (window). He returns shortly thereafter to Vienna with his balance regained.

Afterword

1. [This is a modified version of "L'occulté de l'occultisme: Entre Sigmund Freud et Sergei Pankeiev–Wolfman" in *Cahiers Confrontations* 10 (Autumn 1983): 153–71.–Trans.]

2. With the kind permission of Judith Dupont and Enid Balint.

3. Karin Obholzer, *Gespräche mit dem Wolfsmann* (Stuttgart: Rowohlt, 1980).

4. [Since the publication of *L'écorce et le noyau* (Paris: Aubier-Flammarion, 1978), which contains all of Maria Torok's clinical essays, she has outlined a new field of historical and theoretical research concerned with the psychogenesis of Freudian psychoanalysis. On this topic see "L'os de la fin: Quelques jalons pour l'étude du *verbarium* freudien," in *Cahiers Confrontation* no. 4. (1979); "Nota Beine" in *Affranchissement* (Paris: Confrontation, 1982); "Melanie Mell par elle-même," in *Géopsychanalyse: Les souterrains de l'institution* (Paris: Confrontation, 1981); "Des inedits de Freud à Fliess: La restitution d'une oscillation," in *Cahiers Confrontation* no. 12. (1984); "La correspondence Ferenczi-Freud: La vie de la lettre dans l'histoire de la psychanalyse," *ibid.* "Restes d'effacement: Emmy von N," in *Cahiers Confrontation* no. 15. In English, see "Unpublished by Freud to Fliess," in *Critical Inquiry*, vol. 12, no. 2. and "The Secret of Psychoanalysis: History Reads Theory" in *Critical Inquiry* Winter 1987–Trans.]

5. Let us return to a section of the letter the Wolf Man wrote to *The Psychoanalytic Quarterly* in 1957: "I was perhaps three or four years old and I cannot imagine anyone's taking a child of that age to the opera." The word "opera" becomes significant in this context if we hear it in Russian: *operetsia*, to lean on someone. The child alternates between leaning on his mother and his nurse. The nurse says that the child saw, the mother replies that a child of three or four cannot see. The letter continues: "Indeed, I do not think the opera was open in summer then." The "opera house," *operini teatr*, is only open in winter. In winter, *zimoi*: the boy. We hear the nurse saying: The scene of *tieret* (*teatr*) took place in front of the boy. The mother replies: the scene could not have taken place since it is now summer and not winter. The boy could not have seen anything; it is summer and the *teatr* (*tieret*) is closed.

6. This idiomatic expression in English also recalls by homophony the word game played by Anna and Sergei Pankeiev that I have quoted earlier: Esanetor. It may now be interpreted in English and Russian. Esnet a tor (isn't it a "tor"), that is, *rote nase* ("red nose" according to the children's interpretation) equals in Anglo-Russian (for the nurse): He knows the *tor* (*tieret*, the rubbing).

7. This paragraph alludes to a Europe-wide counterfeit affair that took place in the 1860s and involved Russian rubles. Austrian and British newspaper reports relate the investigation by the police and Joseph Freud's (Sigmund's uncle) arrest in 1865. Both the newspaper reports and the records kept in the archives of the Austrian police clearly suggest that the headquarters of the forgers was believed to be in England and that Freud's two half-brothers (Philip and Emmanuel, living in Manchester at the time) were suspected. For a selection of documents see Marianne Krüll, *Sigmund, fils de Jacob* (Paris: Gallimard, 1983), pp. 219-22 and 296-7.

Index

Index

Nicolas Abraham, born in Hungary in 1919, emigrated to France in 1938 and a decade later took a degree in philosophy at the Sorbonne, where his work centered on the phenomenology of Edmund Husserl. As a guest member of the Centre National de la Recherce Scientifique, he worked on projects in the phenomenology of poetics and the theory of translation while completing his training as an analyst. Abraham practiced psychoanalysis in Paris from 1956 until his death in 1975. His works are being collected and released posthumously by Flammarion; now available are *L'écorce et le noyau* (1978), *Jonas* (1981) and *Rythmes: De l'oeuvre, de la traduction et de la psychanalyse* (1985).

Maria Torok was born in Hungary in 1925 and emigrated to Paris after the war. A practicing psychoanalyst since 1956, she lived and worked with Abraham until 1975, and on his death assumed general editorship of their common *oeuvre*. She has published essays on Freud, Melanie Klein, and Sandor Ferenczi, and is now at work on a major study exploring the psychogenesis of Freudian theories.

Translator **Nicholas Rand**, also Hungarian-born, earned his Ph.D. in French literature at Yale University in 1981 and currently teaches at the University of Wisconsin-Madison. His articles on the relation between translation and a poetics of hiding in Baudelaire, Heidegger, Benjamin, Freud, and Ponge have appeared in *Poétique, Cahiers Confrontation*, and *MLN*. Rand has collaborated with Maria Torok since 1977 and is English-language editor of Abraham and Torok's works.

Jacques Derrida is professor of philosophy at the Ecole des Hautes Etudes in Paris. His most recent publications are *Parages, Schibboleth: Pour Paul Celan*, and *Mémoires: For Paul de Man*.